THE PENN FAMILY *of* VIRGINIA

From England *to* America *and* Beyond

"Surging like a mighty river, from the Thames to the Chesapeake to the Ohio, and now beyond, the Penn family's passage through time has been a quintessentially American one."

Markus Penn

THE PENN FAMILY OF VIRGINIA
From England to America and Beyond
by Markus Penn

Cover Art: "An Extensive Wooded Landscape" (1670s)
by Philips Koninck

ISBN: 978-0-578-93701-4

BREEZE PRESS
breezepresst@gmail.com

To my parents,
the late great R.A. and Loretta Mae,
with thanks so often unsaid

Contents

Penn Ancestry Chart

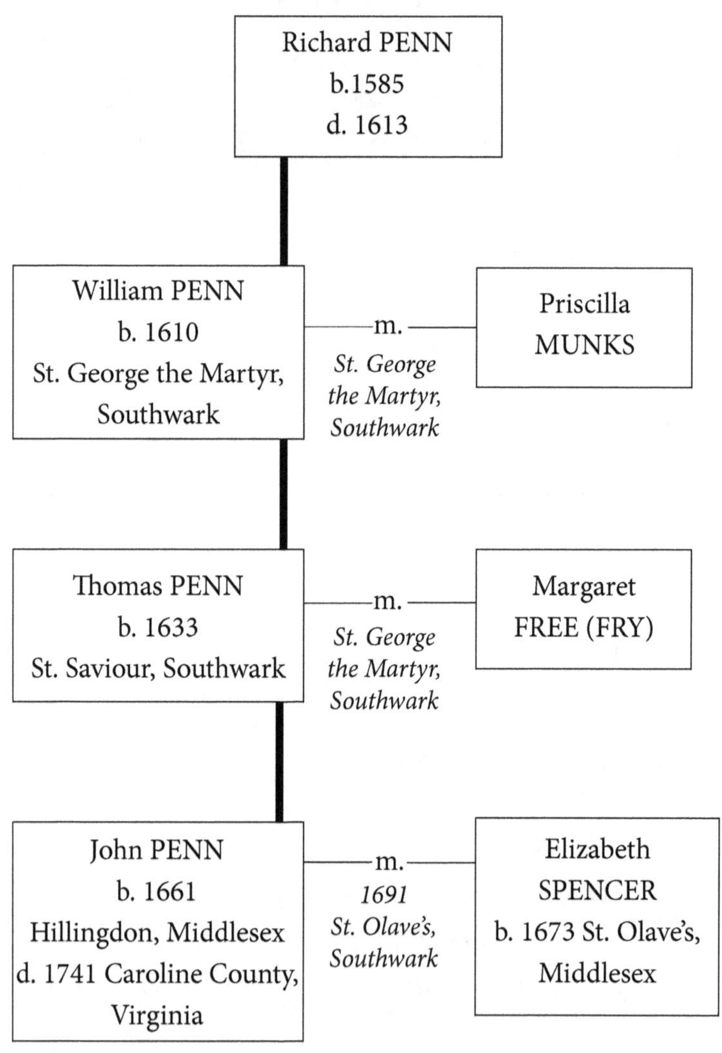

Foreword

The original vision for this work started out as nothing more than a handout for close relatives. I wanted to put to print the history of a single branch in my family tree, that of my surname lineage. Note-gathering that had meandered over decades since my early teens would now come together in one place. But the unforeseen breakthrough of digital transcriptions of formerly nearly-inaccessible original public records brought with it the temptation to dig deeper.

Peeling away one layer of the onion led to yet another, deeper and more saturated. The discoveries of ancestral life events stacked up to a point that the need for fuller presentation nagged at me. I then could see that the sparse genealogy of pedigree charts had morphed on its own into a full-fledged family saga that required a context of social history for each generation.

The miracle of online access to English parish records further expanded this project's original concept to include evidence of the Immigrant founder's origins.

Though arguably circumstantial evidence at best, diligent scrutiny of these and of other British archival material not studied by previous researchers provides the most solid, to-date theory of the Old World source of this bloodline.

Backtracking to stitch together threads of connection frayed by time makes for a slippery undertaking, often proving to be outright dispiriting. Benjamin Franklin found this out when he went looking for ancestors while in England in 1743. Documents, no matter how official, decay, get lost or burned. Witness the irony of systematic torching of county courthouses in the South by rampaging Union soldiers during the Civil War. Those documents that come down to our time may be nearly illegible and/or inaccurate. Private letters disappear but the dry dealings in a land charter survive. Only certain tidbits of life of the past get written down and then usually just for the minority upper crust. Historian Michael Pye laments that records "leave out what everyone knew at the time, what nobody wanted mentioned at the time."

But what does survive in the present case allows for knowing some secrets of the past. Those long gone would likely wish these skeletons had never left the closet. But the warts-and-all approach taken in this book lines up with the desire for a more expressive interpretation of this family's history. Whether one agrees or not, novelist James Baldwin saw it that "we cannot escape our origins, however hard we might try; those origins contain the key—could we but find it—to all that we later become."

This book narrates the story of the English-derived Penn Family of Virginia. This particular line of descent involves not at all the ancestry of William Penn, Founder of Pennsylvania. Though Penn supposedly acknowledged knowing about his Virginia "cousins," his family shares no known link to the lineage that arose in the Upper South. Likewise, this same surname has independent origin outside England. A north German dialect word for tree stump, "pien", has spawned a separate pedigree of the name Penn, again, unrelated to the focus of this book.

Acknowledgments

A nearly decade's worth of research has racked up a now long list of allies who have aided this endeavor.

Endless gratefulness to those unnamed, tireless volunteers who may have lost their eyesight poring through ancient, chicken-scratched parish records and other dusty documents. Their renderings to modern, digitized typescript now lie only a click away. This book would not exist without such fingertip access made possible by these selfless warriors.

For research across the pond for records not yet available online, fortune has brought together a cadre of superb, London-based scholars. Their contributions have made the historical scope of this book possible. Scrutiny of maritime records by Kristina Bedford, M.A., of Ancestral Deeds, has breathed life into otherwise dry details of the Immigrant ancestor's life. The tireless work of Andrew Lewis, Ph.D., in colonial records housed at The National Archives, has turned over stones long forgotten. Judy Lester, M.A. and Susan Moore, M.A. have shed light on time-shadowed lives through probate research.

The staffs at various British repositories have set an exemplary standard for attention to patron inquiries. Foremost among these dedicated professionals have been Andrew Lott at London Metropolitan Archives and Bruno Pappalardo of The National Archives.

Likewise have been counterparts at Library of Virginia, who have remained patiently unflappable even with my at times incessant emails and calls.

Historians and librarians at the local level have provided utterly invaluable insight into the lives and the setting of ancestors for this writer, a descendant long-removed from the colonial heartland. In particular among these experts are Greg Arens of Patrick County, Virginia Historical Museum and Pat Ross of Bassett, Virginia Library.

Cindy Headen of Martinsville, Virginia went way beyond what her assignment called for with voluminous photographic and cartographic documentation of how ancestral lands are presently situated.

Distant kin, all of whom I have yet to meet face-to-face, have generously helped with contributions from their personal archives. Robert Allen has accomplished the monumental task of an extensive list of descendants. Utmost thanks to him for allowing his research to be included as an appendix here. Additions to this listing are the accomplishments of Joe Henderson of Devon, Pennsylvania and of Pete Philpott of Patrick County, Virginia. Brooks Lyles, aside from making referrals to many of those mentioned here, lent his time to edify me on particulars of the Revolutionary War. His sending me in the direction of Cherie Sckorohod led to the lady with all answers about the family's famed forebear, Abraham Penn. Anne Jackson, of Hanover, Virginia, rendered a clear perspective of military exploits of some of Abraham's descendants.

An all-too-short afternoon with the late Jeanne Penn Lane remains a highlight. The rustic backdrop and Jeanne's tales of family lore told from the porch of Penn's Store in Gravel Switch, Kentucky, lifted me back into time. May her daughter, Dawn Osborn, carry on the family tradition.

The learning curve to have been able to mold the manuscript that has become this book would have been too steep a climb for me. Eternal thanks therefore to the infinitely sagacious Saskia Raevouri for handily pulling off this task.

Markus Penn
26 October 2020

CHAPTER 1

England

The surname PENN[1] in England originates from the ancient Celtic language spoken in Britain before Anglo-Saxon settlers from northern Germany brought the dialect that would evolve into English. The word *penn* meant hill or headland. In Wales, where the old British tongue survives as modern Welsh, the word "pen" yet signifies a head or prominence.

The word persists as a place name. The village of Penn sits on a high point in the Chiltern Hills of Buckinghamshire. The town of Penkridge in south Staffordshire developed near a now-gone tumulus from a settlement of likely the Cornuvii tribe. Called in the old language *penn-crug* (say "penn-krik"), the name described the habitation's location near a "head on the ridge or chief hill or mound." Occupying Roman forces partially Latinized the place to *Pennocrucium*.[2]

Under the far-reaching government arm of Norman England, several locations named *penn*,[3] that may have already existed for several hundred years, start showing up in official documents in the 1100s: a farm near Newport in Shropshire, a croft at Symond's Hall in Gloucestershire, a manor in Buckingham, a church in the diocese of Lichfield in Staffordshire.

And the earliest record of what can be interpreted as the Penn surname turns up with Nicolas and son Colin de la Penne[4] of Buckinghamshire in the early 1200s. Colin paid for having driven a stake through the head of Henry de la Sere by forfeiting his property at Mowbray Estate in 1224. Through his more sensible brother, Adam, the Penns held onto the family land at Beaconsfield, which came to be called Penland[5] Manor, before it passed to the Butler clan by 1421. Likely related James Penn took possession of what became the separate Penn Manor nearby at the village of Penn, Buckinghamshire, near 1222. The wife of a descendant, Sybil Penn, 300 years later would serve as Lady of the Bed Chamber to Elizabeth I. The manor stayed within this branch of the family until 1735.

Very soon ever-increasing record-keeping was tracking Penn(e) families in Cornwall, Hertfordshire, Norfolk, Northamptonshire and Wiltshire. Once the word was adapted as a last name it spread throughout much of England. By the end of the 12th century "almost a third of the counties were involved" according to British genealogist, Oliver Hogg, a descendant through the female line of William Penn, The Founder of Pennsylvania. The ubiquity of the name makes it "extremely unlikely that all Penns sprang from a common source."

In the 1250s a Hugh de la Penne, "a Gascon,"[6] served as controller for Queen Eleanor's wardrobe budget. (Both Gascony and a site, *Penne-d'Agenais,* lay within the old French province of Guyenne.) Though these earliest instances to incorporate the place name penn as a last name likely represent Norman nobles, its rapid and far-flung spread hint that quite likely native English took up the name, too. Roger and Simon Pen (*sic*), as well as Geoffrey and John atte Penne, are the

An early written entry of the surname, that of Geoffrey Penne, 1310

earliest recorded residents of London[7] with the surname, as recorded in patent rolls of 1327. John Penne served as clerk to the Mayor of London in the 1350s. Rauf Penn stands as the first of this family name found just south of the Thames in Surrey during the early 1500s.

Generally, those persons by the name Penn in seventeenth and eighteenth century English parish records, as the age of colonization began, clustered to two regions—Worstershire/Herefordshire/Warwickshire, near the Welsh border, and Buckingham/Middlesex/London in the southeast. The first name of John, important to the founding of the Virginia Penns, was maddingly common in both groups, mak-

Artist's interpretation of a medieval London street scene. Persons of the last name Penn were living in the city by 1327

ing for knotty unthreading of family links. As laid out below, steadfast rooting through erstwhile public records leans toward a mariner of that name from the latter region as the English sire to the Old Dominion lineage.

London bustled at this time as the center of national markets that seamlessly meshed with the international. In 1700 more than 12,000 Londoners earned their livelihood though trade overseas. Thousands more worked on ships. Sailors and their families clustered in East End parishes such as Stepney, Wapping, Shadwell and Ratcliff (like Thomas Penn of "new gravaillane" mentioned below), as well in south bank Southwark neighborhoods of Rotherhithe and Bermondsey. Mariners of the surname Penn[8] lived at the time in each of these neighborhoods.

A stated age of thirty-six[9] in a court document from summer 1697 narrows the birth of the suspected immigrant founder John Penn to 1660-1661. That he married and baptized his firstborn[10] at St. Olave Church in Southwark one assumes he had been born in the same area. No baptisms for this time frame of a John Pen(n)(e) turn up in Southwark.[11] A John Pen, son of John, was baptized, a world away for the time, fifty miles south at Hardham, Sussex, 1 November 1661. Closer to ground zero, two infants, one John Paine and the other John Pain, have christenings listed for St. George the Martyr Church in Southwark for 1659 and 1661 respectively. The original handwritten notation clearly shows the surname is Pain(e) and not Penn. Clerks seemed to have been consistent in distinguishing between the two monosyllables, only varying the spelling of each separate name. However, a scribbled entry in the parish register of 27 January 1660 from St. John the Baptist, a distant sixteen miles from Southwark, at Hillingdon in Middlesex, records the arrival in the world of a boy whose name can be interpreted from the poor handwriting as John Pans or John Pann. Parents were Thomas and Margaret. No further listing is found in parish records for Thomas and Margaret Pan(n)s. However, several crop up for a Thomas and Margaret Penn at St. George the Martyr in Southwark, where a Thomas Pen (*sic*), son of William, was baptized 21 April 1633. William himself had been christened a few blocks away at St. Saviour Church 6 October 1610, his father having been Richard Pen (sic). The earliest

Penn in Southwark is the burial of a William Pen (sic) 8 February 1577, also at St. Saviour.

The only Penn couple of that first name combination in the region at that time, Thomas Penn married Margaret Free at St. George the Martyr 10 March 1654. In a strange turn of events a few years later, they buried a son, Charles, at St. Olave in Southwark February 1657. The couple baptized a newborn, Charles, 8 April 1657, three miles away at St. Giles in the Fields, Holborn, to renew their marriage vows back at St. George the Martyr the following 21 May. The Penns may then have resided temporarily at Hillingdon in nearby Middlesex, when a second son, John, was baptized in January 1660, the deemed immigrant to Virginia. Thomas and Margaret next baptized a daughter, Mary, June 1666 at St. Olave, the work of Thomas put down at that time as "maryner." Their apparent last child, Thomas, received his first church blessing, also at St. Olave, 15 August 1669. The younger Thomas may be the lately deceased individual the subject of a grant of administration filed in Prerogative Court of Canterbury January 1691. Thomas had died the preceding year "in the king's ship[12] the 'Advice' on the high seas." A Hannah Penn from St. Olave, and of unknown relation to Thomas, took responsibility for settling the twenty-year-old's affairs. Later that year John Penn, assumed son also of Thomas and Margaret, married local girl[13] Elizabeth Spencer at St. Olave. No relevant records surface as to enable one to trace what turns the lives of Thomas Sr. or Margaret took after the birth of son Thomas. The tale of John Penn before he married likewise bides mute.

At this time, as the city was undergoing a population explosion, civility waned. An 18th Century traveler wrote that "If towns were to be called after the first words which greeted a traveler on arrival, London would be called 'Damn It!'[14]." In sharp contrast to present deference the British public largely shows the monarchy, citizens of Stuart England time hooted the king[15] and the royal family during public appearances.

Amid the rough manners, sprawl and homelessness one historian of London's past contends that a vigorous job market prevailed at that time to support the presence of guilds. Guilds, in turn, sustained a strong middle class to prevent "violent polarization[16] between rich and poor." In fact, segregation by social strata in terms of housing was much less evolved. The mansion of the rich often shared the same street as travelers' inn, taverns and cramped servant class quarters.

London and adjacent Southwark hamlets were veined with mostly unpaved, slop-covered, narrow alleys, all sodden from the nearly incessant rain. Everyone had the same idea of skirting nefarious puddles by walking closely to building fronts. Such avoidance led to "jousting for the wall"[17] and ensuing fights and killings. Gangs of youths, usually apprentices, roamed sections of the city, targeting strangers, foreigners and tax collectors. Blood sports of pitting bulls against bears and dogs, as well as cock fighting, served as routine public entertainment. Further avenues for diversion were afforded by open-air hangings and maiming for vagrancy or heresy. As historian Ian Mortimer puts it, "Elizabethans [were] no soft touch."[18]

As if to offset such barbarism, as the age of European exploration began, regular welfare payments[19] were slowly becoming the norm for certain segments of the poor, especially children. English society showed a definite move away from "the late medieval practice of providing only occasional aid."

London of the early seventeenth century possessed a capable policing apparatus.[20] Within hamlets, grids averaging 120 square yards, formed tiny precincts looked after by constables and night watchmen. Churchmen shepherded parishioners, attempting to stamp out drunkenness, illegitimacy and illicit sex.

Branded and burned at first as a heresy, William Tyndale's Bible translated to English soon emerged as the lynchpin for England's great Reformation changeover. Creed in the homeborn tongue "helped fuse the English identity[21] with the Protestant faith." Henry VIII's self-serving split from the Catholic Church pushed along the turnover. To help suffuse the public's consciousness with the new way of thinking, he decreed that every church must have chained in the open an English Bible which any commoner could peruse. The King also put into place first mandate in 1538 that every church list each baptism, marriage and burial, a move by Henry mostly meant at the time to track taxpayers, but in centuries later to be a boon for family history researchers.

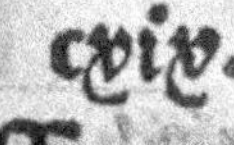

cxix.

The Gospell off
Sancte Jhon.
The fyrst Chapter.

IN the begynnynge
was that worde/ ãd that
worde was with god: and god
was thatt worde. The same
was in the begynnynge wyth
god. All thyngs were made by
it/ and with out it/ was made
noo thĩge/ that made was. In
it was lyfe/ And lyfe was the
light of mẽ/ And the light shy-
neth ĩ darcknes/ ãd darcknes cõprehẽded it not.
There was a mã sent from god/ whose name
was Jhon. The same cã as a witnes/ to beare
witnes of the light/ that all men through hĩ my-
ght beleve. He was nott that light: but to beare
witnes of the light. That was a true light/ which lighteneth all men that come ĩto the worlde.
He was in the worlde/ ãd the worlde by hĩ was
made: and the worlde knewe hym not.
He cã ĩto his awne/ ãd his receaved hĩ not. vn-
to as meny as receaved hĩ/ gave he power to be
the sõnes of god: ĩ that they beleved õ his name:
which were borne not of bloude nor of the will of
the fleshe/ nor yet of the will of men: but of god.
And that worde was made fleshe/ and dwelt
amonge vs/ and we sawe the glory off yt/ as the
glory off the only begotten sonne off the father/

A page from Tyndale's English language bible, 1526

The urban environment[22] of London in the 1600s would have pommeled one's hearing as much as does any modern megalopolis. Wagons with iron wheels clattering over cobblestones, snorting animals driven to market, neighing horses, foul-mouthed draymen, creaking signs, clamoring children, barking dogs, squalling cats and chirping birds all mounted an onslaught to a level of distraction.

What the modern world recognizes as Cockney,[23] the accent peculiar to East End London, already branded the speech of the area. Having developed out of East Saxon, the dialect had gradually been displaced from central London by influx of merchants from the Midlands. Late 16th century phonetic rendering of spoken language, in an era yet lacking standardized spelling, distills the sound of estuarine Middlesex from the time when the founding immigrant of the Penn Family in Virginia was born: " . . . greytt necklygence of our pysshеners"; "on of servand was so freyd that ys here stod up, and yt wyll never come down synes." Further flavor is imparted when considering "texes" for taxes, "towled" for told, "owlde" for old, "cyynes" for chains, "im" for him, "usse" for house, "sawgers" for soldiers, "hoathe" for oath, "suthe" for south, "rile" for rail.

If the local accent[24] remains much unchanged daily vocabulary has undergone major shifts: "swive" for fornicate, "cup-shotten" drunk, "jakes" toilet, "beldam" old woman, "nice" stingy, "cute" sharp, "lawn" high quality linen, "slops" items of clothing and "puke" bluish-black color.

Each district gave off its own stench,[25] based on local concentrations of animal waste, sewage, lime kilns, rotting vegetables, burial grounds, sweat, halitosis and tobacco. The abodes of most classes cached under rush-strewn floors accumulations of "spittle, vomit, scraps of food, and leakage of dogs and other animals. In areas like . . . Stepney some of those animals were pigs." As England's forests dwindled, wood fuel fell out of reach even for the well-off. The pall of coal smoke now enshrouded the mishmash of smells.

The availability of meat may have varied by class and locale. But common people in England lived on a dependable diet of "peas and

Still-standing house, and former tavern, that survived the London fire of 1666, Prince Henry's Room, Fleet Street

beans,[26] greens, parsnips, turnips, carrots and beets . . . milk, butter, cheese . . . chicken and eggs . . . apples, plums, and berries."

Before the Great Fire of 1666, that destroyed most of the City within the Wall, London was a sea of typical medieval, "Tudor-Style,"[27] timber-framed houses. A two- to three-hearth plan was most common, though dwellings of six rooms or more, spread over two or three stories, were not rare. A cluster of two or three seemingly separate singled gable houses might be linked on the inside as one large household. A sterling example of just such a habitat, with upper stories jutting out over the ground level, survived until 1881. Alleged to have been his London residence, the so-called Sir Walter Raleigh House[28] in Blackwall, just east along the River from Wapping, later served as lodging for immigrants bound for the colonies.

A late-surviving medieval structure, Sir Walter Raleigh's House at Blackwell

An inventory from 1686 of the personal effects of a John Penn,[29] a barber who owned a house on Grub Street in Cripplegate Without (i.e., outside) the wall of the City, lends a glimpse back in time of an average household. The account also divulges the layout of the then-typical, bi-level, four-room dwelling. "In the kitchen 13 pewter dishes with ould plates . . .a pr. Of Candlesticks, a sauser, a bed pan . . . a warming pan, a morter with loose ould brass . . . one greate with fire shovel and tongs . . . in the back room behind the kitchen three barbers dishes . . . shears, a looking glass . . . in the shop and empty counter . . . in the room over the kitchen one bed, coverlid and curtains, one chest of drawers, two caine chears . . . a pears of belowes . . . two pears of ould sheets with table linin and towels, two ould Shutes of mens wearing apparel . . ."

Residing on "new gravaillaine"[30] (now called Garnet Street), another and likely related Thomas Penn, and wife Christian Billard Penn, lost the first of their offspring, daughter Margaret in May 1656. Five years later two other girls, Abigale and Elizabeth, died within a few months of the other. Like many men in his raffish neighborhood, Thomas also trolled the seas during his working life as a mariner.[31] For a brief period in early 1661 though he held down a clerical job as an "examinator."[32] In August 1662, son George, the only of their children to survive to adulthood, was baptized at St. Dunstan's, Stepney. George would take up an apprenticeship as a cordwainer[33] (shoemaker) in 1688 after the death of his parents. The Penns' residence was recorded as Ratcliff Highway at the northern boundary of Wapping, in sight of Southwark across the Thames. When George's brother Tristam succumbed in October 1665, the family had apparently moved round the corncr to "old gravaillainc."

Entry for his burial stands out from the hundreds of others set down that week. Tristam Penn[34] was specifically listed as *not* a victim of plague raging through the City that year. Ruling out accidents (most commonly for children of that time, drowning in wells, trampling by horses or head injuries from falls), possible maladies to take the lives of George's siblings, at a time when 30% of all children in Britain died by the age of fifteen, would have been bloody flux (dysentery), scarlatina (scarlet fever), whooping cough, influenza, smallpox and pneumonia.[35]

Plagues had been recorded[36] in London since the seventh century. Between 1563 and 1603 alone three outbreaks had erupted, killing 30,000 people. Likely no one was ever entirely well in a city filled with pits and gutters streaming with excrement, dead animals and rotting food scraps. Having lost the know-how of sewage upkeep when the Romans had pulled out 1200 years before, the Thames, like all waterways in Europe, slogged along its course as an utterly undrinkable "monster soup"[37] of contagion.

What would come to be called The Great (and final) Plague[38] started out slowly in May 1665 at St. Giles. With a June heat wave the pestilence spread to other slum suburbs. Never grasping the identity of the true carrier, residents exterminated dogs and cats, who otherwise would have helped to curb the culpable and odious rat population. The backlog of corpses piling up on the streets required mass graves lined with quicklime. Usually catty diarist of the day, Samuel Pepys was humbled to grieve that "the plague mak[es] us as cruel as dogs one to another."

Painting created soon after the Great Fire of 1666

The next catastrophe descended a year later.[39] Likely neither the Penn's of Southwark nor north bank neighbors had much sleep the first week of September. Watching an enflamed western horizon as The Great Fire swept through the walled part of London, flames reached as far as the Tower of London directly across the River from St. Olave Church. By the second night of the fire, September 3, flames licked at London Bridge, ready to fan out into Southwark. But a wide space between buildings broke the fire as it had done during a lesser conflagration in 1632. An orange glow brightening their faces in the night, Thomas, holding the hand each of his little boys Charles and John, Margaret clutching infant Mary, the young family gazed spellbound across at the blazing cataclysm unfolding before them. Burned out citizens fled to the River or streamed to open spaces at Moorfields and Finsbury Hill to set up refugee camps. An eyewitness recounted that "poor pigeons were loath to leave[40] their houses, but hovered about the windows and balconies till they burned their wings and fell down." That part of the wall at Aldgate and a westerly wind kept outlying areas to the east unscathed.

Indentured servants[41] supplied the labor to keep British business interests humming in the Chesapeake and in Barbados. An industry in itself arose[42] to feed this demand with the vast pool of young unemployed and homeless in London and Bristol. "The trade that developed[43] involved large organizations that allowed investments by individuals interested in obtaining large profits through legal or, at times, illegal means such as kidnapping or fraudulent promises."

Kidnapping in the rough-and-tumble hamlets along the Thames River was rampant during the periods 1657-63 and 1675-84, "when men, women, or children were lured[44] on board ships and sold in Barbados or Virginia."

Whether forced into service on the galley of a ship or packed off to slave overseas, many colonists did not go of their own accord

A Katherine Penn was one of precious few[45] who escaped a kidnapping attempt early in the summer of 1648. Already held captive on a ship in the Thames, she lived to tell her tale, likely through the intervention of her employer, Thomas Smithe, a milkman of Oldstreet near St. Katherine's Tower. Miss Penn herself "affirmeth" before Justice of the Peace, Josias Berners, in Middlesex Court, that accused professional "spirrittes," John and Christiana Chetrost, had enticed her with the promise of "six pounds sterling per annum" as a servant for an unnamed party, but had instead hustled her onto the ship. Delivered from bondage, this lucky girl was quite likely the "Katheryne" baptized 6 March 1624 at the now-leveled church of St. Alphage London Wall, daughter of a Thomas and Joane Penn.

CHAPTER 2

The Immigrant

Between 1620 and 1772 at least forty persons of record[1] by the last of Penn went from England to the New World and nearly all of these to Virginia. Though ages were rarely recorded most were likely in their teens or 20s. Staking a claim in America was for the young and ignorantly fearless, not for the many who went without choice. Probably the youngest of Penn migrants was an urchin,[2] pulled from the streets of London. Like many children accused of nothing more than vagrancy, he was one of many "packte up and punnyshed alyke in Brydewell with rogues, beggers, strompets and pylvering theves." Bridewell Royal Hospital was a former royal residence donated by Henry VIII's son Edward VI to the City for use as both a prison and orphanage. The last record of the child's existence from 26 April 1633 states, "Richard Penn, by constable, Kifith Candleweek (i.e. Candlewick Ward), to goe (*sic*) to Virginia." Given that he survived the horrendous crossing of the Atlantic, this abandoned child likely ended up living a short and brutal existence as little more than a field slave.

A downturn in rural economy at the beginning of the 17th century had driven many from the provinces to London. The ensuing torrent of bereft squatters taxed the City's capacity and patience. A callous attitude soon settled in on the part of authorities. The dean of St. Paul's[3] Cathedral played up in a sermon the official policy to roundup undesirables for shipment to the New World: "It shall sweep your streets, and wash your doors, from idle persons, and the children of idle persons, and employ them . . ." One modern author quotes from muster records that of the first 300 children shipped between 1619 and 1622, only twelve were still alive in 1624.

One of the first girls arrested, in February 1619, for homelessness was Elizabeth Abbott.[4] Sent to Virginia she survived disease, heat and the Indian massacre of 1622 only to be whipped to death by her master in October 1624.

The first known Penn in Virginia was a Robert Penn,[5] who at the stated age of 20, arrived on the *Ship Abigale* in 1620. He is likely the Robert baptized in 1600 in Northhamptonshire, son of Marke and Margery Penn. At least there is no other child recorded with that name in British parish records available for that time period. This Robert also survived the Indian uprising of 1622 and ensuing plague, when two-thirds of colonists perished. In 1625 he was working as a servant on the James River plantation of Captain Samuel Mathew. He last appears as a witness in a local court proceeding of May 1629, his lot improved during nine years in Virginia to that of planter.

Of the several persons by the name of Penn coming to Virginia during the early to mid-seventeenth century, surviving meagre documentation fails to show any left descendants or, at least, progeny bearing this surname. In the case of Robert Penn, the dearth of womenfolk during the first decades of the colony may have resulted in his dying childless. In the first seventy to eighty years of the Colony, the sex ratio was 500 men to 100 women. As a result most men died single, though immigrants to Virginia were younger compared to those to New England or to the Delaware Valley.

The starting point for attempting to establish a colonial progenitor in Virginia leans heavily on the lucky survival of colonial land patent records. At that time the process of land distribution had evolved to the *headright* system.[6] In theory, each person who came to Virginia was given 50 acres. But if that person were unable to pay for transportation to the colony, the fifty acres would be transferred to the person who had paid the cost. This person, known as the patentee, would obtain a certificate of importation from the court that listed names of each individual for whom the patentee had arranged passage. Not every person on such a list was indebted, as some people arrived in the status of landholder.

As an example, the name of Roger Penn,[7] again with no provable line of descent to present times, appears on a list of fourteen other Englishmen whose transportation was arranged by a George Clapham. The patent record is dated 24 December 1652. From the same date is record of an actual land grant, which stated that Clapham had headright "and Roger Penn another" to 670 acres on the south side "of the Yorke, River, in the Narrowes . . . " This would strongly suggest that Roger Penn had arranged for his travel to arrive on sure footing to start off as a landowner.

On occasion an individual would sign up a group of persons to then accompany them to the colonies. There the organizer would claim headright on himself and the others. The entrepreneur could then sell land or servants or try his hand at growing tobacco. Networks[8] for acquiring indentured servants existed, replete with forms and advertisements announcing planned arrivals of servant ships. Ships would ply waterways to sell their human cargoes.

Presence of a name as a headright on a land patent only shows that a person of a certain name had entered the Colony of Virginia prior to the date of the patent. The patent does not prove when the person actually arrived or who received the headright. Frequent instances of fraud,[9] however, undermine reliance that can be placed on this resource.

A George Penn,[10] perhaps erroneously transcribed from some colonial clerk's scrawl as "Denn"[11] by modern-day extractors, appears on a land patent dated 1 October 1679, as one of a dozen other men and women brought to the Colony. Analyzing the long-dead scribe's formation of various letters of the alphabet throughout the original document leans one toward reading the name as "Penn."

Popular theory[12] proposes this George of arguable surname to be the man to give rise to the Penns of Virginia. His "transporters," John Pigg and Francis Crane, claimed headrights to land on the Mattaponi

River in then-New Kent County for having brought in the group that included George Penn. The same area 100 miles from Chesapeake Bay, at the upper end of this York River tributary, was where the Penn family would become established within the quarter century as landholders.

This otherwise rational inference drawn from the thin evidence available disintegrates[13] with the discovery that this same list of twelve persons, including a "George P(D)enny," was used several years earlier for land acquisition in another county. This sham, not an uncommon deed in the loosely-governed backwater of colonial Virginia, along with the obfuscated last name, undermine any reliance on this entry.

Another long-accepted fallacy needs be laid to rest. An Essex County, Virginia deed of 15 January 1699 has long been held forth as first evidence[14] for the presence of the established progenitor of the Penns of Virginia. The name of one witness dangerously resembles that of "John Penn." Matching up capital letters in the albeit old-fangled penmanship pushes past wishful thinking. The last name of the witness is in truth "John Fenn,"[15] a recently married contemporary resident of Richmond County. Whether or not he is the John with this unusual surname baptized 10 November 1670 at St. Olave Church, Hart Street, London (not St. Olave, Southwark), the Fenn name had been in Virginia since at least 1637.

The surname of "Denn" did exist at that time in England. And two instances of it occur in colonial land records of Virginia. However, the first instance from 1637 of a "Christ. Denn,"[16] if the name is again not a misreading of "Penn," likely represents reference to a female, since the given name Christian in that time was used for women. The second instance from 1658 is a nearly illegible entry interpreted in modern times as possibly "Roger Denne,"[17] a notation that may actually refer to the Roger Penn first recorded in 1652. Persons named Denn(e) fail to show up in later in the annals of colonial Virginia. Whether or not these two entries are in actuality references to persons named Penn rather than Denn is a moot point. Arrival dates are too early for either to link with the Penn line of descent to later evolve in Virginia.

Within the decade after notation of this George "Denn" on land records, the names of two other persons of the Penn surname appear as persons transported—"Bath." Penn[18] in 1684 and Robert in 1688. The patentee in each case was associated with coastal Middlesex and with Norfolk County respectively, at the opposite side of the colony from the Mattaponi backwoods where the Penn family eventually appeared.

Opportunities for bonded workers to become established as free citizens would shrink by the beginning of the 1700s. But in the first several decades of colonial life indentured servants did indeed often work off their debt of passage to establish an independent life, as had Robert Penn[19] in the 1620s. A 12 year-old indentured boy named Crispiani Penn[20] arrived in Accomack County, Virginia in 1664. In 23 short years, as he already neared the end of his life, ensuing work as a planter in Northampton County had built up an estate sufficient to provide for his surviving wife and two daughters.

Besides Robert Penn of the 1620s and later arriving Roger Penn, a few other men by the surname, like Crispiani above, who preceded the Immigrant who would found the Penn Family in Virginia, have left evidence of their lives as more than just a name of someone imported from England.

A William Penn, not the Founder of Pennsylvania, was living in James City[21] County during the 1650s. It is he, along with a Thomas Penn, who were in the colony by 1652 as two passengers brought over by Theo. Hoane. In another example of the shady nature of early land dealings, this William's name was used as credit five years later for an Edmond Peeters to take possession of 750 acres for supposedly having transporting a group at that time. Whether he left heirs or not, by the time this William was dead by 1683 twelve acres he had managed to acquire went by grant of the James City court to William Briscoe. As with most names of persons listed on land patent records as those transported, the name of Thomas Penn never surfaces again in this time period in any surviving documents.

Another Penn settler in the generation before the Immigrant progenitor arrived, who made well for himself, but left no descendants, was John Penn of Lancaster County.[22] Court of 12 March 1661/62 declared that "comeing into this Countrey without Indenture [he] is ordered to serve seaven yeres from this daye [as] servt. to the Widd. of Dan. Johnson." Penn dwelled the remaining fifteen years of his life in Lancaster offshoot of (Old) Rappahannock County. He inherited the estate of Richard Simms in 1672/3, who, without wife or offspring, ordained "my well beloved Friend John Pen (*sic*) to be my sole Executor." A short four years later, as his own life drew to a close, a wealthy, but also single and childless John Penn, had in hand a "plantation," servants, livestock, 450 "pounds sterling money of England" and "what else either in Virginia, Mariland (*sic*), England or elsewhere" to bequeath to nine different persons, none with the last name Penn.

Still another co-existent John Penn of mid-seventeenth century Virginia was he of that name imported to Charles City County[23] by 1657. Faint hint puts forth that this particular colonist may have left descendants. This lineage would be the only other Penn pedigree established in colonial Virginia and distinct from the subject of this work. Possibly a grandson, John Penne, one of few with an English surname counted among a French Huguenot majority, lived a few miles away during the 1720s in King William Parish of adjacent Henrico County. Yet within a twenty-five mile radius of where John of the 1650s had disembarked, a John Penn acquired 400 acres in Prince George County late 1749. His spread lay at the head of Mawhiponock Creek on a branch of Bear Swamp, land formerly part of Charles City. The next year, in the same county of Prince George, a Phillip Penn acquired 200 acres from William Hulme, the latter of Amelia County, Virginia. After another quarter century gap in the record, this Phillip Penn leaves a will with several named offspring in the recently created Prince George partition of Brunswick County. The Penn surname would persist there until 1830.

Facts for one London-based John Penn of the 1690s, however, push evidence that he is the Immigrant founder of the lineage traced here.

This John Penn married Elizabeth Spencer[24] 11 October 1691 at Thames-side St. Olave Church in Southwark, Surrey. Colonial Virginia annals make record of an Elizabeth Penn, wife of John by the 1720s. When the Virginia founder, and assumed immigrant, John Penn, Sr.

died around 1741 in Caroline County, Colony of Virginia, his named executrix was named in the will as Elizabeth Penn. At the same time there is a disappearance from the English record of any twosome of the name John and Elizabeth Penn.

Thereafter documentation demonstrates that this John Penn likely left four sons. Following the general, but by no means hard fast English custom common at the time of naming the first son after the father, the eldest of Immigrant John's sons was the John baptized 4 September 1692,[25] also at St. Olave, place name trace[26] of the neighborhood's pre-Norman Danish past. The newborn's mother is listed as Elizabeth. The clerk's scrawled, one-line jotting, crammed between marks for weddings and burials of the same day, notes John Sr.'s work as that of mariner. In fact, two days after his marriage the Royal Navy had taken warrant for the appointment of John Penn to be Boatswain[27] of the *St. Albans Prize*. The *Prize* had earned its name. Some months earlier the vessel entered service in the Royal Navy as booty captured from the French fleet.

Chasing a thin paper trail that leans heavily maritime logs, seaman the Immigrant John Penn connects again to late seventeenth century Virginia as the individual who witnessed a will and later gave deposition[28] in an ensuing case at the court of All Hallows Barking

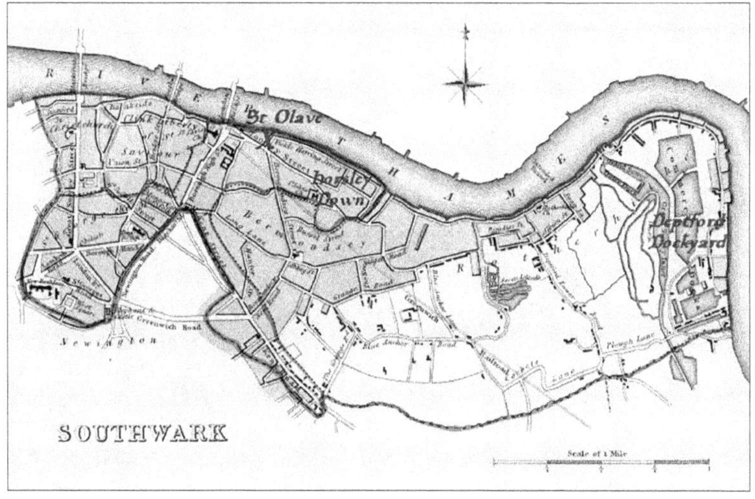

Horseley Down noted on an old map

in London for a Bernard Hunt, fellow mariner who had died at sea in 1693. Details in the deposition of 21 August 1697, pinpoint that "boatswain" Penn, thirty-six years old, "more or less," dwelled at that moment on the Southwark street of Horseley (Horsey) Down (a horse pasture[29] until about the time of John Penn's birth) at the eastern end of the riverbank neighborhood of Bermondsey. The Penns may have

St. Olave Grammar School where the Immigrant may have been a student

St. Olave's Church as it still looked before the Immigrant, John Penn, left England

lived in a brick row house[30] that stood on the short north-south street. A block of them had gone up there in 1662 at the behest of the governors of St. Olave Grammar School to specifically house seamen. A set of stairs[31] put in perhaps during the time of Henry VIII (and still standing!), but already listed as "old" in 1682, allowed watermen a ready path from the street down to the tidal flow of the Thames. A ten-minute walk of about a mile west[32] from Horsley Down along Tooley Street brought one to the door of St. Olave's,[33] one of four like-named churches in London harking back to the Norwegian Olaf Haraldson. A Christian convert, he had helped King Ethelred to drive Danes out of England. His martyrdom in 1029 had forever rooted his sainthood into the English pantheon. Turning right at the corner just beyond this Norman edifice, one came to the entrance of London Bridge[34] and the teeming village that had long since overtaken this only span over the river.

London Bridge at the time the Immigrant's father was born

John Penn's avowal of knowing not only that Hunt had died at sea, but that the ship's Captain Poulson died a few years later at the Chesapeake Bay home in Norfolk County of William Wilson bids the likelihood that this John Penn had been on Virginia soil before settling there. Indeed, folios of maritime business, set forth that the *St. Albans Prize,* having parted company with the *Richmond* east of Cape May, New Jersey arrived at York River,[35] Virginia 7 October 1693. Held over at James River the next summer, Boatswain Penn sent letters to the Navy Board in June and September to make demand for sea stores.

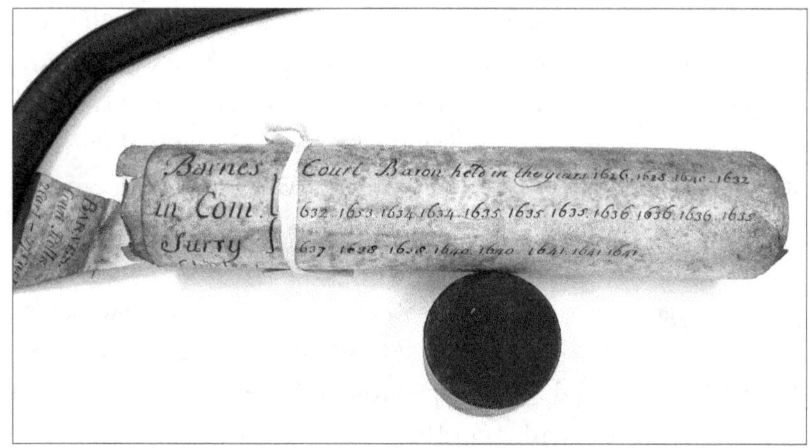

One 17th century document examined

Five months after the deposition in the summer of 1697, during which time he would have been at home in Southwark, John Penn was then posted to Portsmouth[36] Dockyard in Hampshire, ordered on admiralty business to London at least twice at the end of February 1698, before being reassigned to the *Betty* 3 March, as the *St. Albans Prize* went up for sale. The job on the *Betty,* however, never came to pass. The Navy dismissed[37] John Penn on 30 March.

His ousting grew from investigation of a William Baskerville,[38] once a Minister of the Navy. The Navy Board convicted Baskerville of

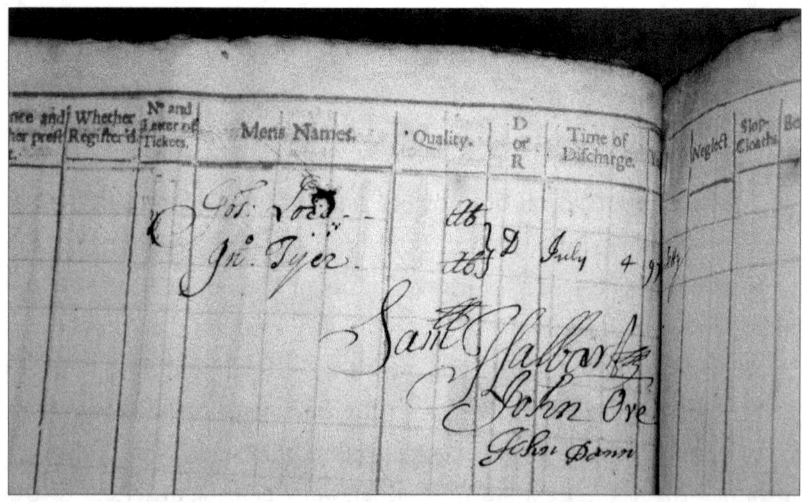

Signature of the presumptive immigrant, John Penn

having forged letters for the *St. Albans Prize,* faking names of sailors never onboard, when the ship had departed Plymouth for Virginia, a scheme to filch money from royal coffers. This scandal involved as well a load of timber missing from the ship's cargo since May 1695. The board immediately pulled the in-process boatswain warrant for Penn's move to the *Betty* when discovered he was "one of them."

British records research expert Kristina Bedford[39] devoted dozens of hours to unindexed, musty, hardbound tomes of Navy correspondence and Pay Books at London's National Archives and Maritime Museum to trace whereabouts in the 1690s of John Penn, boatswain, the Immigrant. She concludes that likely Captain Poulson was in on the fraud, but died before the shenanigans surfaced. John Penn may have acted on captain's orders. This would explain," she feels "why he (Penn) and the Master were dismissed without further prosecution," for what otherwise would have been grounds for court martial. "Court martial records survive, and there are none for John Penn," Bedford reports.

Perhaps pressured by corrupt higher-ups to sign off on ship's correspondence, but without sufficient evidence before the court of forthright wrongdoing, John Penn's career in Royal Navy for the moment came to an end. Suggestion though that Penn may have gotten himself[40] reinstated crops up in Navy Board entries from 1701 and 1702 that list a John Penn as master of the ketch from the warship Barfleur at London's Deptford dock, two miles from home on Horsley Lane.

Soon founding ancestor John Penn corralled means, crew connections and firsthand experience of Virginia to start over in the Colony, like many, leaving "tarnished reputations and economic failures behind."[41] Savings from his Navy pay would have provided for the then-going rate of two to fifteen pounds[42] per person for overseas passage.

With no subsequent trace in Southwark, by 1704 likely it is his name that appears in colonial records, written down as John "Pann," when he paid quit rent[43] that July on 200 acres in King and Queen County, in the Colony of Virginia. That no record exists in Virginia land patent records of his name means that either Penn had rented this tract or had acquired the property through a private party[44] rather than

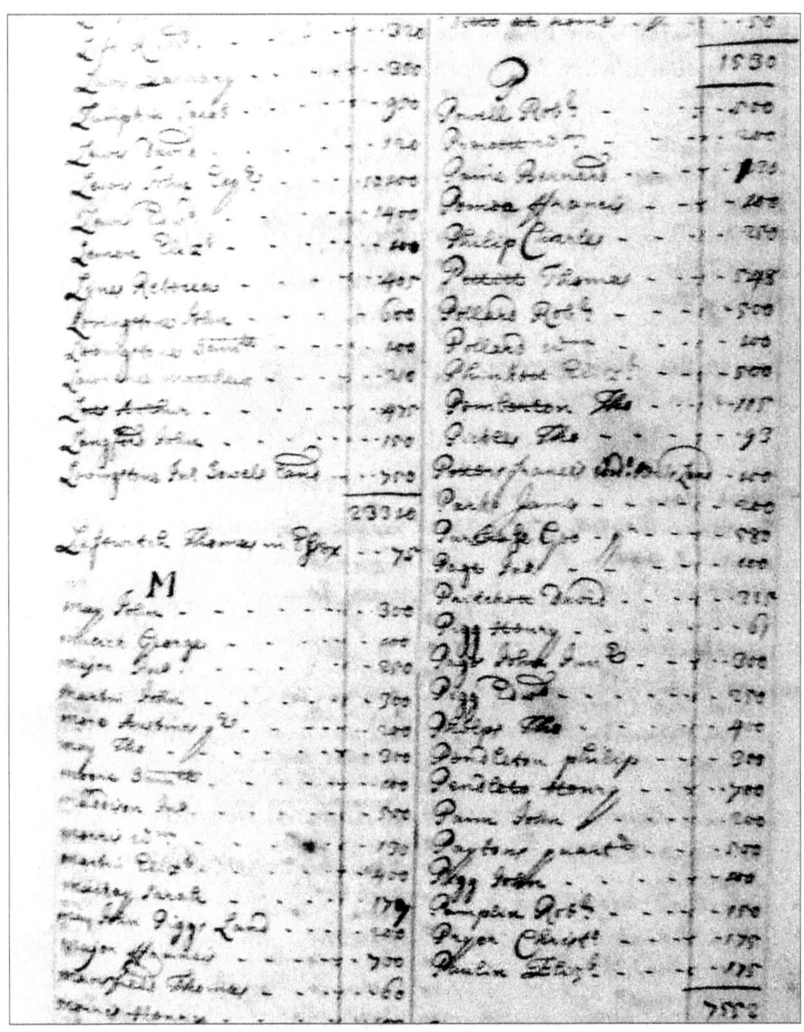

The Immigrant listed as John PANN on the Quit Rent Roll of 1704

through royal decree. Large landholders[45] likely bought to sell small parcels. King and Queen County citizen John Walker, that year serving in the House of Burgesses, topped out, of the total 408 persons taxed, with 6,000 acres. That so many small farms outnumbered the large plantations suggest a middle class had taken root (soon "doomed by slave labor"[46]). Could the upper crust Walker have been the party through whom just-off-the-boat John Penn got his first footing to building a new life?

With some details that had become distorted[47] by time, a liked-named descendant set down family legend in his journal of 1858. He recalled that great-grandfather John Walker[48] had come from England "with a man named Penn some where (*sic*) about the year 1700 or thereabouts." Though it would have been actually the great-great-great surname grandsire who was living when John Penn the Immigrant came to King and Queen, memory of an old connection carried on in the Walker Family tradition. A grandson of John Penn[49] the Immigrant, Abraham Penn, would buy his first acreage in Amherst County, Virginia in 1767 from the journal writer's grandfather, Baylor Walker.

CHAPTER 3

TO VIRGINIA

For the ocean crossing,[1] daily diet relied mainly on bread, oatmeal and molasses, with Sunday allowance of meat, peas and port. Vinegar[2] countered scurvy. Jamestown founder, John Smith,[3] mentioned stores of beef, pork, oil, aqua vitae, beer, butter cheese, biscuits, meal and oatmeal. Though some ships' captains may have been stingy with rations, the intention remained to feed passengers well enough so that they arrived healthy[4] enough to work. Masters at sur-

17th Century English merchant ship, by Wenceslaus Holler

vival, sailors adroitly beefed up the menu. Using what must have been a spear-like tool, sea dogs snagged with a "fish-gigg"[5] anything from fish, birds, seaweed and dolphins to seals, sharks and turtles. There was little drinking water[6] to be had, which is why voyagers used hats to catch rainwater. To head off ill effects of too much time under deck with the noise and stench of livestock,[7] every four hours those being transported had to go above to stand watch with sailors.

The company of seamen would have rattled the grit of even the most hardened wayfarer. Brusque and coarse-talking, their bearing swayed steeply between self-possessed capability to unbridled recklessness. With faces scarred and wrinkled by unrelenting exposure to nature, work-related hazards left many maimed.[8] Bodies gnarled with missing fingers, crooked backs and bellies bulged with hernia deepened the seamy setting onboard. The unyielding drudgery and hovering presence of death over life at sea gave rise to belief in forebodings and spooks and of scorn toward the church. Much of the swearing wafting on deck was unadulterated blasphemy.

Romanticized vision of an 18th century English sailor taking leave of his family

"Jack Tar,"[9] eighteenth-century English slang for sailor, first took to sea as a teen or twenty-something. Rarely out of a sense of adventure, many lower-class youths, whether from the country or from London, ended up as mariners when abducted by press gangs or shut out of craft apprenticeships. As long as he survived a sailor would earn good, if at times delayed, pay. But the thinking of the day held that "those who would go to sea for pleasure would go to hell for pastime."

The first sight of Virginia young John Penn and his shipmates saw, as it entered Chesapeake Bay, was likely Cape Charles at the southern tip of the peninsula known as the Eastern Shore. Another thirty miles and the heaving ship moored at the settlement of York (just as the place was taking on the name Yorktown), at the mouth of the liked-named river. Having set sail from Plymouth,[10] England 30 July 1693, the *St. Albans Prize*, on which John Penn served as boatswain, arrived at York River 8 October.

Under the ship's captain the pecking order[11] lined up as master, mate, carpenter, boatswain, gunner, quartermaster, maybe a cook and four or five sailors. Like the mate, the boatswain acted as a foreman.[12]

He may have had the duty to call the crew to work, but his main job centered on maintaining the rigging—lines, cables, sails and anchors. John Penn's responsibilities included ordering supplies. At this time the ever-in demand position of boatswain paid about two-and-a-half pounds monthly, fifty percent more during wartime. Penn's pay[13] for the first ten months of 1691 amounted to a predictable 25 pounds, 1 shilling and 5 pence. Little more than a year later, still during peacetime, he had copped a take-home of 124 pounds, 7 shillings and 1 pence.

While the *St. Albans Prize* was stationed at Long Reach in England October 1692 to February 1693, her crew was made up of approximately twenty five Englishmen,[14] among them Commander Christopher King, boatswain John Penn, gunner Ralph Hindson, carpenter William Fange, cook Peter Phillips and sailors Francis Lee, Michael Short, William Ward, Andrew Ward, John Potter and William Waterford.

With so many creeks and rivers indenting the coast of Virginia the lay of the land impeded establishment of fixed ports. Ships from overseas in the early days of the colony dropped anchor at six makeshift landings:[15] Accomack, Lower James River, Upper James River, York River, Rappahannock and South Potomac. Mariners harbored at Lower James quartered in Hampton, those at York River in Yorktown and those at Upper James in Williamsburg.

The *St. Albans Prize* may have continued beyond York to the Mattaponi's confluence with the Pamunkey River, to dock at Port Richmond West Plantation, near present-day West Point. Seventy years earlier the Indian town of Cinquotek stood on the same spot. With the natives now pushed to north of the York River, former colonial Governor John West had himself acquired the 3,000-acre tract twenty-five years earlier "for [having provided] the transportation of forty and nine persons to the colony." John Penn took in the sights, not even thinking at the time he would someday dwell near the Mattaponi. With yet little buildup along its shores, the mostly tidal river features to this day "tea-colored water,[16] green marshes and spots of nearly white sand on its bottom and banks."

The first sight of the unspoiled Chesapeake landscape must have appeared "like a forest in water"[17] to the wayfarers. The sea of trees would have soothed body and soul wracked by half-starvation, nausea and homesickness of the weeks-long Atlantic crossing. But the region could be deadly.[18] Mosquitos and raw sewage endemic to the Bay led to summer epidemics of malaria and typhoid.

Settlers soon discovered that the nearby highlands were not only healthier, but gave some feel of home, with quiet estuarine expanses bounded by low wooded hills. Here, in the upper reaches of the Mattaponi River, John Penn of Southwark, England would start a new life.

The then unbridled expanse allowed settlers plenty of space. At the time of his arrival, the entire population of the Chesapeake, an area half the size of England, would have matched that in one London parish alone. The Algonquian chiefdom, Tsenacomoco,[19] had stretched from the sea inlets of the south bank of the Potomac to the James River and inward to the base of the Piedmont foothills. In a hundred years this aboriginal homeland had irretrievably morphed into a British province. The original "ancient general Burroughs,"[20] Henrico, James

City, Charles City and Elizabeth City, alone spread over thousands of acres 100 miles and more up the James River. "Towns"—scattered clusters with no more than a church, barns and a few houses—lay few and far between encompassing plantations and woods. So much elbow room may even have curbed the development of towns. One contemporary observer put forth that early Virginia colonists "had a taste for living solitary and unsociable (lives)[21] . . . confused and dispersed." A world away from familiar stomping grounds, newcomers would certainly have been homesick for markets, fairs, theater and inns. As scholar James Horn points out, "Getting used to[22] the absence of significant aspects of everyday life that were taken for granted in England was probably the most difficult part of adapting to conditions in the Chesapeake."

Gloucester Point,[23] a plantation on the bank opposite York, typified a settlement of the time. The planter's house occupied the upper central portion of the community, with other small farms, a tavern and a church scattered amid fields on a mostly wooded peninsula. Tidewater plantations were in fact laid out on lines of an English manor—one large house surrounded by servants' quarters. Such a system had been in place in England since before the Norman Invasion and particularly entrenched in Wessex, whence a fair share of migrants to Virginia had come. An enclosed quarter acre provided protection for settlers and livestock in case of attack.

Earliest structures of settlers relied on primitive wattle-and-daub[24] construction of sticks covered in clay set between posts and covered with thatched roofs. Floors were of dirt and interior lighting non-existent.

From a shaky beginning at Jamestown in 1607, the colony of Virginia had slowly taken hold, with a population of now nearly 40,000 persons by the time John Penn set foot in the Colony. But Jamestown had teetered on the brink of disappearing for the first forty years of its existence. First arrivals were a lazy lot,[25] former town dandies balking at the very idea of crop-raising. They pushed the work off onto starved settlers, many of whom who fled the labor camp conditions

Artist's interpretation of Jamestown, Virginia in the first decade of its existence

Aerial View of Jamestown, 1614

to maroon themselves among the Indians. Mutiny hung in the air[26] born of the tyranny of the so-called gentlemen class. If three resupply ships just arrived with Lord De La Warr from England June of 1610 had not intercepted haggard Jamestown survivors sailing downstream to head home, the colony would have evaporated as had the earlier attempt at nearby Roanoke and of the Popham Colony in Maine.

Once founding colonist John Rolfe[27] hit upon a viable strain of tobacco, to establish a cash crop for export, the colony commenced a

Harvesting tobacco in colonial Virginia

viable economy. Shiploads of colonists, nearly all from England, began docking every few weeks.

Tobacco was soon turning a high price in England, followed very closely for a while by sassafras.[28] The frantic crush to cash in on profits, and a rising work force, launched the haphazard stripping of land. Each new clearing inch-by-inch encroached on tribal lands. Borderlines were vague. The world of the natives and of the settlers "permeated each other."[29]

Comings and goings from each side flowed instinctively, the English visiting Indian settlements and natives traipsing between plantations. Descriptions survive of colonists feeding Indian neighbors and lodging them in their own sleeping areas. Engulfed with Europeans and their trappings culture in the Chesapeake "was no longer purely Indian[30] . . . neither was Jamestown purely English."

But any peaceful relations engendered by Rolfe's marriage to native, barely teen-aged Pocahontas, and by this at-first, easy comingling between the races soon dissipated. The burgeoning presence of white people and the unceasing squeeze on the Powhatan people's land led to two major bloody uprisings. The uncle of Pocahontas, Chief Opechancanough, having failed diplomatically to stem the growing and increasingly aggressive English tide, set out to obliterate England's grand business venture of establishing settlement in the New World. Fanning the flames of discontent[31] among his up-

Indians and Colonists; an imagined scene from Virginia, 1692

rooted people, he engineered in 1622 a massacre of one-third of the settlers.

Again, almost twenty-two years to the day later, another Indian assault, instigated by a now elderly Opechancanough, had lesser effect on the now-doubled immigrant population, with a tenth of colonists killed. Opechancanough's soon-subsequent capture and murder set the stage for three decades of peace. But it also marked the rapid dissipation of Native culture.

The transplanted Old World society into which John Penn the Immigrant landed was equally fraught. The social inequalities of the old country persisted in Virginia. Though royalty stayed in England, the Virginia gentry, derived from landed, but not noble, lineage, perpetuated a system dependent on "deference from inferiors[32] and condescension from the elite." The top tier of Tidewater society, occupied by the Berkeley and Byrd families, lorded over a majority composed heavily of indentured servants and landless tenants, with their "damn-you-get-out-of-the-way gallop."[33] They welded power through debt.

No one could plant a crop without credit. Commoners were forced to borrow tools, seed, livestock from gentlemen planters. Loans were paid back in tobacco, the basis of the entire economy.

In contrast to English middle class-derived New England colonists, most early Virginians, as seen, originated at the "bottom of the middle[34] ([often] rural) ranks" or from the "unfortunates of the squalid teeming underworld . . ." Living under dire circumstances many persons were forced to sign for indenture, "more sinned against than sinning."[35]

Though attempts have long existed to whitewash the seamy origins of many white Virginians, the truth is that "instead of being composed of[36] the best elements of English society [the population] was composed to a considerable extent of the worst." At least fifteen percent of settlers were prisoners, whether men, women or children, shunted from English jails, often for the most minor of offences. "Descent from the *Mayflower*[37] is stressed by genealogists; but the fact is forgotten that many unknowing present-day Americans of colonial antecedents derive their New World beginnings from the consignments sent in duress."

Historian Bernard Bailyn, in his vast survey of colonial America, *The Barbarous Years: The Conflict of Civilizations, 1600-1675,* also points out how later generations would "gentrify" the peopling of British North America: " . . . but there was nothing genteel about it.[38] It was a brutal encounter—brutal not only between the Europeans and the native peoples, despite occasional efforts at accommodation, and between Europeans and Africans, but among the Europeans themselves . . ." Surfeit riff-raff offloaded across the sea existed solely to bolster Old World money. English colonies served to widen the empire as well as to relieve social ills at home.

Reprieve from prison or even from the gallows meant "pardon" to be sent into bondage to the colonies. Felons were usually freed in seven years. But that space of time might be beyond even the strongest to survive. Often fed on nothing more than maize bread and water, Virginia colonial court records are stuffed with references to cases of abuse by masters against indentured servants. Whereas a maltreated laborer in

England could flee to another region, the essentially enslaved bonded colonist had little option for taking flight. Recent evidence to surface confirms colonial account of "Whereas the private[39] burial of servants & others give occasion of much scandal against diverse persons and sometimes not undeservedly of being guilty of their deaths. . . ."

A shallow grave[40] unearthed in 2001 at the foundation of a colonial-era storage cellar in Anne Arundal County, Maryland contained the skeleton of a European-born young male. A large piece of ceramic milk pan lay over the chest that had been used to dig the hole into which the flexed corpse had been placed. Lab examination of the remains revealed back trauma, malnutrition, dental infection and fracture of the right wrist. Forensic experts concluded that "the hidden circumstances of his burial and evidence in his bones suggest abuse and wrongful death." Wracked with illness, the boy's ensuing weakness and inability to work further must have enraged the sadistic landowner into a murderous frenzy.

The brutal lives of colonial English "white slaves" mirrors the apparcnt and abiding cxpcndablc naturc of humankind. Many, likc thc battered youth whose remains were found in the ancient cellar, whose name history has seen fit to erase, died in poverty and obscurity. But a multitude did indeed survive servitude to at least become modest freeholders, if not independent planters.

Three classes of indentured servants existed: prisoners, kidnap victims, and freewillers (those voluntarily serving out the cost of their passage). John Penn the Immigrant from St. Olave's parish in Southwark, however, seems to have arrived unencumbered by any contract of servitude. By 1704 he was paying rent on acreage in Virginia. These circumstances thus insinuate John Penn likely stepped off a ship from London with means, and connections, to begin homesteading.

A potential peer group cousin of John Penn may have been the Edward Penn[41] appearing as owner of 100 acres seventy miles to the north in Baltimore County, Maryland. Of the fourteen English baptism entries for boys named Edward Penn during the span of 1660 to 1680, all but one maintain an ongoing presence in their birth locales during the next two and three decades, as traced through baptism/

marriage records. The sole exception is for the Edward born at Putney in Surrey. This parish lies within a few miles west of adjacent Thames south side parish of Bermondsey in Southwark, whence John the Immigrant hailed. Descendants of Edward were those post-Revolution Penns who would settle in northern Ohio River Valley counties of Kentucky, somewhat before the Virginia branch would migrate to the south central region of that state.

Contemporary observers saw 17th century Virginia, with perhaps of a bit of jaundiced eye, as a place where "none but those of the meanest quality[42] and corruptest lives went . . ." Travelers observed a weak plebian work ethic in the humid Virginia summers and a frivolous upper class that frittered itself into heavy debt. "The climate and external appearance[43] of the country conspire to make them indolent, easy, and good-natured: extremely fond of society, and much given to convivial pleasures."

Durand de Dauphine,[44] a French Huguenot exile, visited the Rappahannock Valley in 1684. Looked upon as a possible recruiter for settlers from his homeland, locals hospitably buttered up the foreigner. At a wedding celebration in Gloucester County Dauphine was placed at the head table crammed with twenty four people, who gorged half-a-day on meat of every description. The regaled Frenchman observed that "they did nothing afterwards for the rest of the day and all night, but drink, smoke, sing and dance." Among the hung-over partiers the next morning, he "did not see one who could stand straight."

By the time John Penn the Immigrant arrived in Virginia, economic conditions in England[45] had begun to rise out of the slump that had commenced some sixty years earlier. Agricultural output (and wages) had ramped up to a level that the nation's labor force was needed at home. The ensuing ebb of workers to Virginia and steadily shrinking pool of the indentured as these servants worked off their terms of service spurred the shift to reliance on African slaves.

At the same time the most desirable lowlands had been taken. Some researchers note that already colonists were moving on to greener pastures in the Carolinas and in Delaware. Others were beginning to trickle toward and over the Fall Line, river rapids that split the coastal plain from the Piedmont at the foot of the Blue Ridge Mountains and which prevented boat travel farther into the interior. Based on where his sons held land, John the Immigrant would have settled along the still waters of the Mattaponi River, at the threshold of the surging Fall Line, in the extreme west end of terrain that yet lay within King and Queen County, turf carved out of New Kent County a decade earlier. The original county, set up in 1654, girded territory that had taken in western parts of both the Lower Peninsula and Middle Peninsula of the upper Chesapeake. That section of the Middle Peninsula on the north bank of the Mattaponi became King and Queen County. Since Penn property by default would become part of the future Caroline County, a jurisdiction to lie at the western extreme of the river, the original stakes set down by Immigrant John would have been located well into the hinterlands. Like hundreds of other families, the first Penns of Virginia lived in isolation.

Acreage spread over vast areas difficult to fathom nowadays, the nearest neighbors five or ten miles distant. Attendance at churches in the woods and sporadic contact with agents or with big plantation owners, who marketed the tobacco crop, would have been coupled with recent news. However, pastors often had to contend with half-full pews and children not "catechized"[46] due to the remoteness of the Upper Chesapeake.

Gatherings as well, whether for wedding or funeral, were vital to break up loneliness of life off the beaten path. Overindulgence was the core[47] of the cure. Though Virginians ate very little bread, they were avid meat-eaters, particularly of venison, which often ended up in pies as well. Not having wine, they devised their own libation, which consisted of a mixture of beer, brandy, sugar, nutmeg and cinnamon. And everyone smoked, "men, women, girls and boys[48] from the age of seven years . . . while working or idling," even outside the church before and after the preaching.

When now-colonist John Penn settled up the York River, Indians were still stalking colonists.[49] Most strife involved hit-and-run raids inflicted by displaced hostile Iroquois from the north rather than on-

Carving a niche in the wilderness of Virginia

going warfare with dwindling numbers of local Algonquian or Souian natives. But encounters could erupt into outright slaughter. From *The London Times*[50] 19 July 1700: "[A]bout 20 miles above Middle Plantation (on the verge to soon being renamed Williamsburg), upon York River, a Party of Indians came upon a Planter's House, killed all therein, and afterwards plundered and burnt the House, as also 2 large tobacco Ware-houses."

Pirates were known on occasion to slink up rivers and raid settlements as well. Non-human menace took the form of rattlesnakes and wolves, atavistic perils for which the old country provided no experience.

Besides the nagging unease of what lurked in forest shadows, a restlessness must have pervaded the at-times overwhelming woodland stillness. Dreary, mud-soaked downtime days of dank weather and long nights made all the more black by the spectral hooting of an owl led to much rumination. The mood, worsened by human nature's abiding uncertainty about the future, was one of longing. Nearly a century since the settlement of Jamestown, wistfulness for England resided as a communal state of mind. Ships brought letters, lace, tea and other magical trinkets from across the sea to briefly lift the doldrums of rough-hewn colonial monotony.

Historian David Hockett Fischer ventures the thought[51] that this anxious nostalgia for the bustle of Albion's shores fostered provincial detest of persons and things not English. Francis Louis Michel,[52] a Swiss visitor to Virginia in 1702 lost his way while trekking on foot through Essex County. When two locals spotted the wanderer and heard his alien accent, they took him for an escaped indentured servant and apprehended him. When Michel was able to provide the justice of the peace with the name of the ship on which he had arrived and of its captain, he was set free to continue his perambulations. Michel later recounted his surprise that the poor in Virginia provided travelers with better food than did those well-off.

The sound of day-to-day discourse[53] itself would have soothed subliminally any fanciful hankering for the homeland. Voices in the Colony echoed quite clearly the speech of southern England. Grammatical artifacts of this region sprouted in the Colony along with the tobacco and sassafras: "he was took bad; he was drove to it; I be; you be; she ain't; I hain't." Also a direct import was such standard vocabulary of "innards, lay-off, wud (for with), bide, dis and dat, mess of greens, moonshine, passel, skillet, chittlins, no-count, dawg (dog), poke and whopper." In contrast to the clipped, nasally rasp of New England, "Virginia's speech was a soft, slow, melodious drawl that came not from the nose, but from the throat." For a feel of the talk of Penn forebears a generation or two removed from England consider ha-alf for half, gyarden for garden, ke-er for care, holp for help, fuust for first, Aah'm for I'm, acrost for across, wid or wud for with and yaller for yellow. Thomas Jefferson's daughter, Patsy, wrote of the stained-glass "winders" that she had seen in Paris, forensic trace of the Virginia soul of a voice long-since vanished.

It would be near the time of the Revolution that a distinct divide would arise[54] between pronunciation of the Mother Country and that of the colonies. Namely, the dropping of the "r" sound when not at the beginning of a word swept most of England in the late 1770s. This key shift in speech grew out of English *nouveau riche* commoners' need to clearly separate themselves from the working classes. This fad became entrenched as "received pronunciation" or the "Queen's English." The English were now saying in their newly acquired non-rhotic accent "hahd wintuh" instead of the former rhotic "hard winter." The affectation seeped into certain American regions, namely port cities which felt strong British influence after the Revolution, such as, obviously, Boston, New York, Richmond and Savannah. The American accent has changed but little. That of England has undergone sharp enough change that pre-colonial English might well understand more clearly descendants who ended up across the pond.

Dwellings at all community levels cloned the British pattern in terms of materials and layout. Not at all unlike the floor plan described earlier for London abodes of the time, a French eyewitness to Virginia in 1687 reported an unyielding pattern, no matter the social class, of two rooms on the ground floor and two or three on a second story, the entire structure divided in the middle by a stairway. This "hall and parlor" design[55] intrinsic to Virginia society was squeezed into a foundation of sixteen-by-twenty feet. Most often built of wood, these residences of the time usually stood with a chimney at either or both gable ends. A larger plantation mansion depended on this same blueprint, as preserved at Mount Vernon. The home of Patriot Abraham Penn,

Buildings standing at the time of the Immigrant's arrival: [above] Christ's Cross, New Kent County, and [below] Warburton House, James City County

Poplar Grove[56] in Patrick County, Virginia, existed as a three-story version of this essentially medieval pattern passed down to the first colonists. The no-nonsense, two-tiered box, cleaved by a set of stairs in the middle, persisted through the 1800s in the farm houses of Penn descendants who settled in the hilly backwoods of Kentucky.[57]

As based on the pre-Norman English manor[58] configuration, even smaller farms included out buildings. These outlying structures provided space for sheltering indentured servants (often referred to as "Christian slaves,")[59] and negro slaves, as well as for cooking and for the drying of tobacco. Though doors of Virginia homes were open to strangers, field slaves were forbidden to enter. At the same time, house slaves slept in the bed chamber with their owner.

Furniture included at most bed rolls, benches, a table, chests for storage and pewter and wooden dishes. Bed frames and chamber pots were rare. People relieved themselves outside near the walls of the rickety dwelling called home. For all the hardships immigrants had endured just to come to the colonies, nearly all ended up with a standard of living at or below the lowest in England.[60]

Interior of a colonial farmhouse. Most abodes were likely not so cozy

Darkness of night was eased only by smoldering, smelly candles made of animal fat. The absence of artificial light brought sleep to most as the sun set. After this "first sleep,"[61] reawakening of an hour or two arrived around midnight. This roused interlude supplied a break for praying, writing, urinating or fornicating until sleep returned before dawn and another day's labor.

Though writing of the period of United States history directly after the Revolution, author Daniel Walker Howe's description of day-to-day existence in pre-industrial America befits equally well survival in colonial times. "People spent most of their waking hours[62] working, with scant opportunity for the development of individual talents and interests unrelated to farming." As can be imagined, clothes and shoes were hard to come by. Few owned more than a change of outfit and many walked barefoot. White people rightly so believed[63] the sun bad for the skin and swaddled themselves even during the sweltering summers in heavy apparel. Preparing bath water was labor-intensive itself. People settled for a sponge bath or a dip in a nearby creek as their world-weary lives allowed. The populace in its entirety stank. Whiff of a modern-day street vagrant could conjure a step back in time in this regard.

Skeletal remains of Jamestown[64] and Maryland colonists reverberate the toll of their physical existence. Spur-riddled spines, rotten teeth and hobbling, badly-healed fractures cut across societal levels. Analysis of wisps of head hair yet clinging to the skull of an older woman, who died at St. Mary's City, Maryland in the 1690s, betray that her system was laced with arsenic, side effect of then *en vogue* medications. A late teenaged male, who died of a bone-splintering musket lead shot wound to the lower leg early on at Jamestown, stood in life at five feet, nine inches tall, ". . . slightly taller than the average[65] Englishman of the period."

Humankind's legacy of predictably shortened lifespan to result from an earthly domain of overwork, exposure to the elements, food of precarious supply and quality and lack of hygiene persisted in early Virginia. This predicament shaped cultural mores. The ever-presence of death gave rise to a tradition of elaborate funerals. Serial marriage, as another example, stood as tenet of society. The term "now wife,"[66] to differentiate from past and future ones, occupied a place in standard parlance. Coupled with the high child death rate, family cohesion came to rest in many cases more on a collective of step-relatives,

"In some secluded corner . . ." Penn Family Cemetery, Patrick County, Virginia

orphans and servants rather than on a nuclear family. This mindset of extended kin carried over to private burials, "in some secluded corner[67] of the farm or plantation." The will of the John Penn of Old Rappahannock from the late 1670s, outlined above, personifies strong ties beyond consanguinity.

But bloodlines remained of utmost importance. The hard-fought struggle to acquire property lodged heavily in clan memory. This was especially true for descendants of indentured servants. Preserving land holdings motivated staunch practices. "Children of the elite[68] were bred to one another in a manner not unlike dogs and horses," reported one foreign observer in 17th century Virginia. Though Puritans in the north had forbade the practice, Virginians carried on with the English custom of cousin marriage as a device for preserving freehold. A Virginia colonial explained to a visiting Englishman "either by blood or marriage,[69] we are almost all related . . ."—

CHAPTER 4

Four Sons

Far removed from the assiduous record-keeping of Church of England clerks, account of baptisms, marriages and deaths mostly lapsed in the backwater of colonial Virginia. Of any parish entries created by the far-flung, tiny churches to spring up in the Chesapeake during the 1600s, only a trifling sample survive. In fortuitous instances, pivotal life events survive in isolated bible records, account books or in provincial matters mentioned in English documents.

By then established in Virginia, lawyers would likely have testified on behalf of John the Immigrant and Elizabeth Penn in a Chancery Court case of 1710, when they, along with her father and a brother, John Spencer, filed suit against Spencer[1] and other named relatives/associates over dispute of property in Huntspill and Burnham, Somerset, England. But lack of further filing activity insinuates the case never went to court.

Property transactions, however, remained of utmost importance on the western Atlantic fringe of European civilization. These exchanges, whether preserved in land deeds, wills or in court case books, add up to the backbone database for tracing colonial ancestors.

Those shires of New Kent, King and Queen and Caroline County, where the Penn family first settled, share the onerous legacy, with most other original eastern districts, as "burned record counties."[2] This ill-boding designation refers chiefly to catastrophic document loss incurred by Union Army destruction of court houses during the Civil War. But other acts of theft, vandalism and arson by local citizens, recorded back as early as the 1700s, affect most counties. Caroline enjoys the lucky happenstance of survival of circuit court chancery copies of wills and deeds, as well as of court order books.

Gleanings from both public and private records of the time make possible the determination of the spouse and of four sons of John Penn the Immigrant. First evidence surfaces in the registry pages of the bible of Ambrose and Frances Taylor Madison,[3] he the son of immigrant John Maddison. Maddison[4] had established presence in Gloucester County, Virginia by 1654. Ambrose was the grandfather of fourth United States president, James Madison, Jr. Ambrose names an Elizabeth Penn as one of two godmothers of his children James and Frances, the latter born 6 March 1726/7.

From the same time the personal account book[5] of Ambrose Madison provides the first solid reference to offspring of John Penn. Among the names of his Madison relatives and Taylor in-laws, Ambrose records also that his business dealings in 1726 and 1727 included John Penn Sr., John Penn Jr., and George Penn.

Another contemporaneous proceeding suggests family ties.[6] John Chew, married to a Martha Taylor, deeded 614 acres in bordering Spotsylvania County 5 March 1727 to John and George Penn, "of Parish of Drysdale and County of King and Quenn (*sic*)" on the Mattaponi River, adjacent to land of namesake and recently supplanted lieutenant Governor Alexander Spotswood. Among witnesses to this transfer were James Taylor and John Penn, the latter likely John, the Immigrant.

Not until after the formation of Caroline County in 1728 from westernmost sections of Essex, King and Queen and King William does initial reference of another Penn son come to light. A Caroline Court Order book item of 10 May 1733 states, "Lucy, a negro girl[7] belonging to Joseph Penn is adjudged to be 12 years old."

The fourth son[8] makes his first appearance in written history eight years later, at the time of the death of John Penn the Immigrant. In Caroline court held 8 May 1741 his last and will and testament was presented by Elizabeth Penn and Moses Penn. The court book entry details that the now no-longer surviving will had been "proved by the oath of John Taylor . . . and Edward Taylor" and that the executors "had entered into Bond of Law with George Penn their surety."

Though marriage listings for colonial Virginia exist, record of unions for the Penns of Caroline are absent in these annals. Strictly from his own probate activity, wife of John Jr. is known to be Mary, her surname not having been ascertained. Tradition holds that George Penn married Ann, daughter of Charles Fleming and Susannah Tarleton. But this "rumor" is unfounded, since Ann Fleming, daughter of Charles, shows up in records as having married Josias Payne. Whatever her maiden surname, Ann Penn would outlive first husband George Penn by nearly forty years.

Younger brothers[9] Joseph and Moses Penn married daughters of John Taylor and Catherine Pendleton Taylor, Joseph to Mary 3 Feb 1734/5 and Moses to Catherine 4 July 1739. These dates were entered, along with many others, in the bible of their mutual father-in-law, John Taylor.

Whether the family of John and Elizabeth Penn included daughters will likely never be known. Through their four sons alone thousands of descendants, bearing the surname or not, have scattered to filter out of the Tidewater homeland over the ensuing 300 years.

By this time in the early half of the eighteenth century, with the flow of English immigrants considerably slowed, the old headright system of acquiring land for transporting immigrants into the Colony was giving way to conveyance by treasury right.[10] For the cost of five shillings paid to the secretary of the colony's land office, the colonist could purchase the right to patent fifty acres. An additional 100 acres could be bought for each tithable person (i.e., indentured servants and negro slaves) living on the homestead.

The Penns may have had some pull with then-reigning royal ruling governor Sir William Gooch. George Penn[11] received a relatively large tract of 1,000 acres in contiguous Spotsylvania County 28 Sep 1728 at the base of the Blue Ridge Mountains. But as Caroline County historian T.E. Campbell lays out in plain language, "the favorites,"[12] who managed, "by hook or crook," to bend homestead laws, to acquire huge tracts in one fell swoop, were only "minor gentry, who had been lucky enough to worm their way into favor" of those in current power under royal appointment. The prospect of taking possession of the vast and remote parcel to seat ownership must have soon proved daunting. George deeded the land[13] two years later to a David Williams.

The Mattaponi, "an at-times shallow, twisting rivulet"

At the same time of these property dealings the House of Burgesses was setting up the County of Caroline.[14] The nearly landlocked position of King and Queen County parishes of Drysdale and St. Margaret's forced local planters to rely on the at-times shallow, twisting rivulet that was the Mattaponi as their sole trade route south to port on the York River. Life would become much easier sending goods overland to market through Port Royal nearby to the northeast on the Rappahannock. However, such a path would have to cut through dense physical and political obstacles that at that moment took in parts of King William, Essex and King and Queen Counties. This sore need to lay down a road directly to Port Royal fueled a grassroots movement to establish a new county as a means to loosen these constraints. Williamsburg at first ignored petition from citizens of Drysdale and St. Margaret's for a new county. But when light dawned for one faction of Burgesses that the commoners' appeal could be appropriated to gerrymander rivals from office, the idea gained traction. Action moved fast after the bill was introduced early in February 1727 to create a new county from the heads (i.e., western ends) of Essex, King and Queen and King William. Caroline County, named for German-born Caroline of Ansbach, the popular, then-reigning Queen of Great Britain, as wife of King George II, became Virginia's newest county on 12 March that year.

Though a Penn was not among the eighteen men Governor Gooch appointed that spring as Caroline's first king's magistrates, their close associate and family friend Ambrose Madison did receive such distinction.

The first order of business for the new county was to carry through with the very inspiration for its existence, that of construction of a

A hogshead

main arterial, through the heart of Caroline, to Port Royal. Three types of roads then existed—bridle path, cart trail and rolling road. The latter provided for moving a hogshead,[15] an enormous oak barrel used to store and transport liquid, foodstuffs or, most often, tobacco. Weighing nearly 1,000 pounds, the rounded contours of these huge casks made easy their movement over rolling roads to warehouses. Perpetually soggy areas in the Mattaponi Valley hampered construction on the road to Port Royal, which ultimately took four years to complete.

The influence of a local patrician, Robert Beverley,[16] dated back nearly twenty years. His estate, Beverley Park, lay near the head of the Mattaponi in northwestern King and Queen County. By this time retired, Beverley, of the same generation as John Penn the Immigrant had built his fame and fortune from holding high ranking chief clerkships and serving in the House of Burgesses. He settled political scores, in which he had lost land and office, by publishing at London in 1705 his *The History and Present State of Virginia, In Four Parts*. The book not only detailed history and life in the Colony, but provided the soapbox for Beverley to expose current corruption maintained by Beverley's main adversary, Governor Francis Nicholson. Beverley's legacy was set. His tome, the first published history of a British colony written by a born North American, set in motion Queen Anne's booting Nicholson out to replace him with reform Governor Alexander Spotswood.

Beverley, though a part of the elite, in essence opposed the control of rich planters over politics of the Colony. The off-the-record agenda of the ruling clique, headed by the Byrd and Berkeley families, was to end migration of whites to Virginia. The grand scheme envisioned control of all land and importation of African slave labor. Caroline County historian T.E. Campbell contends that Beverley's *History* "saved Virginia and the entire South from becoming another Haiti . . ."[17]

Beverley's wealth and triumphs gave him the power to indulge in "primitive baronial splendor"[18] that included viticulture. It also accommodated his aim to decide the ilk of the populace living near him. Owning at least 30,000 acres in King and Queen, Beverley hand-picked settlers to whom to sell his excess holdings from those who were like-minded free thinkers, innately at odds with the treacherous, blue-blood aristocracy. Beverley granted deeds to not only German immigrants, whom he had invited to the Mattaponi Valley, and colonists moving in from just over the Rappahannock, but to some residents who, like John Penn Sr., had lived in the north end of St. Stephen's Parish from before Beverley took up living there.

The Beverley mindset likewise contended that the church was further means to oppress the poor. One can arrive at the conclusion that those who bought land in the Beverley enclave must have also agreed with their benefactor on this point. Soon after Robert Beverley died in 1722, his political pull removed that had formerly blocked such subdivision, authorities halved St. Stephen's Parish, the upper part now to be called Drysdale Parish.[19] This annexation gave rise to an inconvenient b-shape sector. With no center, towns and trading posts failed to develop in Drysdale. The parish's sole church, Joy Creek Church, lay near

Eastern Shore Chapel, dating to 1754

Caroline County's eastern border with King and Queen, at least thirty miles from its uppermost northern stem. This isolation, if not apathy alone, may have early on led to authorities abandoning enforcement of mandatory church attendance. Where consistent tracking of such an infraction is plain to see in court order books for Caroline's sister parishes of St. Mary's and St. Margaret's, it is non-existent in Drysdale.

Twenty years later, shortly before the death of George Penn, with population growth, improved roads and apparently changed public attitude, George's brother, Moses, and William Pendleton oversaw the construction of Drysdale's new Ivey Church[20] near Marocossic Creek.

Time has blurred the exact boundaries[21] that once hemmed Drysdale Parish. Most certainly the locale took in high ground in King and Queen County, starting a few miles northwest of the modern day community of St. Stephen's Church at Biscoe. Robert Beverley described his Park estate as occupying the riverbank near Newtown that was not in Drysdale. The lower end of the parish followed the road to Todd's Bridge at modern Dunkirk, up the Rolling Road to Mattaponi Run (likely represented nowadays by Chapel Hill Creek) to the Essex County line.

Now a century since ships from England had first come ashore, land in Virginia's Tidewater brimmed with ypeople. The crush propelled the surge toward the mountains and beyond to the Shenandoah Valley. But hard scrabble survival in yet-untamed parts like Caroline County may have slaked the push for the time being.

Scourge beset the early 1730s.[22] A silent outbreak of caterpillars soon fanned out as a massive feeding frenzy to strip all native flora. This loss of plant life forced deer to graze on crops. This displaced foraging set in motion a year-round open season as farmers took to killing deer in droves. Carcasses littered fields, enticing wolves to move in for easy pickings. Soon inured to human presence, the wolves began preying on livestock and children.

Burgesses set a bounty of 100 pounds of tobacco for each wolf scalp. (A field slave could harvest at most thirty pounds of tobacco in one day.) For some years many settlers made a living as wolf hunters.

But by the end of the decade disruption from this serial calamity had subsided as business returned to the mundane. County court, for instance, appointed George and John Penn Jr. appraisers in 1737 for the estate of John Stone.

Though a few families held great wealth from plantations of several hundred acres, far more lived hand-to-mouth, clearing trees and stumps and sowing crops for others. Probably half the population owned no property, either being indentured servants, headrighters or slaves. The Penns apparently occupied a tier in society just below the small but powerful gentleman class (who were of landed but not noble lineage) known as freeholders.[23] Defined by the Colony of Virginia voting law of 1736, a freeholder was a white male, at least twenty-one years old and who owned at least 100 acres of unimproved or twenty-five acres of improved land, with a house and a "plantation." Required to vote, the freeholder could serve on juries and hold office. John Penn, Jr. sat on three juries between the years of 1732 to 1745. His civic sense bordered on bravery.[24] In 1741 he took on the dangerous position as county constable. Enforcing unpopular laws often set one up as a moving target and most appointees gave the job up after a year.

Since John Jr. had not yet moved to land in Spotsylvania that he had acquired in the preceding twenty years, and that nephew John (son of Joseph) already resided there, Caroline records from the mid-1750s refer to him or to his own John son (born ca. 1725). A John Penn was fined for selling rum[25] without a license in 1755. The next year either the elder John Jr. or son John was appointed to replace John Burk as county deputy.

Freeholders could perhaps afford to own a few slaves. Caroline records from 1732 and 1734 divulge that during this time John Penn acquired two slaves[26] and his brother George Penn one. Whether or not the same slave he bought at this time, in June 1740, a negro girl named Candis[27] belonging to George Penn, was "adjudged" by the court to be ten years old.

By the first quarter of the eighteenth century slavery was fully anchored in colonial society.[28] In the hundred years since the first African[29] captives were brought to Virginia, a gradual entrenchment to a harsher system had unfolded. Some of those first Africans at Jamestown in 1619, Christian converts that they were, eventually moved on in life as free citizens. "For a brief time[30] belief in Christ overpowered slavery, but the Virginia Assembly began to close this religious loophole in 1667," when baptism would no longer necessarily exempt a person born a slave from bondage. By 1682, all "negroes, moors, mulattoes or Indians"[31] imported to Virginia were deemed permanently enslaved.

As economic conditions shifted[32] in England at the beginning of the 1700s, the royal government grasped that it now needed to hold on to its own cheap labor, rather than jettisoning lower class excess and convicts to the colonies. Figures exist[33] that 1500 to 2000 white indentured servants streamed in yearly during the 1680s. In 1715 only 100 had made the trip. Virginia planters were forced to ramp up the flow of African slaves to maintain a work force.

Even as the official stance tightened, colonists exerted in day-today life free will in the burgeoning, novel racial landscape. Masters often freed slaves and, as a matter of nature's course, people intermarried.

Historian Phillip D. Morgan leaves no stone unturned in succinct re-creation of Virginia's proletariat of the late seventeenth century: "… in spite of the blacks' debased status,[34] race relations in early Virginia were more pliable than they would later be, largely because disadvantaged blacks encountered a group of whites—indentured servants-who could claim to be similarly disadvantaged … Not only did many blacks and whites work alongside one another, but they ate, caroused, smoked, ran away, stole, and made love together."

The forward-thinking planter Nathanial Bacon[35] had led a rebellion of low-class whites and blacks against his in-law Governor William Berkeley in May 1676. The revolt, like much strife in the human experience, grew out of coveting land. Bacon sought land to distribute to the poor that belonged to Indians. At that particular moment the government was protecting the Natives. Civil War raged all summer, with Jamestown torched in September. Bacon was dead soon after, as Berkeley regained control, shortly before being ousted.

Annette Gordon-Reed, author of *The Hemingses of Monticello,* points out that the uprising by the mixed masses taught the power elite that a permanent schism between races had to be put in place and that a "thoroughly subjugated work force,[36] i.e., the slaves, must be put in a position to block their demand for benefits within society." By 1736,

The burning of Jamestown during Bacon's Rebellion

the scheme was set. Ruling class planter William Byrd II rued that year the adversely altered mindset of the people. "I am sensible[37] of many bad consequences of multiplying these Ethiopians amongst us. They blow up the pride and ruin the industry of our white people, who, seeing a rank of poor creatures below them, detest work for fear it should make them look like slaves."

In 1685 the estimated white population of Virginia of 38,100 dwarfed that of 2,600 blacks. By the time John Penn Sr. died[38] in 1741, 148,300 white people lived along with 85,300 slaves. By the time of the Revolution thirty years later the population of African-derived persons was nearly seventy-five percent of the white segment of 279,500.

A society enmeshed in slavery spawned a convoluted rationale of handling the reality of a motley populace. As early 1662 the House of Burgesses addressed the status of mixed-race children. The planters demanded that the "increase" of slaves likewise be slaves. As a consequence of legislation then passed, no matter "how a slave woman became pregnant[39]—whether it was by her owner, his son, his overseer, a white neighbor, a servant, a slave, or indeed anyone . . ." her offspring were forever consigned to her same bondage.

Mary Chesnut's Civil War, published in 1981, excerpts diaries of Mary Boykin Chesnut, a planter's wife who lived in South Carolina during the War Between the States. In one entry she speaks openly about intimate integration in an otherwise highly segregated society. "Like patriarchs of old[40] our men live in one house with their wives and their concubines, and the mulattoes one sees in every family exactly resemble the white children—and every lady tells you who is the father of all the mulatto children in everybody's household, but those in her own she seems to think drop from the clouds—You see, Mrs. Stowe did not hit on the sorest spot. She makes Legree a bachelor."

During the 120 years of importation of African slaves to Virginia, circumstances of Native Americans not unexpectedly precipitously declined. When Chief Totopomoy was killed in 1656, his wife Cockacoeske[41] took over as ruler of the Pamunkey tribe for the next thirty years. Unable to turn the tide against the tidal wave of relentless European settlement, Cockacoeske worked a deal with the English whereby the tribe relinquished claim to ancestral lands in turn for protection from hostile tribes and with guarantee of a "limited amount of reserved land" for her people. Her rational thinking during time of such great upheaval amounted to the establishment of the first Indian reservation, which miraculously exists to this day.

But throughout the 1700s most tribes of Virginia lost their lands—the Rappahannock by 1700, the Chickahominey in 1718 and the Nansemond in 1792. Before her end Cockacoeske was struggling to keep white ways off the reservation and to keep members of the tribe from leaving to acculturate into white society.

The first of John Penn the Immigrant's sons to die[42] was George Penn. Likely not quite yet fifty, his untimely death left fatherless several children, the youngest two-year-old Moses, named after George's youngest brother. Widow Ann Penn presented her late husband's will in Caroline Court 12 August 1749. Ann Penn remarried Thomas Dudley and after the death of her second husband she and many of her offspring and their Penn cousins made the monumental decision to move 150 miles southwest from Caroline to the newly forming Piedmont Region County of Amherst by 1760. She died there in 1794[43] near the age of ninety.

Moses Penn also passed[44] at a young age a decade later, his sole offspring son John Penn. This John would practice law, lead a radical anti-royalist faction in Caroline and would, as a delegate from North Carolina, sign the Declaration of Independence.

Both John Jr. and Joseph Penn[45] had also relocated by 1760 to west-bordering Spotsylvania County. Younger Joseph died by 1767 and perhaps the eldest of the four Penn sons, English-born John, by 1772, each man leaving numerous sons and daughters.

CHAPTER 5

Generation of Revolution

The Caroline era for the Penns of Virginia drew to a close as the French and Indian War approached.[1] The budgetary throes fomented by that conflict, heightened by a simultaneous decade of drought, set off a surge for greener pastures elsewhere.

British colonial presence continued during the 1700s to mount in then-French territory of the Ohio Valley. Settlers had steadily trickled in as squatters for decades. By the early 1730s this influx swelled with newly-arrived Scots, Scots-Irish, Welsh and more Germans streaming into the Valley Of Virginia and west of the Alleghenies. Tales of massacre by Indians egged on by the French fanned hostilities. But jockeying for control at the confluence of the Allegheny and Monongahela forks of the Ohio, where stood Fort Duquesne (now Pittsburgh), proved to be the eventual boiling point for violence to erupt. The first battle of a long war took place 28 May 1754. Virginia militiamen under a very young George Washington ambushed a French patrol at Jumonville Glen, near present-day Unionville, Pennsylvania. Washington, a peer of John Penn the Immigrant's grandchildren, had been born forty miles away from Caroline, in Westmoreland County.

The war between England and France shut down completely the market[2] for Virginia tobacco in Europe. Nearly drained ponds from the lack of rain brought mills for grinding of grain to a standstill. Hard times led to a crime wave of theft and to a ferment of lawsuits. No one was much interested in the war with the French dragging on 300 miles away.

Reaching their rope's end, with no inkling of better things to come, many families pulled out of Caroline County. The Penns were part of the flight. With rainfall better on the frontier, migrants traded the drought for "the hazards of living among the Indians."[3] (Campbell, p. 150) When rain returned in 1760 and the French and Indian War ended in 1763 the Penns had already vacated beleaguered Caroline. Surviving sons of the boatswain, John Jr. and Joseph, moved with their offspring to adjacent Spotsylvania, to land they had acquired several years earlier. The large brood of the late George Penn, with their mother, Ann Penn Dudley, trekked *en masse* 150 miles to the southwest to newly forming Amherst County. The sole child of Moses, John Penn, was the last Penn to leave Caroline. A radical patriot,[4] purported anti-royalist statements caused life to be difficult for him in Caroline. After found guilty by a Caroline jury of "stirring up rebellion" and fined one penny, John soon relocated just over the border in Granville County, North Carolina in 1774, as reported in the *Virginia Gazette* that May, where Taylor relatives of his had already resettled.

Deed books of Spotsylvania County[5] first note presence there of John Jr. and of younger brother Joseph by 1762. Perhaps as their own readying to pull up stakes, George's son Phillip and wife Martha[6] (Crutcher), still residing in Caroline, conveyed 220 acres in St. George Parish of Spotsylvania County to John May 6 September 1762. Brother Gabriel Penn's sale to his uncle John of 130 acres of Spotsylvania ground in 1764 record Gabriel's residence as Amherst County,[7] first proof of offspring of George Penn in that county, just as he was serving as a sergeant in the First Virginia Regiment at the end of the French and Indian War.[8] During the Revolution,[9] he supplied patriot forces and even recruited younger men for the patriot cause. Gabriel had cajoled an Isaiah Giles[10] into a tour of duty, that would include the Siege of Yorktown, by allowing the twenty-something Giles to simply drive the wagon of the elder Giles to work off his service commitment.

Gabriel Penn, unlike some of his brothers, remained for his life in Amherst, living along the Buffalo River, as a substantial landholder and slave owner. He placed an ad in the *Virginia Gazette* August 1774 in hopes of retrieving Sally Grey,[11] a mulatto slave who had run away that summer.

Several years later Molley,[12] a neighbor's slave, fled to Gabriel's plantation. He stepped in on Molley's behalf by writing a stridently stated letter to her owner, William Crawford, about overseer Vaughn's harsh treatment of the woman. Though Penn by this time owned forty slaves himself, perhaps his coming forth to help Molley hints at a kind nature.

Abraham Penn, Gabriel's younger brother, is the next to show up in Amherst. As a newlywed he purchased 136 acres in 1767 from Baylor Walker[13] of King and Queen County on the south branch of Harris Creek. Four years later Abraham doubled his tract along the same stream.

In the generation of John Penn the Immigrant's grandchildren, the first wave of descendants to stream out of the ancestral Mattaponi homestead, record of marriages is sporadic. Though most maiden names of brides have come down through time, precise dates of espousal more often than not are nonexistent. Those few marriages to which a specific time can be attached retain such distinction from happenstance of hit-and-miss county registration, if not from the lucky entry in a family bible. But this loose state of affairs may have come about from not only yet behindhand bureaucracy in the newly-formed counties, but from varying social attitude. Public record of many marriages may never have been created in the first place, if the couple had chosen not to make official their union before a bondsman. The stance of some may have held that people themselves called the tune for their own nuptials, bypassing recognition by clergy and state. Such nonconformity harked to the "little weddings"[14] of England's peasantry, folkway to persist in Virginia of the late colonial period. The more recent experience of out-in-the-open loose to lapsed church attendance in Caroline's Drysdale Parish may have continued to incline hearts toward free spirit thinking.

One such instance intersects the lives of two siblings. Grandsons of John the Immigrant, Phillip Penn and Abraham Penn both removed to Amherst County. Tradition holds that the older Phillip married Martha Crutcher by 1760, a date deduced by the ages of their offspring, but without support documentation ever to surface. Archival collections of the Virginia Historical Society make reference to their "being a married couple"[15] without date or location. The name of Abraham Penn, however, and of his bride, Ruth Stovall,[16] specifically appear in the register of marriages for Amherst County of 3 March 1767.

The association between the Crutcher and Penn families[17] elucidates the depth of entwinement that evolved between colonists, perhaps only at first neighbors. Phillip's eldest sibling, sister Frances, married near the same time to Phillip's brother-in-law Samuel Crutcher. When Phillip's son Gabriel wed Charlotte Crutcher 20 December 1794, after both families had moved to Patrick County, Gabriel took a wife who was both his first cousin through the Crutchers and a first cousin-once-removed through the Penns. Whether such consanguinity, most certainly known to the involved parties, came about with the aim to solidify assets or out of clannishness growing from comfort with people and places familiar remains an open topic. Everyone knew one another and their business. "You weren't going to move away[18] and it was hard to settle disputes or reason out crimes when everyone was involved with everyone else."

A new life farther into the Piedmont could not stave off Virginia's impending showdown with England. Earliest immigrants' pining for home had by the 1760s festered into bitterness of being under the Crown's thumb. This brewing discontent argued that colonists served as nothing more than as debtors to the British. Most arrived owing with their progeny never freed of the burden. Even wealthy planters George Washington and Thomas Jefferson lived lives deeply in the red beholden[19] to London dealers or to shark Glasgow "tobacco lords."[20] Grandson of the Immigrant, through son Joseph, Phillip Penn of Spotsylvania County mortgaged against 237 acres left by his late father to pay a debt of 77 pounds to McCall, Smillie and Company,[21] merchants in Glasgow, January 1773. One writer maintains that "declaring independence[22] was a way of cancelling those debts." As the tide turned, all civil proceedings, including the collection of debts, ceased in Virginia courts[23] 12 April 1774.

A dark mood[24] moved over Virginia during the summer of 1774. A bizarre killing frost in May had severely set back crop growth. Dissolution of the House of Burgesses, flare-up with Indians on the frontier and martial law put into place at Boston kept everyone on edge. Both church and state called for days of fasting in June to impress on the mind of the public the grave state of affairs. Amid the tumult, the first Continental Congress, a coalition of delegates from the thirteen colonies, first met that autumn at Philadelphia.

Gearing up for battle, the Virginia Convention established the first military draft July 1775, requiring most free males "above the age of sixteen,[25] and under fifty years" to enlist in the militia. A year later patriots brought down royal control in Virginia, with the defeat of Lord Dunmore[26] near the mouth of the Rappahannock. At the same moment colonial delegates, among them John Penn, son of Moses,

Portrait of John Penn, signer of the Declaration of Independence

signed the Declaration of Independence at Philadelphia. The authors, still English citizens, modeled the document after earlier proclamations in England's history dating back to 1327, whereby the reign of a living king was brought to an end for his having overstepped limits of power, in this case James II, for having acted "utterly contrary[27] to the knowne Laws and Statutes and freedome of this Realme."

The British made two, oft-forgotten overtures[28] for peace early on during the conflict. Fervent colonial leaders brushed off these schemes, baring that deepest motivation for independence "ran deeper than mere 'taxation without representation.'"

Aside from presence of John Penn at Philadelphia that momentous summer of 1776, first cousin Gabriel Penn, with William Cabell, served as Amherst County representative at the fifth convention[29] in Williamsburg. This assembly passed the resolution urging the Continental Congress to declare the United Colonies free and independent. Gabriel's younger brother,[30] William Penn, joined the Virginia Dragoons, commissioned as first lieutenant, in June, to rapidly rise to Captain of the First Continental Dragoons by November. Mentioning that he was "going into the service," William with foresight, if not foreknowledge, submitted his will in August. He died of smallpox at Trenton, New Jersey the next March.

Another Amherst County Penn[31] brother would go on to mark his place in Virginia history as soldier and statesman. The times in which he lived milked to full expression the singular talents of Abraham Penn. In his late twenties he sold his Amherst spread to his oldest sister's second husband, Drury Tucker, and struck out 100 miles farther south to settle in the western part of Pittsylvania County that soon became Henry County. Abraham's estate took in land later occupied by Beaver Creek Plantation, three miles north of present Martinsville. He and Robert Hairston were delegates from just-formed Henry County for the House of the General Assembly[32] in 1777. Abraham reprised this duty again in 1779 and in 1789. He later moved to and was one of the organizers of adjacent Patrick County. There he served in later life as a magistrate in his own home, for the jurisdiction's inchoate court system.

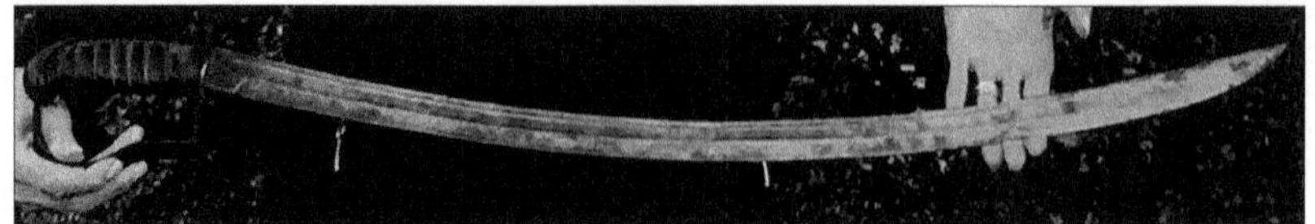

Sword of Patriot leader Abraham Penn

Revolutionary War militiaman

For service he may have put in[33] as a youth near the end of the French and Indian War, he was referred to as Lieutenant Penn[34] by 1768. In 1776 Abraham Penn led a company of Minute Men to guard Jamestown,[35] as Lord Dunsmore was defeated. Now Major Penn, Abraham then organized and commanded a Henry County contingent of horseback-riding riflemen[36] to protect the frontier against Indian attacks. He fit the mold of "competent and charismatic leaders[37] (who) floated to the top." Governor Thomas Jefferson raised Penn to rank of Colonel[38] in 1780 just as Penn took over as County Lieutenant, which entailed recruiting soldiers. That autumn Colonel Penn marched patriot troops[39] to Yadkin River, North Carolina, whence several Tory (loyalist) prisoners[40] had been taken a week earlier. At a low point[41] during the Revolution, Thomas Jefferson himself called upon Abraham Penn in May 1781 to pull together a body of troops from his distant region in Henry and Patrick Counties to reinforce General Nathanael Greene's efforts to beat back the British in the Carolinas. Abraham managed to muster[42] a local contingent though by this stage in the war guns and fighting spirit were scarce.

The end could not have come[43] at a better time. By 1781, with depreciation of paper money and heavy taxation, the will to fight among Virginians was heavily strained. Brigades walked off from the battlefront as soldiers went home to harvest crops. Muster rolls lay bare the fact that native-born white Americans left the bulk of the fighting to Negroes, Indians and to just-arrived immigrants from Britain and Germany. Home born commoners put forth they had nothing for which to take up the fight. Rich planters and overseers payed their way out of service, while farmers put their lives on the line for pittance and no advancement. That the Americans, with their wavering patriot drive, had overcome the prowess of the British Army stands out as all the more remarkable in that loyalist favor among colonists ran at about fifty percent. Eventually back-country militias wore down the Redcoats with "actions in which they excelled:[44] small battles, raids, ambushes, and assassinations." The ceaseless war's[45] mounting cost and growing ill will toward it in Britain sealed its fate.

Profiteering[46] by some farmers from the sale of foodstuffs to enemy troops, who could pay more, further undermined the patriot cause. Record of public claims in Amherst County near the end of the Revolution, however, suggest that citizens there had provided goods[47] in direct support to the quest for independence. Gabriel Penn had supplied beef and bushels of wheat, brother George brandy, oats, "flower," and corn, cousin John bacon, rye and services "driving publick beeves" (i.e., cattle).

Patriot soldiers excelled at small battles, raids, ambushes, and assassinations

The relentless drive of kinsmen Abraham aside, the main of Amherst Penns abided a homebody spirit during the Revolution. Sole evidence[48] of military service by any of the Penns, excluding Abraham Penn, rests with a single page in a county order book. The entry lists payroll of Captain William Tucker's Company, which served 72 days in the war effort, 14 January to 26 March 1781. Slim inference suggests that the Phillip Penn, who served as one of five corporals, was Abraham's first cousin, rather than his older brother Phillip Penn. Though the latter also resided in Amherst at that moment, that he was nearing his mid-forties favors his liked-named, younger cousin as the one who served. The presence of the younger Phillip's brother, Thomas Penn, in the same unit as a private, abets this notion. The National Archives possesses no evidence of Revolutionary service for any Phillip Penn, in military service, pension or land bounty records.

Stock rehash of the American Revolution glosses over the slaughter[49] that broke out between fellow colonists. This internecine feud matched any spilling of blood from battle with the British. Patriot Whigs clawing for independence and Tories holding fast for the Crown each carried out atrocities on the other. Hangings, severing limbs, ear loppings, urinating on corpses and then stripping the dead for souvenirs (all often in view of relatives of victims) give a gory picture of what otherwise self-assuming civilized persons, future citizens of the United States, were capable of against neighbors. Hasty, scantily covered burials drew in droves of carrion-feeding wolves and hogs. A synchronous outbreak of what likely was rabies resulted in having to put down half of the dog population. In many regions, particularly in the Carolinas, the mayhem made for a surreal netherworld of people afraid to venture outside their homes. In eighty-five years the past would repeat itself.

CHAPTER 6

AMERICANS

War past with France and, for now, with England left the ex-colonists to their own devices. Growing pains made a quick appearance. Sprung from the grip of royal say-so, a fervid rebound for democracy rippled along the seaboard commonwealth. In the decade-and-a-half after the Declaration of Independence, but before the Constitution, the new autonomy fragmented the envisioned union of former colonies. The rule by the majority free-for-all decentralized any effect of a national government, each individual state legislature having set up absolute power for itself. For the first time ever more common people held office than gentry. Fiefdom politics fomented an uproar of inflation, infighting and general "majoritarian confusion."[1] Statesman Alexander Hamilton saw with alarm already by 1778 the low-level character of the American Congress. He wrote George Washington that "Many members[2] of it are no doubt men, in every respect, fit for the trust; but this cannot be said of it as a body. Folly, caprice, a want of foresight, comprehension, and dignity, characterize the general tenor of their actions." James Madison, toughened by three years on the congressional battlefield in the Virginia assembly, drafted the Virginia Plan in 1787, the template for the Constitution, an instrument "to prevent the excesses of localist and interest-ridden democracy."

Penn forebears[3] were in the thick of this tumult. As he had at the end of the 1770s, Abraham Penn served again in the House of Delegates for the General Assembly at the end of 1789. A George Penn, either his son or the son of Abraham's brother Phillip, held a seat in the same body as a delegate from Patrick County during autumn sessions of 1792 and 1793.

As with future post-war eras in the United States, the tumult of the Revolution set in motion great societal changes. The age-old practice of primogeniture,[4] right of the first-born son to inherit all, was abolished in 1776. An even more dramatic reversal came two years later with the ban henceforth of further importation of slaves into Virginia. Any slave brought into the Commonwealth, "contrary to this act,"[5] was free on the spot.

Set apart from the masses[6] by his class and intellect, Thomas Jefferson fantasized the new nation as in a state of "tranquil permanent felicity."[7] His castles-in-the-air dream reflected the degree to which the Virginia gentleman stood out of touch with the hard scrabble survival most endured in the Old Dominion. Jefferson tried to put out of mind postwar depression, foreclosures, squatters, rebellions and rampant vagrancy.

With ties severed with the Anglican England, the new Protestant Episcopal Church now took possession of the glebes[8] of colonial times. At the same moment burgeoning Baptists and Presbyterian denominations quickly offset potential monopoly. These evangelical groups set about divesting the heir apparent Episcopalians of their tax base and property. Separation of church and state now allowed religion to be a choice. Gone were old ways of punishment for non-attendance and of enforced tithing.

Though "nearly all common and middling people[9] in the early Republic still made sense of the world through religion," the intellectual elite, including the "Founding Fathers," despised it. Much as Robert Beverly had espoused in the early days of Caroline County sixty years earlier, the "priestcraft"[10] of preachers, in the "Fathers'" minds, lay in cahoots with despotism. Deists such as John Paine, Benjamin Franklin and Thomas Jefferson looked upon religious fervor as mental imbalance, hemorrhage from "a warmed or overweening brain."[11] Though he opened his will[12] with the canonical, "In the name of God amen," George Washington declared that "religious controversies[13] are always productive of more acrimony and irreconcilable hatreds than those which spring from any other cause . . ." Ona Judge Staines, an escaped slave of Martha Washington, who forever evaded capture, drew into question aggrandizing, posthumous claims of the first president's "piety and prayers."[14] Never once did she see Washington draw himself to worship. Rather, "card-playing and wine-drinking were the business at his parties, and he had more of such company Sundays than on any other day."

During this first decade of the American Republic the two branches of John Penn the Immigrant's descendants dwelt in Amherst[15] and in Spotsylvania Counties. Grandchildren through sons George and Joseph in Amherst formed the largest grouping. Seven Penn Amherst households[16] existed in 1783—the farms of Joseph's sons Phillip, John, Moses and Thomas and those of George's sons George, Gabriel and Phillip.

An unrelated "Penn" family, that of Rawley Pinn, lived on Buffalo Ridge in the county. Presumptively Rawley's male line stemmed from a John Pine[17] settled by 1649 in Lancaster County and from a possible descendant, Thomas Pinn,[18] alive in the late 1690s. By the next generation Pine/Pin had fully shifted to Pinn. As progeny drifted out from stomping grounds near Carter's Creek in Lancaster their mixed blood heritage was a matter of public record. Registers for Wicomico Parish in Northumberland County in the 1730s identified member "Indian" David Pinn.[19] Hezziah Pinn,[20] bound to the Hubbard family in 1748, was the orphan daughter of "Indian" Harry. Thomas Pinn, "a free Negro boy" of about ten was apprenticed in 1764 in Richmond County. Rawley Pinn[21] himself was a "Mulatto" taxpayer in Buckingham County in 1774 and head of an Amherst County household of eight "Mulattos" in 1785. Son Turner Pinn registered as a "free Negro" in 1828, described in his declaration as "of dark brown complexion, about five feet ten inches high aged 46 years born free." Rawley's nephew, in a pension application for service in the Revolution, stated that his father was a "Mustee" (archaic term for white/quadroon cross) and his mother a Cherokee.

A quarter century after the exodus from Caroline, rumblings to move on again stirred in Piedmont society, another aftershock of the Revolution. Armed with war bounty warrants, land titles purchased from the new government or with hazy squatters' rights, the next generation fanned out along and over the Blue Ridge Mountains.

Settlers in the latter group made up the driving force of this latest surge in "manifest destiny." Trespassing on federal property, squatters[22] on blind faith took up land with the hope that grit put out to cultivate it would in the end bring them clear title. Lured by the vision of their own piece of the wide-open spaces, thousands mustered the pluck to head west to seize the chance. With the first permanent settlement set up in June 1774 at Harrodstown (later Harrodsburg[23]), one eyewitness reckoned that 3,000 people had swarmed into Kentucky in the autumn 1779 alone. The border encroachments that had prompted the French and Indian War of thirty years earlier had now swelled into a deluge of humanity. George Washington, again pulled into the thick of the tumult, could see that nothing short of "a Chinese wall, or a line of troops"[24] would stem the tide.

Author Washington Irving used his short story "Rip Van Winkle"[25] as a metaphor to tell of the lightning speed of change which had unfolded in America by 1800. Rip awakened from a twenty-year sleep in the woods that had begun before the Revolution. When he trundles in the direction of his village, the place is now a town with streets thronged with people. One estimate gives that between 1790 and 1820 Kentucky's population[26] alone mushroomed by eightfold.

Visitors' observations are enlightening. Englishman John Heckenwelder,[27] a missionary to Indians in Ohio, described the Kentucky side of the Ohio River at Louisville to already be "thickly settled" in 1792. Fellow English-born Unitarian Minister, Harry (Henry) Toulmin,[28] who became Kentucky's first secretary of state through the pull of Thomas Jefferson and James Madison, pictured the region during his tenure of 1796 to 1804. Threat of Indian attacks were already becoming something of the past, Toulmin himself having traveled 200 miles from Virginia without incident. "The frontiers are often molested," he noted, "but these frontiers are perpetually extending farther from the center of the state." Toulmin also gauged that easternmost settlements in Kentucky by then lay no more than 100 miles from western towns in Virginia and North Carolina. The Secretary boasted that "the post comes and returns once a fortnight and brings a multitude of newspapers."

Transplants from Old Dominion carried with them the standard contemporary practice of bribing votes[29] with liquor. The besotted demeanor of the proceedings dragged one Kentucky election out for three days. The writer George Prentice regaled readers that "during that period whiskey and apple toddy flowed through out cities and villages like the Euphrates through ancient Babylon."

Elias Pym Fordham,[30] later one of the surveyors for the laying out of the city of Indianapolis, set off upon his arrival from England in 1817 on an expedition through Virginia, Kentucky, Ohio and Indiana. Brought up in the English middle class, Fordham's analytical eye must have gaped at the sight of a backcountry gentleman. A scratchy wool blanket overhung the frontiersman's gingham shirt, pants, leggings and coat, "pinned under the chin in Indian fashion and a leather belt suspending a large hunting or scalping knife." The rough exterior aside, Fordham found "more genuine kindness and politeness among these backwoodsmen than among any set of people I have yet seen in America."

Fordham recorded that in Appalachian frontier society, farmers and laborers lived together as equals, though he felt that hunters were more polite than farmers. And though his observations led him to consider Kentucky a "paradise" for them, compared to their lives in Virginia or the Carolinas, slaves were "never supplied with more bedding[31] than a blanket and the kitchen or dining room floor."

Peter Wallenstein, in his book, *Cradle of America: Four Centuries of Virginia History,* declares "When Virginians moved,[32] Virginia changed, in a myriad of ways, and so did the places Virginians moved to." And most former Old Dominion denizens moved west and north

Backwoodsman of the American South, early 1800s

over the Ohio River. By 1850, ex-patriot free Virginians resided in largest numbers in Ohio, Missouri, Kentucky, Tennessee and Indiana.

By the time of the Revolution, only 170 years since the first Jamestown settlers, a distinct, new dialect had arisen in the Colonies. The influx of Scots and Ulster Scots immigrants brought a northern variety of English discernable from the speech that preceding English arrivals had carried from the south of England. Starting in earnest by 1700, Scots and their descendants in Northern Ireland left the religion-inspired bloodshed of the Isles. Saturated settlement in coastal lowlands veered this latest element of the melting pot to the yet-wild mountain valleys in the west. By 1772 reference to the "Scotch-Irish dialect"[33] had appeared in print. In his diary detailing his journey from his plantation in Prince William County to Boone's Fort in Kentucky in 1775, Virginian William Calk's[34] phonetic rendering of his thoughts captures the accent of his spoken word: "Come to a turabel mountain that tried us all almost to death to git over it"; "I got lost Tuesday night and it asnowing"; "we got our house kivered (i.e., covered) with Bark." By this time the speech of eastern Virginians "Tuckahoes"[35] (Tidewater and Piedmont) voiced broad, slow vowels from the back of the mouth and dropped the r-sound (e.g., *palm* and *harm* rhymed). Though Western Virginians (Shenandoah and Appalachia), or "Quo'he's," also gargled some vowels (e.g., *tire* and *fire* identical to *tar* and *far*), they tended more to push such sounds from the front of the mouth and then to draw them out into separate syllables (e.g., *hit* sounded like *hee-it; feet* like *fih-eet*). This drawl, along with a strongly voiced "r" (*hard* for *hired; critter* for *creature; sartin* for *certain*), set apart the talk heard in the hilly hinterlands. In recent times these flavors of American English have acquired the colorful, well-functioning labels of "Coastal Southern"[36] and of "Highland Southern." Present trend of homogenization boils down speech patterns possessing any of the above elements to the encompassing, less illustrative classification "Southern."[37] Though the Elizabethan language of the first English settlers and such local developments as plantation dialect have long since died out, a strong echo of colonial Virginia lives on.

At the time of 1810 Census only four Penn households[38] existed in Kentucky. All concentrated in the north central, Ohio River-bounded area of adjacent Bourbon, Scott and Franklin counties. These Penns, using given names not found among Virginia Penns—Benjamin, Eli, Samuel and Shadrack Penn—were sons of Benjamin and Dinah Acton Penn of Anne Arundel County, Maryland. This line ultimately descends from English colonist Edward Penn,[39] present in that county by 1700. A decade later another small cluster[40] had sprouted in south central Casey, Green and Lincoln counties, representing those of the surname having migrated from Virginia. Gabriel (son of Phillip of Patrick County), and Gabriel's sons James and Thomas, these first Virginians named Penn to come to Kentucky, would be followed within the decade by Gabriel's brothers Abram and Wilson Penn. To cajole men[41] into longer military service, the Virginia Assembly came upon the scheme to award land in Kentucky or Ohio to those having met qualifying time limits. War grants assigned[42] in the 1780s to their uncles Gabriel, John and William for lands in northern Kentucky presumably passed into other hands, such as get-rich-quick land speculators.[43] Post-Revolution depression led to high taxes. Many former soldiers sold off[44] war bounty land grants cheaply to fend off ruin. Frontiersman, politician and himself a land speculator, Squire Boone, brother of Daniel, sold 2000 acres, in that part of Virginia soon to morph into Jefferson County, Kentucky, August 1788 to Patrick Joyes.[45] This huge tract lie adjacent to the original 500 acres granted John Penn in 1783.

The Penn surname's first appearance in Alabama[46] likely derives from the Maryland lineage as well. A William Penn, enumerated in the 1800 Federal Census in Montgomery County, Maryland, had drifted all the way south to the Mississippi Territory by 1810 to settle in what was to become Washington County, Alabama. Of the same generation, a Shadrack Penn,[47] son of John of Maryland, settled in Ohio. Descendants contend that he not only had fought on the side of British in the War of 1812, but had married a daughter of their ally, Indian Chief Tecumseh.

The Immigrant's son John[48] had staked out his territory in the earliest years of Spotsylvania County on land in St. George Parish between the Ni and Po Rivers. Great-grandsons, with perennial Penn given names, here and in England, of George, John, Thomas, William and Edmond, were heads of households there at the time of 1810 census.[49] By the next generation, a century after forebear John, son of the Immigrant, had arrived, the Penn name had disappeared from the county. One of the first to leave was John Jr.'s grandson, William, who settled in Grainger County, Tennessee[50] by 1810. A namesake grandson of George Penn, of the original four brothers, sold the land[51] his father, Phillip, had deeded him in Patrick County, Virginia back in 1789. He resided by 1815 in Smith County, Tennessee. His sons, Creed and Samuel Penn, owned farms there in 1830, where George died in 1834.

A probable grandson, William, also farmed north of the Cumberland and east of the Caney River at the time of the 1850 census.

William and George's second cousin, George Penn (grandson of George of the original four brothers) put down roots sixty miles southwest in Rutherford County,[52] where he died in 1828.

Some progeny of the unallied Penn family of Brunswick County, Virginia, discussed earlier, may have lit briefly the few miles to take them into North Carolina. But after marrying in Brunswick-adjacent Granville County, North Carolina in 1766, Elizabeth Penn and Nimrod Mitchell[53] reared their large brood in Craven County, South Carolina.[54] A Jeffrey Penn,[55] with no connection teased from record to the Caroline Penns of Virginia, resided in the contiguous Newberry District in 1800. Maternal Taylor kin of Signer John Penn had already settled in Granville by the time of the Mitchell nuptials there. But as close as their paths may have crossed, the Penns of Brunswick may never have set eyes on the liked-named strangers of Caroline.

John Penn the Signer's move to Granville County,[56] North Carolina in 1774 marks the first confirmed settlement of the surname in that state. North Carolina issued a land grant to him for 293 acres on the waters of Island Creek in 1779.[57] At the same time he entered a grant for 284 acres in adjacent Orange County. He mentions two offspring in his will[58] of 1784, daughter Lucy and son William Penn. Like his father Moses, John Penn died just before the age of fifty, in 1788. In the years right after his death, son William[59] settled in Edgecombe County. At the same time William made as new assignee of land,[60] for which he had entered claim back in 1783 in distant Rowan County,[61] to a Richard Penn. Only light cogitation is needed to draw the easy inference Richard was perhaps William's brother, though William curiously goes unnamed in John's the Signer's will. During the time the 1790 census was taken, William dwelled in Edgecombe County and Richard 200 miles to the west in Rowan County. Each man had male children under sixteen at the time. That same year the state at last issued to William the grant for the Orange county[62] ground that his father John had first entered claim twelve years earlier. William had taken up living there by 1800[63] near the town of Hillsborough. Head of the Hillsborough Penn household over the next twenty years was William's son John, with three young sons under ten in 1810. That John Penn the Signer may have left offspring bearing his surname has long been disavowed by genealogists.

Richard Penn sold off the acreage[64] along Jacob's Creek in Rowan to Abraham Beanblossom in 1803, just as he must been pulling up stakes to move to Bledsoe County, Tennessee,[65] where a petitioner's list sets down his name in 1815. Richard's presence evaporates thereafter. A son, William Penn,[66] whose obituary gives his birth as 17 April 1786 at Yadkin, Rowan County, North Carolina, had settled by 1840 with wife Elizabeth in Missouri. It is they whose remains lie there in Davidson Cemetery in Dade County, where he died in 1875, leaving five daughters.

After only a decade there, war hero Abraham Penn sold his holdings at Beaver Creek, to move some twenty miles farther west in Henry County, Virginia.[67] Late in 1784 he bought for thirty pounds 343 acres that straddled a stretch of the northern fork of the Mayo River. Here Abraham established his final residence at the estate he dubbed Poplar Grove.[68] The place lay within earshot of old Fort Mayo, which had seen action during the French and Indian War thirty years earlier. Trailing along a straight line, the three-storied, hilltop manor loomed

Poplar grove, Estate of Abraham Penn

amid towering trees. A chimney hemmed each end of the wood frame manse. Another ran down the middle of the house, forming a common wall with a smaller and shorter two-floored wing. Whether of conscious intent, Abraham's wood frame expanse, with its Georgian-inspired pediment porches on one side of the main wing, brands the house in the Federal Style, America's simplified version of English neoclassical architecture popularized at that time by Scotsman Robert Adam. Abraham's home mirrored his lofty outlook in life.

An inventory of his estate at the time of his death in 1801 gives a peek inside the manse[69] at Poplar Grove, an upper middle-class dwelling of the time. Within the walls of the rambling house stood twenty-seven chairs, nine beds, two black walnut folding tables "and two square ones," one black walnut cupboard, one old cherry desk, glassware, books, looking glass, one black walnut bedstead and furniture, curtains, chests, a tea table, looms, money scales and weights.

Intimation of brotherly fondness[70] comes to light when that next summer 1785 older sibling Phillip Penn bought an initial 200 acres in Henry just a few miles to the southwest of Abraham Penn. Phillip had

No Business Mountain: land once belonging to Phillip Penn

likely already moved his family two years earlier. Eldest daughter Frances Penn[71] married in Amherst County April 1783. Just three months later, younger daughter Sarah Penn became the wife of John Norton, but in Henry County. These events pinpoint timing of migration for these Amherst County Penns to uproot 130 miles south to the border county of Henry in the summer of 1783.

Phillip decided upon domain[72] that took in flat and inclined pastures squeezed between thick stands of woods. A shallow creek called to this day Gray's Fork, the northern branch of Mill Creek, the latter a western tributary of the North Mayo, cleaved Phillip Penn's holdings. Off in the distance the chain of rounded green hills known as No Business Mountain swept along the western horizon. With two acquisitions over the next two years Phillip's spread grew to nearly 800 acres. He parsed his holdings[73] in 1789, "for the love and regard for my son George Penn, to "give, grant and confirm and release a parcel of land on the head of Gray' s Fork, by estimate 200 acres more or less . . ."

A grandson each of Abraham and of Phillip established businesses to bear the name Penn's Store.[74] Thomas Jefferson Penn, son of Abra ham's James, perpetuated family fortunes by his stake in the lucrative tobacco industry. Surfeit channeled by Thomas's several sons during

Penn's Store, Virginia

Aurora, the Penn Mansion, Patrick County, Virginia

the latter half of the nineteenth century brought about "Penn's Store," a bustling commercial village near the southern boundary between Patrick with Henry County. Thomas Jefferson Penn's lovely two-story carpenter Gothic house in light pink, "Aurora," listed on the National Register of Historic Places, is a highlight of the unincorporated modern Penn's Store community.

Phillip's son Wilson, born at the outbreak of the Revolution, uprooted with evident strong motivation from Patrick in the spring of 1829. "Leaving our business unsettled,"[75] he and Abram trekked with their families 350 miles to the stand-alone, steep hills of the "Knobs" in south central Kentucky. Starting a new chapter in the last five years of his life, he made a new home along Frey's Creek in Casey County.

Two decades later a younger son of Wilson, Gabriel Jackson Penn, acquired the isolated region's main way station, a wood frame sloped-roof cabin with porch, huddled in a dell hemmed by towering hillocks. Straddling the boundary of Casey and Boyle County at a junction of two creeks, Penn's Store grew to be an important supply station and post office. The still out-of-the-way location has not thwarted Penn's

Martin Wilson Penn, son of the founder of Penn's Store, Kentucky

Penn family home, established in the early 1830s, Casey County, Kentucky

Penn's Store, Kentucky, founded in 1845, the oldest country store in America still in ownership and operation by the same family

Store current guise as a tourist center and as the oldest country store in the United States "in continuous operation by and (in) ownership of the same family," direct descendants of Gabriel Jackson Penn.

At the same moment, other Penn cousins fell in with the surge out of Amherst. Though the Immigrant's eldest son John remained there, Joseph Penn's younger son Thomas Penn was the first to carry the name to Georgia, the last colony set up before the Revolution, "to carve out[76] a middle ground between the extremes of wealth that took hold in the Carolinas, and to serve as a barrier against the Spanish in Florida." There public records note[77] his presence in contiguous Elbert and Wilkes Counties by 1787. Inflamed with land fever as well, droves from Amherst[78] were headed to the same turf, especially the families of Higginbotham, Hilley, Morrison, Rowsey, Rucker, Sandidge, Satterwhite, Stinchcomb and Upshaw. Thomas served under Captain John Hodge[79] in Company 8 of the Elbert County Militia in 1791. The brother of Thomas, the "other Phillip," who had served in the Revolution, had also made the move, witnessing a sale of property in Elbert from Thomas and wife Winifred[80] to William Spears in 1798. Their sister, Catherine, and her husband i[81] also removed to Elbert County, where they died about 1806. The Penn surname disappears in Elbert County after 1870.

In the first decade of the 1800s Phillip's sons Thomas, George Penn and Joseph had settled thirty miles north[82] in Franklin County. Their younger brother, William, married Abigail Wilson there in 1813. Phillip's eldest, daughter Elizabeth,[83] as the young widow of the late Samuel Leake, married in 1788 Turner Hunt Christian[84] in Amherst. Goochland County managed to acquit Christian the previous year in the deemed accidental shooting death of his first wife, Anna Payne, even with suspicion cast of infidelity by testimony from Rhoda Hix, who stated she was carrying Christian's child. With even more of an impetus for a fresh start elsewhere, the couple joined their relatives and neighbors in the leaving for Georgia in 1791.

Thomas and Phillip's brother, Moses, planted his legacy in the same neck of the woods hugging Georgia's northern boundary with South Carolina, in adjacent Oglethorpe County.[85] Though Moses died by the end of 1795, his wife Frances lived on until 1838. Their presumptive offspring, as extracted from Oglethorpe marriage, census and/or land lottery records from the beginning of the 1800s, include David, Edmond, Franky, Jennie, Jeremiah, Moses and Thomas.

CHAPTER 7

A House Divided

The Revolution melded the schism of loyalist and patriot antagonism. The tidal wave of opportunity that had followed independence dulled memory of differences. If not always the Revolutionaries themselves, their offspring streamed west from once-colonial confines to new landscapes and to the radiant blur of the future.

As the early part of the nineteenth century rolled onward and those who had been born during the break from England began to die off, knowingness of a new time seeped into the public's mind. A news article of the late 1830s, detailing the "wonderful state of preservation"[1] of the corpse of George Washington upon its reinternment thirty years post-mortem, "reveals how intensely dependent Americans still were on the revolutionary past that was slipping from their fingers."

Technology unimaginable[2] to patriot farmers 50 years earlier, but which had incubated with the need to arm the colonies, had already taken root in daily life. The era's brainchild explosion took in a nascent web of railways, the first daguerreotypes, crackling telegraph lines, vulcanized rubber and Hoe mass printing type. The modern age had dawned.

The long-fomenting contention over abolition of slavery now approached a tipping point. The brief but bloody slave rebellion led by Nat Turner and retaliatory aftermath in 1830 caused sufficient pause momentarily for the government of Virginia to ponder doing away with a state-sanctioned captive work force. But such drastic changeover in society would demand more-than-imagined sacrifice yet to unfold. As Abraham Lincoln gave his first speech at Springfield, Illinois, a significant coincident stirring of things to soon come arose as Puritan descendant John Brown[3] began his transition from failed businessman to fervent and eventually violent abolitionist.

Lip service toward ending slavery in British North America had murmured since the first African captives were dragged ashore. Enslavement gnawed at the core of Christian conscience of some. But the rapid and insidious entwinement of plantation economy with chattel labor sealed an inescapable dependence. Any background noise about freeing slaves in the South remained idle talk mostly confined to New England parlors. Even those intellectuals arguing for emancipation knew slavery to be "the nursing mother of the north."[4] The hand-in-hand symbiosis of slavery and of free states drove United States capitalism. Abolitionist William Lloyd Garrison branded the North as "a partner in iniquity."[5] Clothes from slave-grown cotton[6] rested on the backs of New Yorkers just as Louisiana sugar made life a little sweeter in the White Mountains of New Hampshire. As succinctly stated by a recent scholar, "Southern nationalists lambasted northern sanctimoniousness."[7] After all, who, without qualm, sold shoes and cloth at good profit to southern planters but Yankees?

Lincoln's pledge[8] to keep all new U.S. territories and incoming states slave-free put slave-holding interests on guard. His election as president, without his name having even appeared on the ballot in most southern states, due to Democratic Party infighting, set a match to the smoldering powder keg. The South took Lincoln's ascendancy as confirmation that Washington had turned its back on the region. Six weeks after Lincoln came to office, South Carolina became the first of seven slave states to sever allegiance to the United States. The Union's fear of a trend of further fractioning by states to form separate countries commenced the grueling build-up for war in an attempt to pull together once again the shredding republic.

The internecine warfare about to explode between the American States took on fratricidal overtones in some families. Mixed border state sentiment spawned a tightrope of divided loyalties. The Prentiss brothers[9] of Baltimore embodied this predicament. They parted ways over slavery in 1857, each to take up the banner for opposites sides after the secession of the South. Tearful reconciliation came on an early April day in 1865, as each lay mortally wounded on a battlefield during the siege of Petersburg, Virginia. So too family ties at the White House unraveled. As a disheartened Lincoln spearheaded the Union's war, Mary Todd Lincoln's three brothers[10] fought for the Confederacy.

Of the then fourteen southern states, Alabama, Arkansas, Florida, Georgia, Kentucky, Louisiana, Maryland, Missouri, Mississippi, North Carolina, South Carolina, Tennessee, Texas and Virginia, all, save South Carolina, also mustered battalions[11] for the Union cause. Sympathies split as well as wavered. George W. and Stephen Penn of Alabama[12] saw action for their state in infantries of the Confederacy and in the Union First Cavalry. Comrade William H. Penn[13] remained loyal to the Confederate cause. He enlisted as a teenager in the Mississippi 36th Infantry early 1862. He was captured the next summer and paroled through a prisoner exchange later in the year. By spring of 1865 William once again was taken prisoner at Fort Blakley, Alabama to be pardoned the next January as the war had ended.

Though likely many were unrelated, about 340 men by the last name Penn fought in the War Between the States, 210 in the Confederate Army and 130 in Union forces. The most numerous southern Penn contingent of 30 soldiers hailed from the ancestral bedrock of Virginia, while those 29 from Ohio made up the greatest enlistment for the North. One wayfaring[14] Pickaway County, Ohio native, John W. Penn, signed on with the Colorado Territory 63rd Infantry before he deserted some months later. One Iowan recruit, Hiram Penn,[15] put in service on a round trip supply caravan that trudged about thirty miles a day over the 1100 miles from Nebraska City to Fort Union, New Mexico.

Virginia's Confederate "muster rolls resembled genealogical tables,"[16] so many related families from the Shenandoah Valley and Piedmont counties of the southwest had sent menfolk into battle. Descendants of Revolutionary-era brothers Abraham and Phillip Penn, yet concentrated ninety years later in cousin counties of Henry and Patrick, joined this wave. Uniformed in light-colored,[17] nine-button, single-breasted frock coats with dark plumb collar, John S. and William A. Penn stood behind seated older brothers Joseph G. and Thomas G.

Four Penn brothers from Patrick County, Virginia

Colonel John Edmund Penn

in a pre-deployment portrait. They would all soon march off to the north as part of Patrick County's Company H of the 42nd Virginia Infantry. The Volunteers from Patrick County drafted the brothers' cousin, John Edmond Penn,[18] as captain of the unit. No doubt with knowledge of exploits of great-grand sire Abraham Penn to carry him through, John Edmond went on to distinguish himself a leader in military and in later public life.

Third cousins likely unknown to the deeply-rooted Patrick County Penns played out their own roles in the saga of the War Between the States. John Edmond Penn's birth in 1837 near Penn's Store, Virginia coincided in the same decade with the arrival in the world of future adversary kin at the soon-to-appear Penn's Store in Kentucky.

Grandsons of Patrick County pioneer Phillip Penn, both namesake favorite Phillip and the younger, Gabriel Jackson Penn, stood well-established in Kentucky's south central Casey County before the nation fractured over abolition. That Phillip named his eldest son after his younger, ambitious brother, who launched Penn's Store, betokens regard between the two. But as the great showdown loomed they drifted apart. First Secretary of State in Kentucky, Harry Toulmin, wrote during his tenure at the very end of the 1700s that already that there was a "great proportion of the people[19] (of Kentucky) with a disposition to abolish slavery." Though Gabriel Jackson Penn yet kept three slaves[20] in 1860, Phillip by 1840 had divested himself of slaves[21] earlier counted as part of his household, whom he had likely brought with him from Virginia in 1829. Sensing the coming storm, Phillip uprooted his family[22] fifteen years later for slave-free southern Indiana. Contemporaries of Patrick County hero, John Edmond Penn, who lost a leg from battle, two of Phillip's sons took up arms for the Union cause. The youngest, teenager Edmond Penn,[23] died May 1863 at home from disease incurred while in the 49th Indiana Volunteer Infantry. Middle son,[24] Gabriel Jackson Penn, served three months at the end of hostilities, the last several weeks hospitalized at Wheeling, West Virginia. Their own suffering personified further bitter irony of the fraternal conflict that was The Civil War. For every soldier killed[25] from battle, two died from sickness brought on by starvation, exposure and typhoid.

This statistical gap stemmed from a deeper source—avoidance of killing one's fellow man.[26] Union soldier and diarist Benjamin McIntyre witnessed a night barrage of gunfire at Vicksburg in 1863. Over a short distance of just "fifteen steps," he was astounded that salvo after salvo caused not one fatality. Boot camp training practice with the black-powder weaponry of the time bore out its clout. Depending on the skill of the soldier and on size of infantry, a kill-rate of hundreds per minute was possible. An average instead of one or two deaths per minute stubbornly persisted. When coming up against a flesh-and-blood foe most soldiers fired over his head.

Epilogue

In the century-and-a-half since the end of the Civil War the diaspora of Virginia Penns has continued. Texas and California now stand as states most populated with this family name, at about 1800 persons each. But reflecting its history as the wellspring for so many with the last name, Virginia holds strong third place with around 1650 Penn households, whether all trace from the Immigrant boatswain or not.

Though the percent frequency of the Penn surname in Australia, Britain and in the United States remains miniscule at 0.004% to 0.008% (i.e., roughly 600 people in Australia, 6800 in the United Kingdom and 25,000 in the U.S.), the name is thus far flung. In the melting pot of the States, where PENN takes 1,765th slot as most common last name, 59% of persons carrying the name classify themselves as white, 39% as black, 3% as Hispanic and the reminder as "other ethnic groups."[1] The incomplete tabulation appended here traces lineages from the four sons of the Immigrant. This catalogue tallies around 200 presently living Penn-named persons. This count does not take into account hundreds of otherwise-surnamed Virginia descendants to whom the Penn name did not pass.

[1] USidentity.com; Locatemyname.com/usa/Penn; Taliesin-arlein.net/names/; Britishsurnames.co.uk.surname/penn/map

The name has assumed household word status from sports and entertainment personalities not related to the Penns of Virginia. One recent offspring of the Old Dominion line, however, has made a name for himself. The late Robert Penn Warren, descended through his mother from soldier/statesman Abraham Penn, holds the distinction as the only person ever to have won a Pulitzer Prize in fiction and a Pulitzer Prize in poetry.

Endnotes

Chapter 1: ENGLAND

1 *the surname Penn:* www.surnamedb.com/Surname/Penn; *The Pennsylvania Magazine of History of Biography,* vol. 14, 1890, "Genealogical Gleanings Contributory to a History of the Family of Penn."

2 *Pennocrucium: Roman Britain,* edited by Tom Stephenson, Odhams Press, Ltd, p.28.

3 *several locations named penn:* discovery.nationalarchives.gov.uk: Newport E329/246, Symonds Hall BCM/A/1/48/3, Buckinghamshire BCM/D/5/3/7, Lichfield sdrc.lib.uiowa.edu/patentrolls, Edward I, vol. 4.

4 Colin de la Penne: discovery.nationalarchives.gov.uk: E40/11535: Colin de la Penne, *Bracton's Note Book,* Vol. 3, p. 470, ed. By F.W. Maitland, C.J. Clay and Sons, Cambridge, 1887: John de la Penne, discovery.nationalarchives.gov.uk, DL 25/773/611.

5 Penland and Penn Manor: *A History of the County of Buckinghamshire,* Victoria County History, Vol. 3, 1925, pp. 155-165, 235-240.

6 *". . . a Gascon": Chapters in the Administrative History of Mediaeval England: The Wardrobe, The Chamber and the Small Seals,* Vol. 1, p. 255, T.F. Tout, The University of Manchester Press, 1920; Hugh de la Penne: sdrc.lib.uiowa.edu/patentrolls, Henry III, Vol. 4,5,6.

7 . . . *residents of London:* sdrc.lib.uiowa.edu/patentrolls, Edward II, Vol. 1,2,4,5; Edward III, Vol. 6.

8 *mariners of the surname Penn:* wills of mariners preserved at The National Archives, London, record set PROB 11/406/668, 11/473/391, 11/559/84, 11/567/195/, 11/761/387.

9 *At stated age of thirty-six:* The National Archives, Chancery Court Depositions, trinity term 1697, C24/1198.

10 *married and baptized his firstborn:* ancestry.com database, *England, Select Marriages, 1538-1973,* marriage of 11 Oct 1691, St. Olave, Southwark, Surrey, England; baptism of 4 Sep 1692, St. Olave, Southwark, Surrey, England.

11 baptisms, marriages and burials for Southwark churches extracted from ancestry.com database *London, England, Church of England Baptisms, Marriages and Burials, 1539-1812.*

12 *"in the king's ship":* The National Archives, London, PROB 6/66, folio 14.

13 *married local girl:* ancestry.com database, *London, England, Church of England Baptisms, Marriages and Burials, 1538-1812,* baptism 24 Sep 1671, St. Olave, Southwark, Surrey, England, Elizabeth Spencer.

14 . . . *"Damn It!": London: The Biography,* Peter Ackroyd, Anchor Books, 2003, p. 177.

15 . . . "hoot the king": ibidem, p. 386.

16 . . . *"violent polarization": London: A Social History,* Roy Porter, Harvard University Press, 1995, p. 58.

17 . . . *"jousting for the wall": From Poverty to Pets, From Medicine to Magic, From Slang To Sex, From Wallpaper to Women's Rights,* Lizabeth Picard, St. Martin's Press, 1998, p. 25.

18 *"Elizabethans were no . . .": The Time Traveler's Guide to Elizabethan England,* Ian Mortimer, Viking Press, 2012, p. 81.

19 . . . *welfare payments: The Economic History Review: a journal of economic and social history,* "Poor Relief in Elizabethan English Communities: An Analysis Accounts," Marjorie K. Mcintosh, Vol. 67, No. 2, May 2014, pp 331-332.

20 . . . *policing apparatus: London: A Social History,* Roy Porter, Harvard University Press, 1995, p. 57.

21 *"helped fuse the English identity": Tudors: The History of England from Henry VIII To Elizabeth I,* Peter Ackroyd, MacMillan, 2012, pp. 131-132.

22 description of London urban environment: *London: The Biography,* Peter Ackroyd, Anchor Books, 2003, pp. 129, 663.

23 *What the modern world recognizes as Cockney:* ibidem, pp. 150-51.

24 *If the local accent: The Time Traveler's Guide to Elizabethan England,* Ian Mortimer, Viking, 2012.

25 *Each district gave off its own stench: London: The Biography,* Peter Ackroyd, Anchor Books, 2003, p. 363, 427; *Coal: A Human History,* Barbara Freese, Basic Books, 2003, p. 30.

26 "peas and beans": *Sir Francis Drake: The Queen's Pirate,* Harry Kelsey, Yale University Press, 2002, p. 6.

27 *Tudor-style:* Pudding Lane Productions, Crytek Off-the-Map, 3-D animation of Pre-1666 London, youtube.com/watch?v=SPY-hr-8-M0

28 Raleigh: *Jamestown, The Buried Truth,* William M. Kelso, University of Virginia Press, 2007 p. 29; british-history.ac.uk/survey-london/vols43-4/pp548-552.

29 *personal effects of John Penn:* London Metropolitan Archives, will inventory, CLC/313/K/C/009/MS19S04/035/51.

30 *new gravaillaine:* burial records of St. Dunstan's All Saints, Stepney, London, microfilm X024/071, London Metropolitan Archives.

31 *mariner:* marriage record of Thomas Penn to Christian Billard 15 Jan 1653, St. Dunstan's, Stepney, London, P93/DUN/267, folio 6, London Metropolitan Archives; baptism of George Penn 10 Aug 1662 St. Dunstan's All Saints, Stepney, London, register P93/DUN, item 258; Ancestry.com. London England Baptisms, Marriages and Burials, 1538-1812.

32 *examinator:* burial record of Elizabeth Penn, 5 Feb 1661, St. Dunstan's All Saints, Stepney, London, microfilm X024/071, London Metropolitan Archives.

33 *apprenticeship as a cordwainer:* transcription of London Apprenticeship Abstracts, 1442-1850, original records at the National Archives London, accessed online at findmypast.com.

34 *Tristam Penn:* burial record, 24 Oct 1665, St. Dunstan's All Saints, Stepney, London, microfilm X024/071, London Metropolitan Archives.

35 *bloody flux (dysentery), scarlatina, whooping cough . . .: The Greatest Benefit to Mankind: A Medical History of Humanity,* Roy Porter, W.W. Norton and Company, New York and London, 1997, page 237.

36 *Plagues had been recorded: London: The Biography,* Peter Ackroyd, Anchor Books, 2003, pp. 194-195.

37 *"monster soup": Colonial Spirits: A Toast to Our Drunken History,* Steven Grasse, Abrams Image, New York, 2016, pp 4-6.

38 *What would come to be called the Great Plague: London: The Biography,* Peter Ackroyd, Anchor Books, 2003, pp. 124-125.

39 *The next catastrophe descended a year later: London's Burning: The Great Fire,* Bruce Robinson, category of British History at bbc.co.uk, 29 March 2011.

40 *poor pigeons were loath to leave:* ibidem, page 213.

41 *Indentured servants: White Cargo: The Forgotten History of Britain's White Slaves in America,* Don Jordon and Michael Walsh, New York University Press, New York 2007, page 126.

42 *An industry in itself: Brides from Bridewell: Female Felons Sent to America,* Walter Hunt Blumenthal, Charles E. Tuttle Company, Rutland, VT 1962; *White Servitude in the Colony of Virginia and Baltimore,* Johns Hopkins University Studies, 13th series, 1895, pp. 35-38.

43 *"The trade that developed": On the Path to Slavery: Indentured Servitude in Barbados and Virginia During the 17th Century,* Timothy Paul Grady, Master Thesis, Virginia Polytechnic Institute and State University, 2000, Page 2.nb

44 "when men, women and children were lured": british-history.ac.uk/report.aspx?compid=22733

45 *one of the precious few: Middlesex County Records, Volume III,* ed. by John Cordy Jaeffreson, The Middlesex County Records Society, Clerkenwell Sessions House, 1888, pp. 99-100.

Chapter 2: THE IMMIGRANT

1 . . . *forty persons of record:* compiled from published ship passenger lists drawn from these sources: Peter Wilson Coldham—*American Wills and Administrations in the Prerogative Court of Canterbury, 1610 to 1657; Bonded Passengers to America; The Complete Book of Emigrants, 1607 to 1660; More Emigrants In Bondage, 1614 to 1775; English Convicts in Colonial America, 1656 to 1775; The Bristol Registers of Servants Sent to Foreign Plantations 1654 to 1686; Lord Mayor's Court of London:* George Cabell Greer—*Early Virginia Immigrants, 1623 to 1666:* Henry B. Hoff—*English Origins of American Colonists:* Nell Marion Nugent—*Cavaliers and Pioneers: Abstracts of Virginia Land Patents, Vol. 1, 1623 to 1660:* Michael Teppe—*Passengers to America:* Beverley Fleet—*Virginia Colonial Abstracts:* Patrick G. Wardell—*Virginia and West Virginia, 1607 to 1870:* Carl Boyer—*Ship Passengers Lists: The South, 1538 to 1825:* R.F. Walker—*Colonial Records of Virginia.*

2 . . . *an urchin: Early Child Immigrants to Virginia,* 1619-1642, Robert Hume, Magna Carta Books, Baltimore, 1986 (copied from microfilm of original records at Bridewell/ Royal Bethlem Hospital Joint Archives, Beckenham, Kent).

3 *The dean of St. Paul's: White Cargo: The Forgotten History of Britain's White Slaves in America,* Don Jordan and Michael Walsh, New York University Press, New York, 2007, p. 85.

4 *Elizabeth Abbott:* ibidem, p. 80.

5 *Robert Penn: The Complete Book of Emigrants, 1607-1660,* Peter Coldham, Genealogical Publishing Company, Baltimore, 1987; *Virginia Immigrants and Adventurers, 1607-1635, A Biographical Dictionary,* Martha W. McCartney, Genealogical Publishing Company, 2007, p. 551; Library of Virginia, Colonial Records Project, *Records from the High Court of Admiralty Examinations, 1629-1630,* Survey Record 03810, p. 2.

6 *headright system:* Library of Virginia Research Notes 20, revised Sep 2009, compiled by Minor T. Weisinger; Library of Virginia (VA-NOTES), "Headrights," Daphne Gentry, Publications and Educational Services Division.

7 *Roger Penn: Cavaliers and Pioneers,* Nell Marion Nugent, Vol. 1, pp. 271, 369; *Virginia Gleanings in England,* Henry Fitz-Gilbert Waters, Genealogical Publishing Company, 1980, p. 106.

8 *Networks: White Cargo: The Forgotten History of Britain's White Slaves in America,* Don Jordan and Michael Walsh, New York University Press, New York, 2007, p. 118.

9 *. . . frequent instances of fraud:* Library of Virginia Research Notes 20, revised Sep 2009, compiled by Minor T. Weisinger, p.2, second paragraph; "Headrights and Head Counts: A Review Article," Edmund S. Morgan, *Virginia Magazine of History and Biography,* vol. 30, #3, part 1, 1972, pp. 361-71.

10 *George Penn: Cavaliers and Pioneers: Abstracts of Virginia Land Patents,* Nell Marion Nugent, Volume Two, Patent Book 7, p. 13.

11 *"Denn":* ancestry.co.uk; familysearch.org; one large family was located during the 17th century in Kent.

12 *Popular theory:* "Descendants of John Penn, Robert M. Allen, http://www.genealogy.com/ftm/a/1/1/ Robert-M-Allen-CA/ GENE3.0001.html

13 *. . . evidence available disintegrates: Cavaliers and Pioneers: Abstracts of Virginia Land Patents,* Nell Marion Nugent, Volume Two, p. 153.

14 *. . . first evidence:* The Library of Virginia, Essex County, Deeds and Wills [#110], 1699-1702 (Reel 3), p. 33 (b)-34(a), William Stone to Francis Merriwether, Deed 250 acres, 15 Jan 1699, recorded, 10 Apr 1700.

15 *John Fenn: Journal of the House of Burgesses of Virginia, 1619-1658,* Vol. Two, Accomoc County, 1682 (John Fenn assisted in capture of runaway Robert West); *Early Virginia Immigrants, 1623-1666,* George Cabell Greer, 1912 (a Samuel Fenn, 1637, James City, William Fenn, 1649, Upper New Norfolk); www.genealogy.com/ftm/b/r/o/Leighanne-L-Brown/GENES-0016.HTML (a John Fenn married Mary Stone, 1698, Richmond County; *Institutional History of Virginia in the 17th Century,* Phillip Alexander Bruce, G.P. Putnam's Sons, 1910 (a John Fenn fined in Accomoc; County for a Sabbath infraction, 1690; London Metropolitan Ar-

chives, microfilm MS28868, baptismal register, St. Olave Church, Hart Street, 1 Nov 1670.

16 *"Christ. Denn": Cavaliers and Pioneers: Abstracts of Virginia Land Patents,* Nell Marion Nugent, Volume One, Part II, p. 75.

17 *"Roger Denne":* ibidem, Volume One, #4, p. 369.

18 *"Bath. Penn":* ibidem, Volume One, Patent Book 7, p. 282.

19 *"Robert Penn":* ibidem, Volume One, Patent Book 7, p. 382.

20 *Crispiani Penn: Colonial Residents of Virginia's Eastern Shore Whose Ages Were Proved before Court Officials of Accomack and Northhampton Counties,* William R.M. Houston, M.D., Jean M. Mihalyka, Genealogical Publishing Company, 1985, p. 79; Library of Virginia, Order Book and Wills, #12, 1683-1689, Reel 27, pp. 298, 302-304.

21 *William Penn . . . in James City: Surrey County Records, Virginia, 1652-1689,* Elizabeth Timberlake Davis, Genealogical Publishing Company, 1980, p. 19; *Virginia Colonial Abstracts,* Series Two, Vol. 5, abstracted by Lindsay O. Duvall, York County Wills, Deeds, Orders, 1657-1659, p. 15; *Cavalier and Pioneers, Abstracts of Virginia Land Patents,* Nell Marion Nugent, Vol. One, Patent book 7, p. 269.

22 *John Penn of Lancaster County: Order Books of Lancaster County, Virginia, 1656-1661,* Ruth Sparacio and Sam Sparacio, The Antient Press, McLean, Virginia, 1993, quoting Lancaster County, Virginia Order Book, 1656-1666, p. 169, 226; *Cavaliers and Pioneers,* Nell Marion Nugent, Volume One, Patent Book 6, p. 107, 514; Library of Virginia: Lancaster County Deed Book, p. 149; (Old Rappahannock County Deed Book, 1665-1677, pp. 205-208; Essex County Deeds and Wills, 1692-1695, pp. 115-118, 193-195.

23 *John Penn . . . Charles City County:* Library of Virginia, Charles City County, Court Order Books, 1655-1658, p. 112; *Virginia Tax Records, Henrico County, Vestry Book of King William Parish,* pp 137, 162; *Cavaliers and Pioneers,* Nell Marion Nugent, Vol. Five, Patent Book 27, p. 301, Vol. 7, Patent Book 37, p. 149, 314; Library of Virginia: Deed 17 Oct 1750, Personal Papers Collection,

accession 29629; Wills and Administrations, Brunswick County, Virginia, 1732-1800, reel 21, pp. 196-198; Brunswick County, Virginia, Deed Book 11, Part 1, 530 (253), Part 2, 662 (404); Deed Book 14, p. 656 (257); *Brunswick County Marriages, 1750-1853,* John Vogt and T. William Kethley, Jr., Iberian Publishing Company, Athens, Georgia, pp. 103, 243.

24 *marriage of John Penn and Elizabeth Spencer:* London Metropolitan Archives, St. Olave, Bermondsey composite register, baptisms, marriages, burials 1685 to May 1716, P71/0LA/012, 11 Oct 1691; ancestry.com, "Select Marriages, 1538-1973," FHL #375307.

25 *baptism of John Penn:* ancestry.com, "London, England, Church of England Baptisms, Marriages and Burials, 1539-1812.

26 *place name trace:* "The Cult of St. Olave in the British Isles," *Saga-Book of the Viking Society,* 12 (1939) pp. 53-80.

27 *John Penn to be boatswain:* The National Archives, London, ADM 33/191, *St. Albans Prize* pay book, 01 Oct 1692, "John Penn, Boatswain, joined the ship on its first day Sea Wages."

28 *deposition:* The National Archives, London, Chancery Court Depositions, trinity term 1697, C24/1198.

29 *horse pasture: A Topographic History of Surrey*, Edward Wedlake Brayley, et al., published by G. Willis, London, 1850, Vol. 5, p. 381.

30 *brick row house: Calendar State Papers, Domestic Series, of the Reign of Charles II,* 1661-1662, Edited by Mary Anne Everett Green, Longman, Green, Longman and Roberts, London, 1861, p. 288.

31 *stairs:* "Watermen's Stairs", en.m.wikipedia.org; *William Morgan's Map of the Whole of London in 1682*, www.british-history.ac.uk/no-series/london-map-morgan/1682/map

32 *a mile west: A Plan of the Cities of London and Westminster, and Borough of Southwark, with the New Buildings 1767,* plan map of London, viewable at https://mapco.net/anon/anon.htm.

33 *St. Olave's: Old and New London,* Edward Walford, Cassell and Company, Ltd., London, Vol. VI, 1893, pp. 100-117.

34 *London Bridge: Old London Bridge: The Story of the Longest Inhabited Bridge in Europe,* Patricia Pierce, Headline Books, 2001.

35 *York River, Virginia:* ibidem, ADM 106/437, folio 270, 18 Oct 1693 (this document records that the *St. Albans Prize* had arrived at York River 7 Oct 1693).

36 *Portsmouth:* ibidem, ADM 106/522, folio 26, 21 Feb 1697/8 ("Portsmouth Dockyard . . . John Penn, Boatswain of the St Albans Prize, to go to London, to attend the Board next day if possible.").

37 *dismissed:* ibidem, ADM 1/3583 ("The Boatsw[ain] Jn Penn (who was one) [who signed said Books], any wages not received to be stopped, and the Master (of the ship) [John Ore] never to be employed again.").

38 *Baskerville:* ibidem, ADM 106/519, folio 76, 16 Feb 1697/8 ("There is a problem with the payment of the St Albans Prize . . . they have Wm Baskerville, once a Minister of the Navy, in custody . . .").

39 *Kristina Bedford:* e-mail from Kristina Bedford, Ancestral Deeds Research and Transcription Services, London, UK, 8 Oct 2017.

40 *. . . may have gotten himself . . .:* The National Archives, London, Admiralty Records, ADM 106/ 541/56, 106/559/332, 106/559/407.

41 *"tarnished reputations and economic failures behind": White Trash: The 400-Year Untold History of Class in America,* Nancy Isenberg, Penguin Books, 2016, p. 14.

42 *two to fifteen pounds: Calendar of State Papers Colonial, America and West Indies,* British History Online, entry 739.

43 *quit rents:* The National Archives, London, within the collection CO 5/1314, part 3, folio 177; *The Quit Rents of Virginia,* compiled by Annie Laurie Wright Smith, 1957, Richmond, Virginia, reprinted by Genealogical Publishing Company, 1975, 1977, 1980, 1987 ("Copy of the Rent Rolls of the Sevll Countys in Virga. for the year 1704 referred to in Col. Nicholson lst: of the 25th July last"); *English Duplicates of Lost Virginia Records,* Louis de Cognets, Jr., 1958, reprinted by Genealogical Publishing Company, 1981, 1990.

44 *acquired property through a private party:* e-mail from Sarah Huggins, Library of Virginia, 15 Nov 2017.

45 *Large landholders: Virginia Historical Magazine,* Vol. 28. Jul 1920,

#S, "Virginia Quit Rent Rolls," 1704.

46 *"doomed by slave labor": The Planters of Colonial Virginia,* Thomas J. Wertenbaker, Russell and Russell, New York, 1954, pp. ii, iv.

47 *With some details . . . distorted:* ibidem, p. 10.

48 *John Walker: In Old Virginia: Slavery, Farming and Society in the Journal of John Walker,* Claudia L. Bushman, Johns Hopkins University Press, Baltimore and London, 2002, p. 13.

49 *A grandson of John Penn:* The Library of Virginia, Amherst County, Land Records, Deed Book C, reel 1, p. 429.

CHAPTER 3: TO VIRGINIA

1 *For the ocean crossing: Brides from Bridewell: Female Felons Sent to Colonial America,* by Walter Hart Blumenthal, originally published by Charles E. Tuttle Co. Inc, Rutland, Vermont, 1962, reprinted by Greenwood Press, Westport, Connecticut, 1973, p. 24; *The Infortunate: The Voyage and Adventures of William Moraley, An Indentured Servant,* edited by Susan E. Klepp and Billy G. Smith, second edition, Penn State University, University Park, PA, 2005, p. 24.

2 *vinegar:* The National Archives, London, ADM 106/437, folio 270, 18 Oct 1693, Capt. Edward Poulson, *St. Albans Prize,* arrived York River, Virginia "the 7th, asks for vinegar to combat scurvy."

3 *John Smith: John Smith, The General History: The Third Book, The Proceeding and Accidents of the English Colony in Virginia, extracted from the author folloing* [sic] *by William Simons, Doctor of Divinity, London,* printed I.D. and I.H. for Michael Sparkes, 1624, reprinted in *Jamestown Narratives, Eyewitness Accounts of the Virginia Colony, The First Decade, 1607-1617,* Champlain, Virginia, Roundhouse, 1998.

4 *arrived healthy: The infortunate: The Voyage and Adventures of William Moraley, An Indentured Servant,* p. 24

5 *"fish—gig": The Voyages and Travels of Captain Nathaniel Uring,* published 1726, edited by Alfred Dewar, reprint 1928, p. 23.

6 *little drinking water: The Infortunate: The Voyage and Adventures of William Moraley, An Indentured Servant,* p. 24.

7 *livestock: Marooned: Jamestown, Shipwreck, and a New History of America's Origin,* Joseph Kelly, Bloomsbury Publishing, New York, London, Oxford, New Dehli, Sydney, 2018, p. 244.

8 *Bodies maimed: The British Seaman, 1200-1860: A Social Survey,* Christopher Lloyd, Associated University Press, Cranbury, New Jersey, 1970, p. 262.

9 *"Jack Tar": Between the Devil and the Deep Blue Sea,* Marcus Rediker, Cambridge University Press, 1993, pp. 12, 24, 83, 153.

10 *Having set sail from Plymouth:* The National Archives, London, ADM 106/433, folio 104; ADM 106/437, folio 270.

11 *the pecking order: The Rise of the English Shipping Industry: In the 17th and 18th Centuries,* Ralph Davis, MacMillan, 1962, pp. 110-113.

12 *boatswain acted as a foreman:* ibidem, p. 112.

13 *Penn's pay:* The National Archives, London, ADM 33/191.

14 *twenty-five Englishmen:* ibidem.

15 *six makeshift landings:* The National Archives, London, CO 5/1441; "Naval Office Shipping Lists for Virginia, 1698-1774," FamilySearch microfilm 007940914.

16 *"tea-colored water": Richmond Times-Dispatch,* "Owners Voluntarily Protecting Land along the Mattaponi," Rex Springston, 11 Apr 2014.

17 *"like a forest standing in water":* "Report of the Journey of Francis Michel from Berne, Switzerland to Virginia, October 2, 1701 to December 1, 1702," *The Virginia Magazine of History and Biography,* XXIV, Jan. 1916, no. 1, p. 16.

18 *But the region could be deadly: Albion's Seed: Four British Folkways in America,* David Hackett Fischer, Oxford University Press, New York and Oxford, 1989, p 251.

19 *Tsenacomoco: Powhatan Foreign Relations, 1500-1722,* "Who Were the Powhatans and Did They Have a Unified 'Foreign Policy,'" Helen C. Rountree, University Press of Virginia, Charlottesville, Virginia, 1993, pp. 1-20.

20 *"ancient general Burroughs": 1619: Jamestown and the Forging of American Democracy,* James Horn, Basic Books, New York, 2018, p. 134.

21 *"had a taste for living solitary and unsociable (lives)": DeBow's Review,* Vol. XXV, edited by J.D.B. DeBow, New Orleans and Washington, D.C., 1858, p. 205.

22 *"Getting used to": Adapting to a New World: English Society in the Seventeenth Chesapeake,* James Horn, University of North Carolina Press, 1994, p. 141.

23 *Gloucester Point: Albion's Seed: Four British Folkways in America,* David Hackett Fischer, Oxford University Press, New York and Oxford, 1989, p. 390.

24 *wattle-and-daub construction: The Barbarous Years: The Conflict of Civilizations, 1600-1675,* Bernard Bailyn, Alfred A. Knopf, New York, 2012, p. 95.

25 *first arrivals were a lazy lot: White Trash: The 400-Year Untold History of Class in America,* Nancy Isenberg, Viking, an imprint of Penguin Random House LLC, New York, 2016, p. 11.

26 *Mutiny hung the air: Marooned: Jamestown, Shipwreck, and a New History of America's Origin,* Joseph Kelly, Bloomsbury Publishing, New York, London, Oxford, New Dehli, Sydney, 2018, pp. 404, 405, 409, 410, 412.

27 *Once founding colonist John Rolfe: Cradle of America: A History of Virginia,* Peter Wallenstein, University Press of Kansas, 2014, p. 22.

28 *Sassafras: The American Plate: A Culinary History in 100 Bites,* Libby O'Connell, Sourcebooks, Inc. 2014, p. 35.

29 *"permeated each other": The Barbarous Years: The Conflict of Civilizations, 1600-1675,* Bernard Bailyn, Alfred A. Knopf, New York, 2012, p. 99.

30 *"no longer purely Indian": Marooned: Jamestown, Shipwreck, and a New History of America's Origin,* Joseph Kelly, Bloomsbury Publishing, New York, London, Oxford, New Dehli, Sydney, 2018, p. 286.

31 *Fanning the flames of discontent:* ibidem, p. 101-102; *Cradle of America: A History of Virginia,* Peter Wallenstein, University Press of Kansas, 2014, p. 22-23.

32 *"deference from inferiors: Albion's Seed: Four British Folkways in America,* David Hackett Fischer, Oxford University Press, New York and Oxford, 1989, p. 385.

33 *"damn-you-get-out-of-the-way gallop": An Imperfect God: George Washington, His Slaves and the Creation of America,* Henry Wiencek, Farrar, Strauss and Giroux, 2003, p. 30.

34 *"bottom of the middle": The Barbarous Years: The Conflict of Civilizations, 1600-1675,* Bernard Bailyn, Alfred A. Knopf, New York, 2012, pp. 171-172.

35 *"more sinned against than sinning": Brides from Bridewell: Female Felons Sent to Colonial Virginia,* Walter Hart Blumenthal, originally published by Charles E. Tuttle Co., Inc., Rutland, Vermont,1962, reprinted by Greenwood Press, Westport, Connecticut, 1973, p. 21.

36 *"instead of being composed of": Harper's Monthly,* Harold Faulkner, Dec 1925, p. 84.

37 *"Descent from the Mayflower": Brides from Bridewell: Female Felons Sent to Colonial Virginia,* Walter Hart Blumenthal, originally published by Charles E. Tuttle Co., Inc., Rutland, Vermont, 1962, reprinted by Greenwood Press, Westport, Connecticut, 1973, p. 7.

38 *"there was nothing genteel about it:" The Barbarous Years: The Conflict of Civilizations, 1600-1675,* Bernard Bailyn, Alfred A. Knopf, New York, 2012, p. xv.

39 *"Whereas the private . . .": The Statutes at Large: Being a Collection of the Laws of Virginia,* William Waller Hening, published by R.W. and G. Bartlow, 1823, Vol. 2, p. 53, Act XV, March 1661-1662, "Buriall of Servants or others privately prohibited . . .."

40 *A shallow grave:* "Written in Bone. Body in the Basement," Chip Clark, *Smithsonian Institution Archive,* Department of Anthropology, Natural Museum of Natural History, 2008.

41 *Edward Penn: England, Births and Christenings, 1538-1975,* index based upon data collected by the Genealogical Society of Utah, microfilm 908518; will of Edward Penn, Anne Arundel County, Maryland, 5 June 1741, liber 26, folio 559, 1742, Box P, Folder 24, Box 44, folder 12.

42 *"none but those of the meanest quality":* from *A Discourse and View of Virginia, First Hand Account, Sir William Berkeley,* London, 1663, reprinted by William H. Smith, Norwalk, Connecticut, 1914, p. 3, digitized by Google Books.

43 *"the climate and external appearance": Burnaby's Travels through North America,* A. Wessels Company, New York, 1904, p. 54 digitized by Google Books.

44 *Durand de Dauphine: A Huguenot Exile in Virginia,* edited and translated by Gilbert Chinard, New York, 1934, pp. 138-139.

45 *Economic conditions in England: Adapting to a New World: English Society in the Seventeenth Century Chesapeake,* James Horn, University of North Carolina Press, 1994, p. 163; *On the Path to Slavery: Indentured Servitude in Barbados and Virginia During the Seventeenth Century,* Timothy Paul Grady, Master's Thesis, Virginia Polytechnic Institute and State University, 2000, p. 19.

46 *children not "catechized":* response to questionnaire, originating with the Bishop of London, by Rev. Lewis Latane, South Farnham, Essex County, Virginia 11 May 1724, reproduced in *Settlers, Southerners, Americans: The History of Essex County, Virginia, 1608-1984,* p. 20.

47 *Overindulgence was the core: A Huguenot Exile in Virginia,* edited and translated by Gilbert Chinard, New York, 1934, pp. 138-139.

48 *"men, women, girls and boys":* ibidem, p. 118.

49 *Indians were still stalking colonists: Colonial Caroline: A History of Caroline County, Virginia,* T.E. Campbell, The Dietz Press Inc., Richmond, Virginia, 1954, 1989, pp. 14, 16.

50 *The London Post:* cited in *Archaeological Investigation of the Remains of Two Early 18th-Century Vessels on the Mattaponi River at Newington Plantation, King and Queen County, Virginia,* Virginia Department of Historic Resources Research Report, no. 18, principal investigator and author Gordon P. Watts, Jr., Ph.D, R.P.A., 2013, p. 13.

51 *ventures the thought: Albion's Seed: Four British Folkways in America,* David Hackett Fischer, Oxford University Press, New York and Oxford, 1989, p. 255.

52 *Francis Louis Michel:* "Report of the Journey of Francis Louis Michel from Berne Switzerland to Virginia, October 2, 1701 to December 1, 1702," part II, edited and translated by William Hinke, *Virginia Magazine of History and Biography,* 24:2, pp. 136-140, Apr 1916.

53 *The sound of day-to-day discourse: Albion's Seed: Four British Folkways in America,* David Hackett Fischer, Oxford University Press, New York and Oxford, 1989, pp. 256-264; *The Hemingses of Monticello: An American Family,* Annette Gordon-Reed, W.W. Norton, New York, 2008, p. 284.

54 *a distinct divide would arise:* www.livescience.com/33652-americans-britis-accents.html

55 *"hall and parlor design": Albion's Seed: Four British Folkways in America,* David Hackett Fischer, Oxford University Press, New York and Oxford, 1989, p. 271.

56 *Poplar Grove:* www.freestateofpatrick.com/revwar

57 *hilly backwoods of Kentucky: A History of Penn's Store (Kentucky),* Jeanne Penn Lane, self-published, revised edition 1993, p. 20.

58 *pre-Norman English manor: Albion's Seed: Four British Folkways in America,* David Hackett Fischer, Oxford University Press, New York and Oxford, pp. 239, 390; *The Architecture of the Old South: The Medieval Style, 1585-1850,* Henry Chandlee Forman, Russell and Russell, 1967, p. 26.

59 *"Christian slaves": A Huguenot Exile in Virginia,* edited and translated by Gilbert Chinard, New York, 1934, p. 119.

60 *below the lowest in England: The Barbarous Years: The Conflict of Civilizations, 1600-1675,* Bernard Bailyn, Alfred A. Knopf, New York, 2012, pp. 171-172.

61 *"first sleep": Dreamland: Adventures in the Strange Science of Sleep,* David K. Randall, W.W. Norton and Co., New York, 2012, pp. 32-36.

62 *"People spent most of their waking hours": What God Hath Wrought: The Transformation of America,* Daniel Walker Howe, Oxford University Press, New York and Oxford, 2007, p. 32.

63 *"White people rightly so believed":* ibidem, p. 32.

64 *Skeletal remains of Jamestown: Written in Bone: Buried Lives of Jamestown and Colonial Maryland,* Sally M. Walker, Carolrboda Books, Minneapolis, Minnesota, 2009, pp. 38, 48, 60, 92, 103.

65 *". . . slightly taller than the average": Jamestown: The Buried Truth,* William Kelso, University of Virginia, 2006, p. 126.

66 *"now wife": Albion's Seed: Four British Folkways in America,* David Hackett Fischer, Oxford University Press, New York and Oxford, 1989, p. 172.

67 *"in some secluded corner":* ibidem, p. 329.

68 *"children of the elite":* ibidem, p. 304.

69 *"either by blood or marriage": An Imperfect God: George Washington, His Slaves and the Creation of America,* Henry Wiencek, Farrar, Strauss and Giroux, New York, 2003, p. 33.

Chapter 4: FOUR SONS

1 *filed suit against Spencer:* The National Archives, London, Chancery Court Records, C 10/454/13; examination by Susan Moore at The National Archives, London, in Chancery Orders and Decrees from 1710 to 1713 shows no answer by the defendant filed with the plaintiff's Bill of Complaint, implying that the case did not proceed, either dropped or settled out of court.

2 *"burned record counties":* Library of Virginia, Research Notes #7, compiled by Virginia Dunne, revised Oct 2009.

3 *bible of Ambrose and Frances Taylor Madison:* Library of Virginia, Archives/Manuscript Collection, #20870, Madison Family Bible Record, 1723-1871.

4 *John Maddison:* Library of Virginia, Land Office Patents, #3, 23 Nov 1653, Reel 12, p. 216.

5 *personal account book:* Shane Collection, Presbyterian Historical Society, Philadelphia, Madison Family Papers, 1717-1753, Box 16, Folder 12.

6 *. . . suggest family ties:* Library of Virginia, Spotsylvania County, Deed Book A, 1722-1729, Reel 1, p. 292.

7 *"Lucy, a negro girl":* Library of Virginia, Caroline County, Order Book, 1732-1740, reel 13.

8 *The fourth son:* Library of Virginia, Caroline County, Order Book, 1741-1746, Part 1, reel 14. pp. 42-43, 46, 53, 121, 123, 143, 147.

9 *Younger brothers Joseph and Moses married:* contents of original bible (since lost) published in *William and Mary Quarterly,* Series 1, Vol. 12, 1903-1904.

10 *conveyance by treasury right:* Library of Virginia, Research Notes 20, revised Sep 2009, compiled by Minor T. Weisinger, p. 2, third paragraph.

11 *George Penn . . . 1000 acres: Cavaliers and Pioneers,* Dennis Ray Hudgins, Vol. 7, Patent Book 36, p. 73.

12 *"the favorites": Colonial Caroline: A History of Caroline County, Virginia,* T.E. Campbell, Dietz Press, Inc., Richmond, Virginia, 1954, 1989, p. 293.

13 *George deeded the land:* Library of Virginia, Spotsylvania County, Deed Book B, 1729-1734, p. 113.

14 *Setting up the County of Caroline: A History of Caroline County Virginia,* T.E. Campbell, pp. 53-58.

15 *hogshead:* ncpedia.org/tobacco/barrels

16 *Robert Beverley: Colonial Caroline: A History of Caroline County, Virginia,* T. E. Campbell, pp. 28-39.

17 *"saved Virginia":* ibidem, p. 33.

18 *"primitive baronial splendor":* ibidem, p. 34.

19 *Drysdale Parish:* ibidem, p. 51-52.

20 *Ivey Church:* ibidem, p. 52.

21 *exact boundaries: The Vestry Book of Petsworth Parish, 1677-1793, Gloucester County, Virginia,* C.G. Chamberlayne, published by the Library Broad, Richmond, Virginia, 1933, foldout map at front of book; e-mail from Page McLemore, King and Queen County Historical Society, 23 Nov 2015.

22 *Scourge beset the 1730s: Colonial Caroline, A History of Caroline County, Virginia,* T. E. Campbell, p. 71.

23 *freeholders:* ibidem, p. 65.

24 *His civic sense bordered on bravery:* ibidem, p. 362.

25 *selling rum without a license:* ibidem, p. 415.

26 *acquired two slaves:* ibidem, p. 330.

27 *"a negro girl named Candis":* Library of Virginia, Caroline County, Court Order Book, 1732-1740, Part 2, 13 June 1740.

28 *slavery was fully anchored: Sons of Providence,* Charles Rappleye, Simon and Schuster, 2006, p. 11.

29 *Those first Africans:* "The First Black Americans," Tim Hashaw, *U.S. News and World Report,* 29 Jan—5 Feb 2007; *Myne Owne Ground: Race and Freedom on Virginia's Eastern Shore,* T.H. Breen and Stephen Innes, Oxford Press, 1980, pp. 7-18, 68-109.

30 *"For a brief time": An imperfect God: George Washington, His Slaves, and the Creation of America,* Henry Wiencek, MacMillan, 2003, p. 42.

31 *"negroes, moors, mulattoes or Indians":* ibidem, p. 42.

32 *As economic conditions shifted: Cradle of America: Four Centuries of Virginia History,* Peter Wallenstein, University of Kansas Press, 2007, p. 34.

33 *Figures exist: An Imperfect God: George Washington, His Slaves, and the Creation of America,* Henry Wiencek, MacMillan, 2003, p. 79.

34 *"In spite of the blacks' debased status": Slave Counterpoint: Black Culture in the Eighteenth-Century Chesapeake and Lowcountry,* Omohundro Institute of Early American History and Culture and the University of North Carolina Press, 1998, p. 8.

35 *The forward-thinking planter: Cradle of America: Four Centuries of Virginia History,* Peter Wallenstein, University of Kansas Press, 2007, p. 33-34; *The Hemingses of Monticello,* Annette Gordon-Reed. W.W. Norton and Company, 2008, p. 671.

36 *"thoroughly subjugated work force": The Hemingses of Monticello,* Annette Gordon-Reed, W.W. Norton and Company, 2008, p. 671.

37 *"I am sensible":* from a letter written by Col. William Byrd, Receiver-General for the Colony of Virginia to the Earl of Egmont, of Georgia, 12 July 1736, reprinted in the *American Historical Review,* New York, 1896.

38 *By the time John Penn died: Cradle of America: Four Centuries of Virginia History,* Peter Wallenstein, University of Kansas Press, 2007, p. 38.

39 *"how a slave woman became pregnant":* ibidem, p. 38.

40 *"Like patriarchs of old": Mary Chesnut's Civil War,* edited C. Vann Woodward and Mary Boykin Chesnut, Yale University Press, 1981, p. 29.

41 *Cockacoeske: Dictionary of Virginia Biography, Encyclopedia of Virginia,* Martha McCartney, 30 May 2014, retrieved from the web 24 Dec 2018.

42 *The first of John Penn Sr.'s sons to die: Colonial Caroline, A History of Caroline County, Virginia,* T.E. Campbell, p. 473; Library of Virginia, Index of Wills, Inventories and Administrations from Caroline County Order Books, 1732-1800, reel 12.

43 *She died there in 1794:* Library of Virginia, Amherst County, Will Book #3, reel 18, p. 302, will of Ann Penn Dudley filed 6 May 1794, probated 2 July 1794.

44 *Moses Penn also passed:* Library of Virginia, Caroline County Order Book, 1759-1763, 13 Dec 1759, p. 87; *Colonial Caroline, A History of Caroline County, Virginia,* T.E. Campbell, p. 477.

45 *Both and Joseph Penn:* Library of Virginia, Spotsylvania County, Deed Book F, pp. 222, 231.

Chapter 5: GENERATION OF REVOLUTION

1 *French and Indian War: Cradle of America: Four Centuries of Virginia History,* Peter Wallenstein, University of Kansas Press, 2007, pp. 55-59.

2 *shut down the market: Colonial Caroline: A History of Caroline County Virginia,* T.E. Campbell, Dietz Press, Inc., p. 145.

3 *"the hazards of living among the Indians":* ibidem, p. 150.

4 *A radical patriot:* ibidem, p. 457 (from Order Book of the Caroline Court, 1772); *The King And Queen County Historical Society Bulletin,* # 44, January 1978 (no sources cited in this article); *Eighteenth-Century Newspapers,* compiled by Robert K. Headley, Jr., *The Virginia Gazette,* 5 May 1774, Genealogical Publishing Company, 1980.

5 *Deed books of Spotsylvania County:* The Library of Virginia, Deed Books of Spotsylvania County, Deed Book F, reel 3; *Spotsylvania County, 1721-1800, being transcriptions from the original files at the county court house, of wills, deeds, administrators' and guardians' bonds, marriage licenses and lists of revolutionary pensioners,* William Armstrong Crozier, New York, publishers for the Genealogical Association by Fox, Duffield and Company, 1905, pp. 227, 228,232, 291, 302, 303.

6 *Phillip Penn and wife Martha . . . conveyed:* The University of Virginia, Spotsylvania County, Deed Book F, reel 3, 6 Sep 1762.

7 *Gabriel Penn in Amherst:* ibidem, p. 231; *Chronicles of the Scotch-Irish settlement of Virginia: extracted from original court records of Augusta County, Virginia, 1745-1800,* Lyman Chalkley, Genealogical Publishing Company, 1989, p. 210.

8 *End of the French and Indian War:* "proof" of this service derived from Land Office Warrant #229, of the Commonwealth of Virginia, issued 4 Dec 1779 to assignee of Gabriel Penn, Joseph Cabell, for Penn's service in the French and Indian War under Col. William Byrd in 1764, document now in possession of the Library of Congress.

9 *During the Revolution: Historical Collections of the Georgia Chapters of the Daughters of the American Revolution,* p. 138.

10 *Isaiah Giles: Virginia Militia in the Revolutionary War: McAllister's Data,* J.T. McAllister, McAllister Publishing, Hot Springs, Virginia, 1913, p. 69.

11 *Sally Grey: Eighteenth-Century Newspapers,* compiled by Robert K. Headley, Jr., *The Virginia Gazette,* 4 Aug 1774, Genealogical Publishing Company, 1987.

12 *Molley:* letter from Gabriel Penn to William S. Crawford, 27 Jul 1792, original in the possession of the Wes McCarty Family, reprinted in *Amherst County,* Vol. II, Walsworth Publishing Company for the Amherst County, Virginia Heritage Book Committee, 2004.

13 *from Baylor Walker:* The Library of Virginia, Amherst County, Land Records, Deed Book C, reel 1, p. 429.

14 *"little weddings": Adapting to a New World: English Society in the Seventeenth-Century Chesapeake,* Omohundro Institute and University of North Carolina Press, 1996, pp. 207, 209.

15 *"being a married couple":* e-mail from L. Eileen Parris, archivist, Virginia Historical Society, 10 Jan 2014.

16 *Ruth Stovall:* The Library of Virginia, Amherst County, Index to Register of Marriage Register, 1763-1854, reel 37; Marriage Bonds and Consents, 1763-1783, Reel 104. P. 1.

17 *The association between:* "Meet Your Cousins: Genealogy of the Samuel Crutcher (Sr.) Family, about 1750-1969," Mildred Holladay Adams Jones, Pecos, Texas, self-published monograph. Locknet.com/crutcher/sources/meetyourcousins.pdf

18 "You weren't going to move away": *The Edge of the World: a Cultural History of the North Sea and the Transformation of Europe,* Michael Pye, Pegasus Books, 2016, p. 141.

19 *in the red beholden:* "I.O.U.," Jill Lepore, *The New Yorker,* 13 Apr 2009.

20 *"tobacco lords": A History of Scotland,* Neil Oliver, Weidenfeld and Nicholson, an imprint Of Orion Books, 2009, p. 25.

21 *McCall, Smillie and Company:* Library of Virginia, Spotsylvania County, Deed Book H, 1771-1774, 21 Jan 1773, microfilm reel #4.

22 *"declaring independence":* ibidem.

23 *ceased in Virginia courts: The Statutes at Large of Virginia,* William Waller Hening, printed originally by R & W & G Barlow, New York, 1823, digitized version by FamilySearch International, 2015, 5: 326-344, 8: 515-516 (referenced in *Westward into Kentucky: the narrative of Daniel Trabue,* edited by Chester Raymond Young, University Press of Kentucky, Lexington, 1981, pp. 162-163.)

24 *A dark mood: Westward into Kentucky: the narrative of Daniel Trabue,* edited by Chester Raymond Young, University Press of Kentucky, Lexington, 1981, pp. 40, 47, 162.

25 *"above the age of sixteen": Statutes,* Hening, 9: 27, 89-90; The Library of Virginia, Research Notes # 8, Minor T. Weisiger, revised Sep 2006.

26 *defeat of Lord Dunmore: Westward into Kentucky: the narrative of Daniel Trabue,* edited by Chester Raymond Young, University Press of Kentucky, Lexington, 1981, p. 163, note 55.

27 *"utterly contrary to the knowne Laws and Statutes and freedome of the Realm": American Scripture: Making the Declaration of Independence,* Pauline Maier, Vintage Books, a division of Random House, Inc, New York, 1997, p. 53 (quoting from the Declaration of Rights of 1689, which ended the reign of James II).

28 *oft-forgotten overtures: Robert Morris: Financier of the American Revolution,* Charles Rappleye, Simon and Schuster, 2010, p. 127.

29 *Fifth Convention at Williamsburg: The General Assembly of Virginia, July 30, 1619-January 11, 1978,* compiled by Cynthia M. Leonard, prepared under the auspices of The Library Board, 6 May to 5 Jul 1776 and 7 Oct to 21 Dec 1776.

30 *Gabriel's younger brother: Amherst County in the Revolution: Including the "Lost Order Book,"* Leonora Higgenbotham Sweeny, J.P. Bell Company, Lynchburg, Virginia, 1951, p. 158; The Library of Virginia, Amherst County, Will Book 1, p. 355.

31 *Another Amherst County Penn brother:* The Library of Virginia, Amherst County, Deed Book B, p. 248, 5 Oct 1767; The Library of Virginia, Pittsylvania County, Deed Book 3, p. 304, 30 Oct 1772.

32 *House of General Assembly: The General Assembly of Virginia, July 30, 1619-January 11, 1978,* compiled by Cynthia M. Leonard, prepared under the auspices of The Library Board, 5 May to Jun 1777 and 20 Oct 1777 to 24 Jan 1778.

33 For service he may have put in: all citations of the military career for Abraham Penn drawn from the monograph, *Abraham Penn's Military Services*, compiled and annotated by C. Leon Harris, as commissioned by Cherie Allemand Sckorohod.

34 Lieutenant Penn: *Virginia's Colonial Soldiers*, L.D. Bockstruck, Genealogical Publishing Company, Baltimore, 1988, p. 3.

35 Minute Men to guard Jamestown: revwarapps.org: S1790, W3656, R2476, R8715, R10387.

36 riflemen: *Virginia Military Records*, Genealogical Publishing Company, Baltimore, 1983, pp. 461, 478, 499, 500, 501.

37 "competent and charismatic leaders": *Patriot Militiaman in the American Revolution 1775-82*, Ed Gilbert and Catherine Gilbert, Osprey Publishing Ltd., 2015, p. 9.

38 rank of colonel: *Virginia Militia in the Revolutionary War*, J.T. McCallister, Heritage Books, Westminster, Maryland, 1913, p. 209.

39 troops against Tories: revwarapps.org: S31558, W8367, W79, S37943, R10395.

40 several Tory prisoners: revwarapps.org/S1597

41 *At a low point: The Works of Thomas Jefferson,* Thomas Jefferson, Federal Edition, New York and London, G.P. Putnum's Sons, 1904-5, Vol. 3. Chapter: "To Colonel Abraham Penn."

42 *Abraham Penn managed to muster:* letter from Abraham Penn to William Fleming, digitized at Library of Virginia, call number: GLR01460.

43 *The end could not have at a better time: Westward into Kentucky: the narrative of Daniel Trabue,* edited by Chester Raymond Young, University Press of Kentucky, Lexington, 1981, p. 184, note 18; *White Trash: The 400-Year Untold History of Class in America,* Nancy Isenberg, Viking, 2016, p. 89; *Valiant Ambition: George Washington, Benedict Arnold and the Fate of the American Revolution,* Nathaniel Philbrick, Penguin Books, 2016, pp. 187-190.

44 "in which they excelled": *Patriot Militiaman in the American Revolution 1775-82,* Ed Gilbert and Catherine Gilbert, Osprey Publishing Ltd., 2015, p. 6.

45 The ceaseless war: ibidem, p. 59.

46 *Profiteering: American History Revised: 200 Startling Facts That Never Made It into The Textbooks,* Seymour Morris Jr., Broadway Books, 2010, pp. 144-145.

47 *citizens had provided goods: Amherst County Revolutionary Public Claims,* Janice L. Abercrombie and Richard Slatten, Iberian Publishing, Athens, Georgia, 2005, pp. 5, 16, 26, 28, 29, 31, 32, 34, 37, 39.

48 *Sole evidence of military service: Amherst County, Virginia in the Revolution, Including Extracts from the "Lost Order Book" 1773-1782,* Lenora Higgenbotham Sweeny, J.P. Bell Company, Lynchburg, Virginia, 1951, p 55-56; *Virginia Soldiers of 1776,* Louis A. Burgess, Richmond Press Inc., Richmond, Virginia, 1929, Vol. 3; National Archives and Records Administration, negative result for search of name Phillip Penn in Bounty-Land Warrant Applications, Full Pension Files, Pre-Civil War Military Service Records, searches performed 10 and 11 June 2014; The Library of Virginia, negative result for name of Phillip Penn in indexes of Dunmore's War Payroll and Service or of French and Indian War Military Bounty Warrants.

49 *glosses over the slaughter: Scars of Independence: America's Violent Birth,* Holger Hoock, Crown, a trademark of Penguin Random House, LLC, 2017, pp. 317-320.

Chapter 6: AMERICANS

1 "majoritarian confusion": *Empire of Liberty: A History of the Early Republic, 1789-1815,* Gordon S. Wood, Oxford University Press, 2009, p. 31.

2 "many members": *A Second Treasury of the World's Great Letters: a Mixed Mailbag Including Intimate Exchanges and Cycles of Correspondence by Famed Men and Women of History and the Arts,* Wallace Brockway, Bart Keith Winer, Simon and Schuster, 1941, p. 242.

3 *Penn forebears were in the thick: The General Assembly of Virginia, July 30, 1619-January 11, 1978,* compiled by Cynthia M. Leonard, under the auspices of the Library Board, 1978.

4 *primogeniture:* "Primogeniture and Entail in Colonial Virginia," C. Ray Keim, *William and Mary Quarterly,* Vol. XXV, no. 4 (Oct 1968), pp. 550 551.

5 *"contrary to this act":* "Bill to Prevent the Importation of Slaves & c." [16 June 1777], *Founders Online,* National Archives, version of January 18, 2018, http://founders.archives.gov/documents/Jefferson/01-02-02-0019. [Original source: *The Papers of Thomas Jefferson,* Vol. 2, 1777-18 June 1779, ed. Julian P. Boyd, Princeton University Press, 1950, pp. 22-24]

6 *set apart from the masses: White Trash: The 400-Year Untold History of Class in America,* Nancy Isenberg, Viking, 2016, p. 87.

7 *"tranquil permanent felicity": Index of the Memoirs, Correspondence, and Miscellanies from The Papers of Thomas Jefferson,* edited by David Widgen, H. Colburn and R. Bentley publishers, London, 1829, letter CXVII to Mr. Bellini, 30 Sep 1785, eremita.di.uminoho.pt/Gutenberg/2/8/8/6/28860/28860-h/28860-h.htm

8 *took possession of the glebes: Cradle of America: Four Centuries of Virginia History,* Peter Wallenstein, University Press of Kansas, 2007, pp. 86-87; *A Brief History of the Episcopal Church,* David L. Holmes, Trinity Press International, Harrisburg, PA, 1993, p. 24.

9 *"nearly all common and middling people": Empire of Liberty: A History of the Early Republic, 1789-1815,* Gordon L. Wood, Oxford University Press, 2009, p. 576.

10 *"priestcraft":* "Thomas Jefferson to Charles Clay, 29 Jan 1815," *Founders Online,* National Archives, version January 18, 2019, http://founders.archives.gov/documents/Jefferson/03-08-02-0181 [Original source: *The Papers of Thomas Jefferson, Retirement Series,* Vol. 8, 1 Oct 1814 to 31 Aug 1815, ed. J. Jefferson Looney, Princeton University Press, 2011, pp. 211-213].

11 *"a warmed or overweening brain": An Essay Concerning Human Understanding,* John Locke, Chapter XIX, Book IV, Section ("What is Meant by Enthusiasm"), 1689, from the Edinburgh Edition, Boston, Cummings and Hilliard and B. Perkins, Hanover New Hampshire, 1822, p. 234, http://books.google.com/books?id=hhdMAAAAYAAJ.

12 *His will:* founders.archives.gov/documents/Washington/06-04-02-0404-0001

13 *"religious controversies are always productive":* "Letter from George Washington to Edward Newenham, 22 June 1792," *Founders Online,* National Archives, version of January 18, 2019, http://founders.archives.gov/documents/ Washington/05-10-02-0324. [Original source: *The Papers of George Washington, Presidential Series,* Vol. 10, 1 Mar 1792-15 Aug 1792, ed. Robert F. Haggard and Mark A. Mastromarino, Charlottesville: University of Virginia Press, 2003, pp. 493-495].

14 *"piety and prayers": The Liberator,* letter to the editor, by Benjamin Chase, 1 Jan 1847, as quoted in "Two 1840s Articles on Oney Judge," ushistory.org and in *Never Caught: The Washingtons' Relentless Pursuit of Their Runaway Slave, Ona Judge,* Erica Armstrong Dunbar, Simon and Schuster, 2017.

15 *descendants dwelt in Amherst: Amherst County Heads of Families—1783,* pp. 48-49, digitized copy accessed via familysearch.org.

16 *Seven Penn households existed in 1783: Spotsylvania County, 1721-1800, being transcriptions from the original files at the county*

courthouse, ow wills, deeds, administrators' and guardians' bonds, marriage licenses, and lists of revolutionary war pensioners; ed. William Armstrong Crozier, published for The Genealogical Association by Fox, Duffield and Company, 1905.

17 *John Pine: Cavaliers and Pioneers, 1623-1666,* Nell Marion Nugent, Press of the Dietz Printing Company, 1934, p. 428, http://www.archive.org/details/cavalierspioneers00nage

18 *Thomas Pinn: Lancaster County, Virginia Order Book 2, 1680-1686* p. 34, *Book 3,* p. 2-3, *1686-1696,* abstracted by Ruth and Sam Sparacio, Antient Press, 1992.

19 *David Pinn:* Library of Virginia, Spotsylvania County, Deed Book F, 1761-1766, 11 Feb 1764, microfilm 3.

20 *Hezziah Pinn, Thomas Pinn: Free African-Americans of North Carolina, Virginia and South Carolina, from the Colonial Period to About 1820,* Paul Heinegg, fifth edition, Clearfield Company by Genealogical Publishing Company, Baltimore, 2005, pp. 942-945.

21 *Rawley Pinn: Amherst Heads of Families, 1783,* p. 47, accessed via familysearch.org; *Pieces of the Quilt: The Mosaic of an African American Family,* Anita L. Wills, self-published, 2008, pp. 125-139.

22 *squatters: David Crockett in Congress: The Rise and Fall of the Poor Man's Friend,* James R. Boylston and Allen J. Wiener, Bright Sky Press, 2009, pp. 27-28.

23 *Harrodsburg: Kentucky Place Names,* Robert M. Rennick, University Press of Kentucky, 1984, p. 132.

24 *"a Chinese wall":* George Washington letter to Secretary of State, 1 Jul 1796, *The Writings of George Washington from the Original Manuscript Sources, 1745-1799,* ed. John C. Fitzpatrick, prepared under the direction of the United States Bicentennial Commission and published by authority of Congress, Vol. 35, 30 Mar 1796—31 Jul 1797, Government Printing Office, Dec 1940 http://www.archive.org/details/writingsof george35wash

25 *"Rip Van Winkle": Empire of Liberty: A History of the Early Republic, 1789-1815,* Gordon S. Wood, Oxford University Press, 2009, pp. 1-2.

26 *Kentucky's population alone mushroomed: Westward into Kentucky: The Narrative of Daniel Trabue,* ed. Chester Raymond Young, University Press of Kentucky, 1981, p. 174, note 8.

27 *John Heckenwelder: Thirty Thousand Miles with John Heckenwelder,* ed. A.W. Wallace, University of Pittsburgh Press, 1958, p. 277.

28 *Harry Toulmin: The Western Country in 1793: Reports on Kentucky and Virginia,* ed. Marion Tinling and Godfrey Davies, San Marino, California, 1948.

29 *Bribing votes: Drinking in America: Our Secret History,* Susan Cheever, Hachette Book Group, 2015, pp. 40-41.

30 *Elias Pym Fordham: Personal Narrative of Travels in Virginia, Maryland, Pennsylvania, Ohio, Indiana, Kentucky and a Residence in the Illinois Territory, 1817-1818,* ed. Frederic Austin Ogg, A.M., The Arthur H. Clark Company, Cleveland, 1906, pp. 158-168.

31 *"never supplied with more bedding":* ibidem, p. 158.

32 *"When Virginians moved": Cradle of America: Four Centuries of Virginia History,* Peter Wallenstein, University Press of Kansas, 2007, p. 122.

33 *"Scotch-Irish dialect": Albion's Seed,* David Hackett Fischer, Oxford University Press, 1989, pp. 652-655, 833.

34 *William Calk: The Wilderness Road to Kentucky,* ed. William Allen Pusey, George H. Doran Company, 1921, pp. 41-42, 49.

35 *"Tuckahoes . . .Quo'hes": Westward into Kentucky: The Narrative of Daniel Trabue,* ed. Chester Raymond Young, University Press of Kentucky, 1981, p. 175, note 15.

36 *"Coastal Southern": Albion's Seed,* David Hackett Fischer, Oxford University Press, 1989, page 833.

37 *"Southern":* "Older Southern American English," http://en.wikipedia.org/wiki/Older_Southern_American_English

38 *four Penn households existed in Kentucky: 1810 United States Census, Kentucky, Bourbon, Scott, Shelby Counties,* NARA microfilm publication M 252, reels 5, 8

39 *Edward Penn:* Will of Edmund Penn, Anne Arundel County, Maryland, 5 June 1741, liber 26, folio 559; 1742, Box P, Folder 24; Box 44, folder 12.

40 *another small cluster: 1820 United States Census, Kentucky, Christian, Green, Lincoln Counties,* NARA microfilm publication M33, reels 20, 22, 24, 25.

41 *To cajole men:* "About the Revolutionary War Bounty Warrants," research guide on website of the Library of Virginia.

42 *War grants assigned: The Kentucky Land Grants,* Willard Rouse Jillson, Standard Printing, The Filson Club publication no. 33, 1925, p. 106.

43 *Get-rich-quick land speculators: The American Revolution: A History,* Gordon S. Wood, Modern Library, 2002, pp. 22-23.

44 *Many former soldiers sold off: White Trash: The 400-Year Untold History of Class in America,* Nancy Isenberg, Viking, 2016, p. 96.

45 *Patrick Joyes/John Penn:* Jefferson County, Kentucky, Deed Book I, 15 Aug 1788, pp. 410-411.

46 *first appearance in Alabama: United States Federal Census, 1800,* District 1, Montgomery County, Maryland, NARA microfilm series M32 , Reel 11, p. 238; *United States census Reconstructed Records, 1660-1820,* ancestry.com database, digitized from *Territorial Papers of the United States,* compilers John Porter Boom and Clarence Edwin Carter, published by United States Department of State, 1962, Vol. 5, p. 441, Vol. 6, p. 760.

47 *Shadrack Penn:* "Shadrack Penn's heir to father's land (now present day Baltimore MD)," http://mvancestry-institution.com/viewer/8aaf8b53-ec31-44f8-8c18-f182 7e389007/5626741/230026141831

48 *immigrant's son John: forgotten Companions: The First Settlers of Spotsylvania County and Fredericksburgh (with Notes on Early Land Use),* Paula S. Felder, History Publications of Fredericksburg, Virginia, 1982, p. 52.

49 *1810 Census of Spotsylvania: 1810 United States Census, Spotsylvania County,* NARA microfilm publication 252, roll 71, p. 102.

50 *settled in Tennessee:* Tennessee Records of Grainger County—tax lists, 1810, Tennessee State Library and Archives, digitized on ancestry.com database "U.S. Census Reconstructed Records, 1660-1820."

51 George Penn sold: Patrick County, Virginia, Deed Book 4, 8 March 1815; Smith County, Tennessee Minutes Book, Nov 1815, p. 154; Abstracts of Deed Books III and IV of Henry County, Virginia, Aug 1784 through June 1792, deed pages 521, 522, abstracted by Lela C. Adams, 1978, monograph at Bassett Public Library, Bassett, Virginia, Phillip Penn conveys land to son George, 27 Apr 1789.

52 *George Penn in Rutherford County: 1820 United States Census, Rutherford County, Tennessee,* NARA microfilm publication M33, roll 124; *1830 United States Census, Smith County, Tennessee,* NARA microfilm publication M19, roll 181, p. 57.

53 *Elizabeth Penn and Nimrod Mitchell:* the date of 25 Dec 1766 is passed from one genealogist to the next and may have existed originally in a family bible; there, however, exists no surviving document of this marriage with either the Granville County, North Carolina Recorder of Deeds office or at the State Archives of North Carolina.

54 *Craven County, South Carolina:* South Carolina Department of Archives and History, Archives ID: Series: S213184, Volume 0009, Page 00241, Item 02; Archives ID Series: S213019, Volume 0018, Page 00443, Item 000; Archives ID Series: S111001, Volume 0008, Page 00523, Item 005, transactions for grant of 200 acres to Nimrod Mitchell on Rayburn's Creek, Craven County, 1769.

55 *Jeffrey Penn: United States Federal Census, 1800,* Newberry District, South Carolina, NARA microfilm publication M32, reel 50, p. 89.

56 *John Penn's move to Granville County: Eighteenth-Century Newspapers,* compiled by Robert K. Headley, Jr., *The Virginia Gazette,* 5 May 1774, Genealogical Publishing Company, 1980; *State Census of North Carolina,* 1784-1787, Alvaretta Kenan Register, Genealogical Publishing Company, 1973, 2001.

57 *1779 land grant:* State Archives of North Carolina, reference: MARS 12.14.66.126; 293 acres entered for John Penn in Granville County, 8 May 1778, issued 24 Sep 1779, "on the waters of Island Creek."

58 *will of John Penn: Holographic Will of John Penn, Granville County, 1784,* North Carolina Department of Cultural Resources, call no. V.C. 23 (digital.ncdcr.gov/cdm/compoundobject/collection/p15012coll11?id/154/rec/1)

59 *son William Penn settled in Edgecombe: First Census of the United States, 1790,* NARA microfilm publication M637, reel 7, p. 397.

60 *made as new assignee:* State Archives of North Carolina, reference: MARS 12.14.107.3629; 100 acres entered for Richard Penn in Rowan County from William Penn, 1 Dec 1783, "on the waters of Jacobs Creek."

61 *In distant Rowan: First Census of the United States, 1790,* NARA microfilm publication M637, reel 7, p. 302.

62 *Orange County:* State Archives of North Carolina, reference: MARS 12.14.95.1895; 284 acres entered for John Penn in Orange County 9 Dec 1778, issued 26 Nov 1790 to William Penn, "on the waters of Little River."

63 *had taken up living there: United States Census, 1800, Person County, North Carolina,* NARA microfilm publication M32, reel 32, p. 197; *United States Census, 1810, Orange County, North Carolina,* NARA reel 41, p. 827.

64 *Richard Penn sold off the acreage:* State Archives of North Carolina, reference: MARS 12.14.107.3629; 100 acres to Abraham Beanblossum, "assignee of Richard Penn, who was assignee of William Penn."

65 *Bledsoe County, Tennessee: Tennessee Census, 1810-91,* compiled and digitized by Ron V. Jackson from microfilmed schedules of the U.S. Federal Decennial Census, territorial/state censuses, and/or census substitutes, Accelerated Indexing Systems.

66 *A son, William Penn:* https://www.findagrave.com/memorial/32725057#view-photo=131591280

67 *Abraham Penn to Henry County: Abstracts of Deed Books III and IV of Henry County, Virginia, Aug 1784 through June 1792,* deed pages 224, 225, extracted by Lela C. Adams, monograph at the Bassett Public Library, Bassett, Virginia, 1978; "Josiah Smith to Abraham Penn, 343 acres, witnessed by Phillip and George Penn"; *The Per-*

sonal Property Tax Lists for the Year 1787 for Henry County, Virginia, Netti Schreiner-Yantis and Florence Speakman Love, Genealogical Books in Print, Springfield, Virginia, 1987, pp. 674, 680.

68 *Poplar Grove:* http://www.freestateofpatrick.com/revwar; analysis of architectural style by Mark Nemger, Professional Landscape Artist, Denver, Colorado.

69 *A peek inside the manse:* "Inventory of the Estate of Abraham Penn," 2 Oct 1801, *Abstracts of Wills, Inventories and Accounts, Patrick County, Virginia, 1791—1823,* abstracted, edited and published by Lela C. Adams, 1973, monograph at Bassett Public Library, Bassett, Virginia, p. 44 of original source material, p. 10 of monograph.

70 *Intimation of brotherly fondness: Abstracts of Deed Books III and IV of Henry County, Virginia, Aug 1784 through June 1792,* deed pages 202, 203, abstracted by Lela C. Adams, 1978, monograph at the Bassett Public Library, Bassett, Virginia, "Phillip Penn paid John Lindsay 100 pounds for 100 acres, 22 Aug 1785."

71 *Eldest daughter, Frances Penn:* Library of Virginia, Marriage Records, Amherst County, Order Book 1782-1784, reel 27, minister's return of marriage, marriage of George Fulcher and Fanny Penn, dated 15 Apr 1783; *Virginia Compiled Marriages, 1660—1800,* ancestry.com database, Henry County, Virginia, Sarah Penn to John Norton, July 1783.

72 *Phillip Penn property description:* from photographs and document research carried out in Patrick County records by Cindy Headen, Martinsville, Virginia, Sep 2013.

73 *He parsed his holdings: Abstracts of Deed Books III and IV of Henry County, Virginia, Aug 1784 through June 1792,* deed pages 521, 522, abstracted by Lela C. Adams, 1978, monograph at Bassett Public Library, Bassett, Virginia, Phillip Penn conveys land to son George, 27 Apr 1789.

74 *Penn's Store/"Aurora": History of Patrick and Henry Counties, Virginia,* Virginia G. Pedigo and Lewis G. Pedigo, Genealogical Publishing Company, 1977, pp. 224-225; https://commons.wikimedia.org/wiki/File:Aurora_Penn%27s_Store_Patrick_County_Virginia.JPG

75 *"Leaving our business unsettled":* Library of Virginia, Patrick County, Deed Book 7, reel 4, p. 218, 29 Nov 1828.

76 *"to carve out": White Trash: The 400-Year Untold History of Class in America,* Nancy Isenberg, Viking, 2016, p. 56.

77 *Public records note his presence: The Reconstructed 1790 Census of Georgia: Substitutes for Georgia's Lost 1790 Census,* Marie DeLamar and Elisabeth Rothstein, Genealogical Publishing Company, Baltimore, 1985, pp. 79, 86, 87, 172; Wilkes County, Georgia, Deed Book DD, 1788-1789, p. 83, sale of property from Charity Bowers to Solomon Ellis, witness Thomas Penn.

78 *Droves from Amherst County:* "Migrations from Virginia to Elbert, Georgia," http://mv.ancestryinstitution.com/viewer/96002b90-de64-413d-ab38-8c175_ae60a2/1918625/-1876572954

79 *Under Captain John Hodge:* http://mv.ancestryinstitution.com/viewer/6560eef4-9348-4c2c-a0db-b05c02ae-3ae9/18050663/596789449

80 *Thomas and wife Winifred:* Elbert County, Georgia, Deed Book E, 1798 1799, p.58, sale of property from Thomas Penn Winnifred, his wife, to William Spears, 1798.

81 *Larkin Gatewood: Georgia, Wills and Probate Records, 1742-1992, Elbert County Probate Court Records,* probate 1 Oct 1802, ancestry.com database.

82 *Thirty miles in Franklin County:* Thomas Penn, Franklin County, Georgia 1803 Tax List, p. 006, Joseph and Sally Penn, Franklin County, Georgia 1808 Tax list, pp. 068 and 069, digitized to *Georgia, Compiled Census and Census Substitutes Index, 1790-1890,* ancestry.com database.

83 *Elizabeth Penn Leake:* Library of Virginia, Amherst County, Marriage and Consent Book (1788-1791), reel 107, 6 Oct 1788, marriage of Elizabeth Leake to Turner Hunt Christian.

84 *Turner Hunt Christian:* Library of Virginia, Goochland County, Court Order Book 17 (1787-1788), reel 27, pp. 46-48.

85 *Penns in Oglethorpe County:* Edmond Penn, Oglethorpe County, 1800 Georgia Territorial Census, *Georgia, Compiled Census and Census Substitutes Index, 1790-1890,* ancestry.com database; *The*

History of Oglethorpe County, Georgia, Mrs. Florrie Carter Smith, Wilkes Publishing Company, Inc., Washington, Georgia, 1970, pp. 167, 266, 267, 271, 280; ibidem, Supplement, p. 237 and Supplement II, p. 101; *Court House Records in Oglethorpe County, Georgia and in Hancock County, Georgia,* "Land Lottery List of Oglethorpe County, Georgia, 1804 an 1806," Martha Lou Houston, Columbus, Georgia, 1928.

Chapter 7: A HOUSE DIVIDED

1 "wonderful state of preservation": *America, Historical, Statistic, and Descriptive,* J.S. Buckingham, Esq., Vol. II, London: Fisher, Son and Company, 1941, p. 380, digitized by University of Connecticut Library.

2 technology unimaginable: *Martin Van Buren: The Eighth President, 1837-1841,* The American Presidents Series, Ted Widmer, Times Books, Henry Holt and Company, 2005, p. 15.

3 John Brown: history.com, originally published 27 Oct 2009, *http://www.history.com/topics/abolutionist-movement/john-brown*

4 "the nursing mother of the north": *De Bow's Review and Industrial Resources, Statistics, etc.,* ed. By J.D.B. De Bow, Vol. XVII, New Series Vol. IV, "The North and the South," by John Forsyth, Esq., published at New Orleans and Washington City, 1854, p. 365.

5 "partner in iniquity": *Fourth New England Anti-Slavery Convention,* held in Boston May 30, 31 and June 1 and 2, 1837, printed by Isaac Knapp, Boston, 25, Cornhill, 1837, p. 45 (quoted in *Slavery's Capitalism: A New History of American Economic Development (Early American Studies),* Sven Beckert and Seth Rickman, University of Pennsylvania Press, 2016, p. 2.

6 clothes from slave-grown cotton: *Slavery's Capitalism: A New History of American Economic Development (Early American Studies),* Sven Beckert and Seth Rickman, University of Pennsylvania Press, 2016, p. 2.

7 "Southern nationalists lambasted northern sanctimoniousness": ibidem, p. 2.

8 Lincoln's pledge: *American Battlefield Trust, A Brief Overview of the American Civil War,* "A Defining Time in Our Nation's History," Dr. John McPherson, www.battlefields.org/articles/brief-overview-american-civil-war

9 *The Prentiss Brothers: The Untold Civil War: Exploring the Human Side of War,* James I. Robertson, Jr., National Geographic Society, p. 22.

10 *Mary Todd Lincoln:* ibidem, p. 94.

11 *also mustered battalions:* compiled from Confederate and Union Civil War Service Records of the National Archives and Records Administration (NARA) at fold3.com

12 *George Penn:* Alabama Confederate Civil War Service Records, 16th Infantry, Union Service Records, Alabama First Cavalry; *Stephen Penn,* Confederate Civil War Service Records, Alabama 54th Infantry and Alabama 55th Volunteers, Union Service Records, Alabama First Cavalry, extracted from fold3.com

13 *William H. Penn:* compiled service record at *mv.ancestryinstitution.com/viewer/8ec383ab-2007-4338-b52a-9c3caa480d97/2219069/-1852685017*

14 *One wayfaring:* Union Civil War Service Records, John W. Penn, Colorado (Territory), 63rd Infantry, fold3.com

15 *Hiram Penn: Monticello Express* (Iowa), "Interesting Events of Iowa News," J.W. Jarnagin, 11 Mar 1937.

16 *Resembled genealogical tables: The Untold Civil War: Exploring the Human Side of War,* John I. Robertson, Jr., National Geographic Society, 2011, p. 94.

17 *Uniformed in light-colored, nine-button:* original photograph in the possession of the descendants of Fred V. Woodson, Martinsville, Virginia.

18 *John Edmund Penn: The Virginia Magazine of History and Biography,* Vol. 3, no. 3, The Virginia Historical Society, Jan 1896, p. 306-307, *www.jstor.org/stable/4241904*

19 *"a great proportion of the people": The Monthly Magazine or British Register,* Vol. IX, no. 71, "Letters from Mr. Toulmin of Kentucky," p. 551, (Jul) 1800, printed for R. Phillips, St. Paul's Church-Yard, London, available on google books.

20 *yet kept three slaves:* United States Federal Census, 1860, Slave Schedule, Casey County, Kentucky, NARA microfilm publication M653.

21 *had divested himself of slaves:* United States Federal Census, 1830, Casey County, Kentucky, NARA microfilm publication M19, reel, 34, p. 286, five total persons in the household of Phillip Penn, 2 of which were listed as slaves; no slaves on 1840 or 1850 census in household of Phillip Penn, Casey County, Kentucky, NARA microfilm publication M704, reel 107, p. 167 and NARA microfilm publication M432, reel 196, p. 288A, Image 8 respectively.

22 *uprooted his family: 1860 United Federal Census, Harrison County, Indiana,* NARA microfilm publication M653, reel 361. P. 85, household no. 565.

23 *teenage Edmond:* 49th Regiment, Company C, Indiana Infantry, Edmond Penn, *Report of the Adjutant General of the State of Indiana, Vol. V, 1861-1865,* W.H.H. Terrell, Samuel M. Douglas—State Printer, 1867; *ehistory.osu.edu/uscw/features/regimental/Indiana/union/49thindiana/history-cfm*

24 *middle son Gabriel Jackson:* ibidem, 144th Indiana Infantry, Company F.

25 *For every soldier killed: The Untold Civil War: Exploring the Human Side of War,* James I. Robertson, Jr., p. 126.

26 *Avoidance of killing: On Killing: The Psychological Cost of Learning to Kill in War and Society,* Dave Grossman, Back Bay Books, 2009, pp. 3,4,10,11,16.

Image Credits

Page 2 *"An early written entry of the surname, that of Geoffrey Penne, 1310"* [The National Archives, London, C66/135, Patent Rolls]

Page 3 *"Artist's interpretation of a medieval London street scene. Persons of the last name Penn were living in the city by 1327"* [Peter Jackson, LookandLearn.com]

Page 7 *"A page from Tyndale's English language bible, 1526"* [Wikimedia Commons, original housed at the British Library]

Page 9 *"Still-standing house that survived the London fire of 1666, Prince Henry's Room, Fleet Street"* [Wikimedia Commons, 17 Fleet Street, London]

Page 10 *"A late-surviving medieval structure, Sir Walter Raleigh's House at Blackwell"* [Wikimedia Commons, photograph of ca. 1890, housed at National Maritime Museum, Greenwich, U.K.]

Page 12 *"Painting created soon after the Great Fire of 1666"* Wikimedia Commons, unknown artist, painting ca. 1675

Page 13 "Whether forced into service on the galley of a ship or packed off to slave overseas, many colonists did not go of their own accord" [Wikimedia Commons, file: Caricature -1780-press gang

Page 21 *"Horseley Down noted on an old map"* [mapco.net/anon/anon.htm]

Page 22 (top) *"St. Olave Grammar School where the Immigrant may have been a student"* [A Topographic History of Surrey, Vol. 5, 1850, p. 384]

Page 22 (bottom) *"St. Olave's Church as it still looked before the Immigrant, John Penn, left England"* [London Metropolitan Archives, adapted from Visscher's 'View of London' 1616, catalogue #p 5352011]

Page 23 *"London Bridge at the time the Immigrant's father was born"* [Yale Center for British Art, Paul Mellon Fund, by Claude de Jongh]

Page 24 (top) *"One 17th century document examined"* [The National Archives, CLC-313-L-033-ms25275-006, London

Page 24 (bottom) *"Signature of the presumptive immigrant, John Penn"* [The National Archives, London, ADM 33-191-189; ADM 106-453-259CU]

Page 26 *"The Immigrant listed as John PANN on the Quit Rent Roll of 1704"* [The National Archive, London, CO 5/1314, part 3]

Page 28 *"17th Century English merchant ship"* [Artist, Wenceslaus Holler; University of Toronto, Wikimedia Commons file]

Page 29 *"Romanticized vision of an 18th century English sailor taking leave of his family"* [Royal Museum, Greenwich, U.K., PAH:py7359]

Page 33 (top) *"Artist's interpretation of Jamestown, Virginia in the first decade of its existence"* [Estate of Sidney King]

Page 33 (bottom) *"Aerial View of Jamestown, 1614"* [Estate of Sidney King]

Page 34 *"Harvesting tobacco in colonial Virginia"* [Estate of Sidney King]

Page 35 *"Indians and Colonists; an imagined scene from Virginia, 1692"* [Artist Keith Rocco]

Page 40 *"Carving a niche in the wilderness of Virginia"* [Estate of Sidney King]

Page 43 *"Buildings standing at the time of the Immigrant's arrival, (top)Christ's Cross, New Kent County, and (bottom) Warburton House, James City County"* [Photographed by Frances Benjamin Johnson, Library of Congress]

Page 44 *"Interior of a colonial farmhouse. Most abodes were likely not so cozy"* [Estate of Sidney King]

Page 46 *"In some secluded corner..." Penn Family Cemetery, Patrick County, Virginia"* [Photo by Cherie Sckorohod]

Page 50 *"The Mattaponi, 'an at-times shallow, twisting rivulet' "* [Wikimedia Commons, photo by Antepenultimate]

Page 51 "A Hogshead" [From *Documenting the American South*, University of North Carolina, Chapel Hill Libraries]

Page 53 *"Eastern Shore Chapel, dating to 1754"* [Library of Congress, photographed by Frances Benjamin Johnson, 1930s]

Page 57 *"The burning of Jamestown during Bacon's Rebellion"* [Artist Howard Pyle; from *Harper's Encyclopedia of United States History: from 458 A.D. to 1905*, Vol. 5, facing page 120]

Page 64 *"Portrait of John Penn, signer of the Declaration of Independence"* [Library of Congress]

Page 66 (top) *"Sword of Patriot leader Abraham Penn"* [Photo Cherie Allemand Sckorohod, courtesy of Edwin G. Penn III]

Page 66 (bottom) *"Revolutionary War militiaman"* [Artist Steve Noon, from *Patriot Militiaman in the American Revolution, 1775-82,* with permission of Osprey Publishing]

Page 68 *"Patriot soldiers excelled at small battles, raids, ambushes, and assassinations"* [Artist Steve Noon, from P*atriot Militiaman in the American Revolution, 1775-82,* with permission of Osprey Publishing]

Page 75 *"Backwoodsman of the American South, early 1800s"* [From *The Great South,* James Wells Champney, 1873, p. 372]

Page 79 *"Poplar grove"* [Estate of Abraham Penn, Patrick County History Museum, Stuart, Virginia]

Page 80 *"No Business Mountain: land once belonging to Phillip Penn"* [Photo by Cindy Headen]

Page 81 *"Penn's Store, Virginia"* [Patrick County History Museum, Stuart, Virginia]

Page 82 *"Aurora, the Penn Mansion, Patrick County, Virginia"* [Wikimedia Commons, file: Aurora, Penn's Store, Patrick County, VA]

Page 83 (top) *"Martin Wilson Penn, son of the founder of Penn's Store, Kentucky"* [Courtesy of Dawn Osborn]

Page 83 (bottom) *"Penn Family Home, established in the early 1830s, Casey County, Kentucky"* [Courtesy of Dawn Osborn]

Page 84 *"Penn's Store, Kentucky, the oldest country store in America still in ownership and operation by the same family"* [Photo by Dawn Osborn]

Page 89 *"Four Penn Brothers from Patrick County, Virginia"* [Original photograph in possession of descendants of Fred V. Woodson, Martinsville, Virginia]

Page 90 *"Colonel John Edmund Penn, in uniform of a Colonel"* [Old Roanoke County Courthouse, Salem, Virginia]

Descendants of John Penn, the Immigrant

Generation 1

1. Children of John Penn and Elizabeth Spencer are:

1. i. John Penn, Jr. B:1692 in Southwark, England, D: 1772 in St. George's Parish, Spotsylvania County, Virginia, M: Mary, Bef. 1757.

   With no baptism uncovered in English records of the relevant time period, one must assume George, Joseph, and Moses were American-born.

2. ii. George Penn, B: Abt. 1706 in King and Queen County, Virginia, D: 1749 in Caroline County, Virginia

3. iii. Joseph Penn, B: Abt. 1712 in King and Queen County, Virginia[3], D: Bef. 06 Jul 1767 in Caroline County, Virginia, M: Mary Taylor, 03 Feb 1735 in Caroline County, Virginia[3, 4].

4. iv. Moses Penn, B: Abt. 1720 in King and Queen County, Virginia, D: 04 Nov 1759, M: Catherine Taylor, 04 Jul 1739 in Caroline County, Virginia.

Generation 2

2. John Penn, Jr.-2(John-1) was born 1692, Southwark, England. He died in 1772 in St. George's Parish, Spotsylvania County, Virginia. He married Mary before 1757.

Children of John Penn Jr and Mary are:

6 i. Elizabeth Penn, B: Abt. 1743, M: Thomas May, Abt. 1763

ii. John Penn III, B: 1746 in St. George's Parish, Spotsylvania County, Virginia, D: 1829 in Virginia, M: Elizabeth Thomas, 10 Feb 1767.
Notes for John Penn III:
He inherited 100 acres from his father's will.

7. iii. George Penn, B: Abt. 1752, D: Abt. 1798, M: Elizabeth Atkinson, Dec 1773.

iv. William Penn, B: Bet. 1751-1757, D: 18 Mar 1781 in Spotsylvania County, Virginia.

8. v. Mary Penn, B: Bet. 1751-1757.

9. vi. Rachel Penn, B: Bet. 1751-1757.

vii. Mildred Penn, B: Bet. 1751-1757.

viii. Sally Penn, B: Bet. 1751-1757.

10. ix. Frances Penn, B: 1758, D: 1841.

x. Thomas Penn, B: 25 Apr 1749 in Caroline County or Spotsylvania County, Virginia[3], D: 08 Jan 1793 in St. George's Parish, Spotsylvania County, Virginia.
Notes for Thomas Penn:
He inherited 70 acres from his father's will.

3. George Penn-2(John-1)[5] was born about 1706 in King and Queen County, Virginia. He died in 1749 in Caroline County, Virginia. He married Ann.

Notes for George Penn:

On March 5, 1727, John and George Penn were deeded 614 acres in Spotsylvania County, Virginia from Thomas Crew.

On September 28, George Penn received a land patent of 1000 acres in Spotsylvania County, Virginia adjacent to Zachary Taylor. On September 1, 1730, George Penn deeded this land to David Williams.

Notes for Ann Fleming:

Moved to Amherst County, Virginia after the death of her second husband Thomas Dudley.

Children of George Penn and Ann are:

11. i. Frances Penn, B: 09 Jan 1735 in Caroline County, Virginia, D: 1812 in Patrick County, Virginia, M: Ambrose Lee, Bef. 1750.

12. ii. George Penn, B: 12 Dec 1737 in Caroline County, Virginia, D: 1790 in Amherst County, Virginia, M: Sarah Lee, Abt. 1760.

13. iii. Phillip Penn, B: 27 Jun 1739 in Caroline County, Virginia, D: Bef. 31 Jul 1806 in Patrick County, Virginia, M: Martha Crutcher, 1762.

14. iv. Gabriel Penn, B: 17 Jul 1741 in Caroline County, Virginia, D: Jul 1798 in Amherst County, Virginia, M: Sarah Callaway, 20 Sep 1761 in Bedford County, Virginia.

15. v. Abraham Penn, B: 27 Dec 1743, D: 26 Jun 1801 in Patrick County, Virginia, M: Ruth Stovall, 03 Mar 1767 in Amherst County, Virginia.

vi. William Penn, B: 09 Apr 1746, D: 15 Mar 1777 in Trenton, New Jersey.

Notes for William Penn:

Conflicting date of birth of 4/9/1745.

Was a lieutenant in the Continental Line of the Revolutionary War for over 3 years before his death. As a result, this earned him right to Military Land Grant for 2,666 2/3 acres of land in the Military Land Grant District of Kentucky or Ohio.

vii. Moses Penn, B: 13 Jan 1748, D: Sep 1774 in Amherst County, Virginia.
Notes for Moses Penn:
Never married.

4. Joseph Penn-2(John-1)[1, 2, 3] was born about 1712 in King and Queen County, Virginia[3]. He died before 06 Jul 1767 in Caroline County, Virginia. He married (1) Mary Taylor on 03 Feb 1735 in Caroline County, Virginia[3, 4], daughter of John Taylor Sr. and Catherine Pendleton. She was born on 30 May 1718 in King & Queen County, Virginia[1, 2, 3, 4]. She died on 13 Sep 1757 in Caroline County, Virginia[1, 2, 3, 4]. He married (2) Elizabeth after 1735.
Notes for Joseph Penn:
The names and birth dates of their children through Thomas Penn born in 1749 were recorded in the abstract of John Taylor Bible (except for the name of their eldest child, born on 13 Dec. 1736 which was obliterated from the abstract of the bible by 1903). For more information about the John Taylor bible see the notes to his son, John Penn. The fact that the child born on 13 Dec. 1736 was their son, John Penn, comes from the William Edmunds journal which states that John Penn (grandfather of his wife) was born on 13 Dec. 1736 and was the son of Joseph Penn and Mary Taylor. Also there is a 1761 Deed from Joseph Penn to John Penn "son of the said Joseph Penn" which proves that Joseph Penn had a son John who was not otherwise listed in the named children in the John Taylor bible abstract.

John Taylor, Sr., the father of Mary Taylor who married Joseph Penn, wrote his will on 16 March 1780 in Granville County, North Carolina on which he leaves property to the children of his deceased daughter, "John, Phillip, Moses, Thomas, Catherine and Mary". John Taylor, Jr., son of John Taylor, Sr., and brother to Mary Penn, wrote his will in Granville County, North Carolina on 23 Oct. 1787 in which he leaves property to the following nieces and nephews, children of his sister, Mary Penn: Moses

Penn, Mary, Fanny Hunt. These two records combine together to add Mary Penn and Frances Penn to the list of children of Joseph Penn and Mary Taylor.

On 7 Sept. 1761 Joseph Penn of Spotsylvania County, and Elizabeth his wife, deeded 200 acres to his son, John Penn, adjacent to John Holladay, Peter Gatewood, Joseph Penn, Dudley Gatewood, Ignatious Turman. Witnesses were William Garrett and Thomas Lane. There is a Memorandum of Possession and Seisen also dated 7 Sept. 1761 as part of the Deed. (Spotsylvania Co Deed Book F, page 222; or 41-43)

Joseph Penn wrote a Trust Deed (substitute will) on 19 September 1763 giving 65 acres and personal property and slaves in which he names his wife, Elizabeth, and his children John, Phillip, Moses, Thomas, Catherine Gatewood, Mary and Frances. Witnesses were Uriah Edwards, James Chiles, Joseph Holladay and Thomas Green. There is reference to a schedule in which his son, Phillip Penn was given the land (i.e., 65 acres). (Spotsylvania County Deed Book F, page 230; 277-279) , This supports the fact that his son Joseph Penn, died prior to 1763 by his name not having been mentioned as a son Joseph in the Trust Deed. It also raises some question about whether Elizabeth Penn and James Penn were living at that time.

His date of birth is an estimate based upon the fact that the first Caroline County, Virginia Court record mentioning Joseph Penn was 10 May 1733 Court Order Book reference of "Lucy, a Negro girl belonging to Joseph Penn is adjudged to be 12 years old. He then got married in 1735 and have his first child in 1736. There is one account from Josephine Easterliln which give an exact date of birth of 11/17/1717 which I doubt is correct.

On 6 July 1767, there is a receipt signed by John Penn which reads —"Rec'd of William Holliday twenty shillings back also, he give him Cr. when I (k)now the sum of money the Gentleman alowd, in his acct. against Jos. Penn, dec'd when they settled the accts. of the sid estate. /S/ John Penn.

Notes for Mary Taylor:

Her birth and death dates and the names of her parents were recorded in the abstract of the John Taylor bible (for more details about this bible see the notes to her son, John Penn).

Children of Joseph Penn and Mary Taylor are:

16. i. John Penn, B: 13 Dec 1736 in Caroline County or Spotsylvania County, Virginia[1, 2, 3, 6], D: 1818 in Amherst County, Virginia[1, 2], M: Elizabeth Munford, 24 May 1756 in Spotsylvania County, Virginia[1, 2, 6].

ii. Joseph Penn, B: 27 Sep 1738 in Caroline County or Spotsylvania County, Virginia[3].

17. iii. Catherine Penn, B: 11 Mar 1741 in Caroline County or Spotsylvania County, Virginia[3], D: Abt. 1806 in Elbert County, Georgia, M: Larkin Gatewood, Bef. 12 Jan 1757.

18. iv. Phillip Penn, B: 08 Feb 1743 in St. George's Parish, Spotsylvania County, Virginia[3], D: Aft. 1802 in Georgia.

19. v. Moses Penn Sr., B: 03 Dec 1744 in Caroline County or Spotsylvania County, Virginia[3], D: 31 Dec 1795 in Oglethorpe County, Georgia[3], M: Frances Richardson, Abt. 1765 in Amherst County, Virginia.

vi. Elizabeth Penn, B: 16 Jul 1746 in Caroline County or Spotsylvania County, Virginia[3], D: 02 Feb 1818 in Laurens County, South Carolina[7].

vii. James Penn, B: 12 Aug 1748 in Caroline County or Spotsylvania County, Virginia[3], D: Bef. 1763 in Amherst County, Virginia[3].

viii. Thomas Penn, B: 25 Apr 1749 in Caroline County or Spotsylvania County, Virginia[3], D: 08 Jan 1793 in St. George's Parish, Spotsylvania County, Virginia.

Notes for Thomas Penn:

He inherited 70 acres from his father's will.

20. ix. Frances Penn, B: 30 Jan 1756 in Caroline County or Spotsylvania County, Virginia[3], D: 1824, M: John Hunt, 05 Aug 1771 in Granville County, North Carolina[3].

21. x. Mary Penn, B: Abt. 1757 in Caroline County or Spotsylvania County, Virginia[3], D: 10 Jan 1830 in Wilkes County, Georgia, M: Joel Walker, 21 Feb 1775 in Amherst County, Virginia[3].

5. Moses Penn-2(John-1) was born about 1720 in King and Queen County, Virginia. He died on 04 Nov 1759. He married Catherine Taylor on 04 Jul 1739 in Caroline County, Virginia, daughter of John Taylor Sr. and Catherine Pendleton. She was born on 30 Dec 1719[4]. She died on 04 Nov 1774[4].

Child of Moses Penn and Catherine Taylor is:

22. i. John Penn, B: 06 May 1740 in Caroline County, Virginia, D: 14 Sep 1788 in Granville County, North Carolina, M: Susannah Lyne, 28 Jul 1763.

Generation 3

6. Elizabeth Penn-3(John-2, John-1) was born about 1743. She married Thomas May about 1763. Children of Elizabeth Penn and Thomas May are:

i. Elizabeth May.

ii. Martha May.

iii. William May.

iv. George May.

v. Sarah May.

7. George Penn-3(John-2, John-1) was born about 1752. He died about 1798. He married (1) Elizabeth Atkinson in Dec 1773, daughter of George Atkinson and Martha. He married (2) Ann before 1773.

Children of George Penn and Elizabeth Atkinson are:

i. George Penn.

ii. William Penn.

iii. John Penn.

8. Mary Penn-3(John-2, John-1) was born between 1751-1757. She married John Pritchett Jr., son of James Pritchett Sr. and Ann Hawkins.

Notes for Mary Penn:

Moved to Albemarle County, Virginia on November 9, 1796.

Child of Mary Penn and John Pritchett Jr. is:

i. James Pritchett.

9. Rachel Penn-3(John-2, John-1) was born between 1751-1757. She married Thomas Pettit.

Child of Rachel Penn and Thomas Pettit is:

i. Susannah Pettit.

10. Frances Penn-3(John-2, John-1) was born in 1758. She died in 1841. She married Henry Carter Sr..

Children of Frances Penn and Henry Carter Sr. are:

i. Sally Carter, B: 03 Aug.

ii. Mary Carter, B: 03 Aug.

iii. John Carter, B: 11 Aug 1780.

iv. Henry Carter Jr, B: 26 Mar 1781.

11. Frances Penn-3(George-2, John-1) was born on 09 Jan 1735 in Caroline County, Virginia. She died in 1812 in Patrick County, Virginia. She married (1) Ambrose Lee before 1750. He died in 1764. She married (2) Drury Tucker on 06 Apr 1767 in Amherst County, Virginia.

Children of Frances Penn and Ambrose Lee are:

i. George Penn Lee, B: Abt. 1750, D: Abt. 1825, M: Elizabeth Shelton, 22 Jan 1772 in Amherst County, Virginia.

24. ii. Francis Lee, B: Bet. 1750-1755, M: Nancy Penn, Nov 1786.

25. iii. Elizabeth Lee, B: Bet. 1750-1755.

iv. Jane Lee, B: Bet. 1750-1755.

v. Nancy Lee, B: Bet. 1750-1755.

25. vi. Susanna Lee, B: Abt. 1755, D: Abt. 1832.

vii. Richard Lee, B: Aft. 1755, M: Frances Harrison, 04 Dec 1780 in Amherst County, Virginia.

26. viii. William Lee, B: Aft. 1755, D: 1785 in Amherst County, Virginia, M: Susannah Dawson, 03 Sep 1770.

Children of Frances Penn and Drury Tucker are:

i. Robert Tucker.

ii. Isaac Tucker.

iii. Littleberry Tucker.

iv. Zachary Tucker.

v. Pleasant Tucker.

12. George Penn Jr.-3(George-2, John-1) was born on 12 Dec 1737 in Caroline County, Virginia. He died in 1790 in Amherst County, Virginia. He married (1) Sarah Lee about 1760, daughter of William Lea and Rachel. He married (2) Mary Lee on 25 May 1783 in Amherst County, Virginia, daughter of William Lea and Rachel.

Children of George Penn Jr. and Sarah Lee are:

27. i. George Penn III, B: Amherst County, Virginia, D: Bef. 01 Mar 1834 in Smith County, Tennessee.

ii. Thomas Penn, M: Behethland Stevens, 27 Sep 1796 in Amherst County, Virginia.

iii. Wilson Penn, M: Frances Taliaferro, 08 Sep 1796 in Amherst County, Virginia.

28. iv. Mary Penn, M: James Harrison, 08 Nov 1780[5].

v. Moses Penn.

29. vi. Frances Penn, B: 1762, D: 06 Oct 1831, M: William Burton, 06 Mar 1780 in Amherst County, Virginia.

vii. Nancy Penn.

viii. Sally Penn.

ix. Lucy Penn, M: Anderson Moss, 13 Dec 1786.

13. Phillip Penn-3(George-2, John-1) was born on 27 Jun 1739 in Caroline County, Virginia. He died before 31 Jul 1806 in Patrick County, Virginia. He married Martha Crutcher in 1762, daughter of William Crutcher.

Children of Phillip Penn and Martha Crutcher are:

i. Frances Penn, B: Abt. 1762, M: George Fulcher, 15 Apr 1783 in Amherst County, Virginia.
Notes for Frances Penn:
She has not been proven to be a daughter of Moses Penn.

31. ii. George Penn, B: Abt. 1763 in Amherst County, Virginia, D: Bef. 22 Aug 1828 in Rutherford County, Tennessee, M: Martha Ferris, 08 Dec 1784 in Henry County, Virginia.

32. iii. Wilson Penn.

iv. Lucy Penn.

v. Gabriel Penn, M: Charlotte Crutcher, 20 Dec 1794.

vi. Millie Penn, M: Nathaniel Ross, 1794.

vii. Cynthia Penn, M: Thomas Sneed, 1798.

viii. Nancy Penn, M: David Taylor, 1800 in Patrick County, Virginia.

ix. Sarah Penn, M: John Norton, 26 Jul 1783 in Amherst County, Virginia.

x. Abraham Penn, M: Elizabeth Chitwood, 1805.

xi. Martha Penn, M: Alexander Philpot, 1807 in Patrick County, Virginia.

xii. Mary Penn.
Notes for Mary Penn:
Not named in the Phillip Penn will of Patrick County, Virginia.

xiii. Elizabeth Penn.
Notes for Elizabeth Penn:
Not named in the Phillip Penn will of Patrick County, Virginia.

14. Gabriel Penn-3(George-2, John-1) was born on 17 Jul 1741 in Caroline County, Virginia. He died in Jul 1798 in Amherst County, Virginia. He married Sarah Callaway on 20 Sep 1761 in Bedford County, Virginia, daughter of Richard Callaway and Frances Walton.

Children of Gabriel Penn and Sarah Callaway are:

i. Elizabeth Penn, M: David Shepherd, 04 May 1778 in Amherst County, Virginia.

33. ii. James Penn, B: Virginia, D: Feb 1823 in New Orleans, Orleans County, Louisiana, M: Margaret Ann Cowan, 20 Feb 1787 in Bedford County, Virginia.

iii. Parmelia Penn, M: Thomas Haskins, Sep 1787 in Amherst County, Virginia.

33. iv. Sophia M. Penn, B: 1771, D: 08 Oct 1844 in Louisville, Kentucky, M: William Sidney Crawford, Nov 1785 in Amherst County, Virginia.

v. Matilda Penn, B: Abt. 1772, M: Abner Nash, Jul 1792 in Amherst County, Virginia.

vi. Frances Penn, B: 11 Dec 1779, D: 07 Mar 1816, M: Samuel White, Dec 1793 in Amherst County, Virginia.

34. vii. Nancy C. Penn, B: 1777, D: Abt. 1822, M: Alexander Brydie, Dec 1795 in Amherst County, Virginia.

viii. Edmund Penn, B: Abt. 1780.

ix. Sarah Penn, B: 27 Feb 1785, M: Thomas Crew, Dec 1804 in Amherst County, Virginia.

x. Catherine Penn, M: John W. Holder, Jul 1808 in Amherst County, Virginia.

15. Abraham Penn-3(George-2, John-1) was born on 27 Dec 1743. He died on 26 Jun 1801 in Patrick County, Virginia. He married Ruth Stovall on 03 Mar 1767 in Amherst County, Virginia.

Children of Abraham Penn and Ruth Stovall are:

35. i. George Penn, B: 06 Jan 1770, D: 12 Mar 1828 in Tammany Parish, Madisonville, Louisiana, M: M. A. Gordon, 23 Nov 1795.

36. ii. Lucinda Penn, B: 03 Sep 1771, D: 04 Sep 1850 in Patrick County, Virginia, M: Samuel G. Staples, 30 Dec 1790 in Patrick County, Virginia.

37. iii. Gabriel Penn, B: 14 Nov 1773 in Pittsylvania County, Virginia, D: 18 Jul 1818 in Patrick County, Virginia, M: Jane Clark, 06 Feb 1797 in Virginia.

38. iv. Horatio Penn Sr., B: 14 Nov 1775 in Pittsylvania County, Virginia, D: Oct 1838 in St. Charles, Ralls County, Missouri, M: Nancy May Parr, 14 Jul 1807 in Patrick County, Virginia.

39. v. Mary Penn, B: 01 Jul 1777 in Henry County, Virginia, D: 1849 in Patrick County, Virginia, M: Charles Foster, 08 Sep 1811.

40. vi. Greensville Penn, B: 16 May 1779 in Henry County, Virginia, D: 20 Jun 1844 in Patrick County, Virginia, M: Anna Leath, Bef. 1811.

41. vii. Thomas Penn, B: 15 Jun 1781 in Henry County, Virginia, D: 29 Mar 1858 in Popular Grove, Patrick County, Virginia, M: Martha Frances Leath, 18 Nov 1805 in Patrick County, Virginia.

42. viii. Abram Penn, B: 14 Mar 1783 in Henry County, Virginia, D: Bef. 1850 in Tennessee, M: Sally Kreitz, Patrick County, Virginia.

43. ix. James Francis Penn, B: 31 Jan 1785 in Henry County, Virginia, D: 1849 in Patrick County, Virginia, M: Catherine Leath, 10 May 1808 in Virginia.

x. Luvenia Penn, B: 03 Apr 1787 in Henry County, Virginia, D: Patrick County, Virginia.
Notes for Luvenia Penn:
Conflicting birth date of 1/8/1787. Died in infancy.

44. xi. Edmond Penn, B: 08 Jan 1789 in Henry County, Virginia, D: 11 Aug 1860 in Kentucky, M: Mary Clark Ferris, 11 Jun 1816 in Patrick County, Virginia.

45. xii. Phillip Penn, B: 05 Mar 1792 in Patrick County, Virginia, D: Tennessee.

xiii. Mary Penn, B: 1795 in Patrick County, Virginia, D: Aft. 1870.

Notes for Mary Penn:

Most researches do not have Mary as a child of Abraham.

xiv. Granville Penn, B: 1797 in Patrick County, Virginia.

Notes for Granville Penn:

Most researchers do not have Granville as a son of Abraham.

16. John Penn-3(Joseph-2, John-1)[1, 2, 3] was born on 13 Dec 1736 in Caroline County or Spotsylvania County, Virginia[1, 2, 3, 6]. He died in 1818 in Amherst County, Virginia[1, 2]. He married Elizabeth Munford on 24 May 1756 in Spotsylvania County, Virginia[1, 2, 6], daughter of Edward Munford and Lucy. She was born on 28 Jun 1738[1, 2]. She died after 1818[1, 2].

Notes for John Penn:

Moved from Spotsylvania County, Virginia to Amherst County, Virginia about 1767.

His birth date and the fact that he is the son of Joseph Penn and Mary Taylor comes from an entry in the William Edmunds journal and from the abstract of the John Taylor bible printed in the William & Mary College Quarterly, Series I, Vol. 12, 1903-1904 (the John Taylor bible information was copied from the bible while it was in the possession of Mrs. Mary Blackwell (nee Taylor) by Joe W. Taylor in 1870. The bible was thereafter destroyed by a fire sometime between 1870-1902). His Will was written 12 Feb. 1718 and was proved in Court 21 Dec. 1818.

On 7 Sept. 1761 Joseph Penn of Spotsylvania County, and Elizabeth his wife, deeded 200 acres to his son, John Penn, adjacent to John Holladay, Peter Gatewood, Joseph Penn, Dudley Gatewood,

Ignatious Turman. Witnesses were William Garrett and Thomas Lane. There is a Memorandum of Possession and Seisen also dated 7 Sept. 1761 as part of the Deed. (Spotsylvania Co Deed Book F, page 222; or 41-43)

He moved from Spotsylvania County, Virginia to Amherst County, Virginia about 1767.

On 10 Feb. 1767, John Penn of Spotsylvania County and Elizabeth, his wife deeded 200 acres in Spotsylvania County,to John Holloday, lands which John Penn purchased from Phillip Ballard and joining the lands said Holloday bought from John Sartin and the lands of William Mays and the patent of Edmund Waller. Witnesses were John Holloday, Jr., and Edward Chapman. Recorded 2 March 1767. (Spotsylvania County Deed Book G, page 253)

On 12 Feb. 1770, John Penn and Elizabeth, his wife, of Amherst County, Virginia deeded 275 acres in Spotsylvania County, Virginia to John Holloday. Witnesses were Henry Gatewood, Jr., John Tureman, Benjamin Holloday, Jr., and Banjamin Perrye. Recorded on 7 May 1770. (Spotsylvania County Deed Book G, page 271)

There are two Amherst County, Virginia deeds, one from John Sandidge to John Penn "of the County of Spotsylvania County" dated 2 May 1767 of 200 acres on the Buffalo River in Amherst County, Virginia and the other from John Roark "of the county of Amherst of the one part and John Penn of the same County" dated 7 October 1771 of 31 acres on Huffs Creek in Amherst County, Virginia.

On 28 May 1778, John Penn "of Amherst County" deeded 128 acres in Spotsylvania County, Virginia, to Benjamin Perry and Elizabeth Perry, "his mother, of Spotsylvania County." The witnesses were William Smith, Thomas Lipscomb, Uriah Edwards and Henry McDaniel. This was recorded 19 Nov. 1778. (Spotsylvania County Deed Book)

It is not known if John Penn actually fought in the Revolutionary War. There is an Amherst County, Virginia Court Order Book record for 2 April 1782 where John Penn, Joseph Penn (his son) and many other make a claim for property impressed or taken for public service in support of the Revolutionary War. I think that this qualifies John Penn for DAR and SAR entry.

On 12 Feb. 1818 John Penn, Senior, "of the County of Amherst" wrote his Will, in which he gave the tract of land which was then in the possession of his son, John Penn on the North side of Huff Creek adjoining the land of Robert Walker, to John Penn. He directed that his plantation on Indian Creek and his mansion house is to be kept for his widow, Elizabeth, and after her decease it is to be sold. He mentions the following children in the Will in the following order: Lucy, Nancy, Betsy, Sally, John William and Alexander. He mentioned his grandsons, Joseph Penn and Robert Alexander Penn. He named Robert Walker, James Powell and his son, John Penn, as executors. Witnesses were John Smith, Leroy Camden, George Tucker and Lewis Powell. The Will was admitted for probate on 21 Dec. 1818. Amherst County (Will Book 6, page 49) It should be noted that his son, Joseph Penn died in about 1792.

Notes for Elizabeth Munford:

Elizabeth's last name, the first name of her parents and her date of birth comes from the entry in the William Edmunds journal.

Children of John Penn and Elizabeth Munford are:

i. Elizabeth Penn, M: George Dillard, 20 Oct 1792 in Amherst County, Virginia[3].

ii. John Penn Jr..

iii. Lucy Penn.

46. iv. Nancy Penn, M: Francis Lee, Nov 1786.

v. Sarah Penn, M: John Dillard, 17 Aug 1791 in Amherst County, Virginia[3].

vi. William Penn.

47. vii. Joseph Penn, B: 22 Nov 1757 in Spotsylvania County, Virginia[1, 2, 6], D: 1792 in Amherst County, Virginia[1, 2], M: Frances Burrus, 04 Dec 1780 in Amherst County, Virginia[1, 2, 3].

48. viii. Alexander Penn, D: 15 Nov 1813, M: Nancy Watts, 11 Oct 1805 in Amherst County, Virginia[3].

17. Catherine Penn-3(Joseph-2, John-1)[3] was born on 11 Mar 1741 in Caroline County or Spotsylvania County, Virginia[3]. She died about 1806 in Elbert County, Georgia. She married Larkin Gatewood before 12 Jan 1757, son of Henry Gatewood and Dorothy Dudley.

Children of Catherine Penn and Larkin Gatewood are:

49. i. Amy Gatewood, B: 12 Jan 1757 in Essex County, Virginia, D: 28 Dec 1826 in Elbert County, Georgia, M: John Upshaw Sr., 07 Mar 1776 in Amherst County, Virginia.

50. ii. Mary Gatewood, B: Abt. 1760, D: Bef. 1809 in Elbert County, Georgia.

iii. Dolly Gatewood, B: 1763, D: 1830 in Feliciana Parish, Louisiana, M: Francis Higginbothom, 02 Dec 1783 in Amherst County, Virginia[3].
Notes for Dolly Gatewood:
Moved to Elbert County, Georgia by 1791.

iv. James Gatewood, B: Abt. 1765, D: Bef. 01 Oct 1802 in Elbert County, Georgia, M: Elizabeth Shoemaker, 1789 in Amherst County, Virginia.

18. Phillip Penn-3(Joseph-2, John-1)[3] was born on 08 Feb 1743 in St. George's Parish, Spotsylvania County, Virginia[3]. He died after 1802 in Georgia. He married Martha Rollins Holloday, daughter of Benjamin Holloday.

Children of Phillip Penn and Martha Rollins Holloday are:

i. Elizabeth Penn, B: 09 Feb 1763[3], M: Samuel Leak, 16 Oct 1783 in Amherst County, Virginia[3].

51. ii. Mary Penn, B: 22 Mar 1766[3], M: Absolam Stinchcomb, 24 Dec 1785 in Amherst County, Virginia[3].

52. iii. Joseph Roscoe Penn, B: 30 Jul 1768 in Virginia[3], D: 27 Dec 1848 in St. Clair County, Illinois[3], M: Sally King, 22 Apr 1790 in Bedford County, Virginia[3].

iv. Citty Penn, B: 22 Jul 1770[3].

53. v. John Penn, B: 10 Nov 1772[3], D: Abt. 1828 in Elbert County, Georgia.

vi. Penn, B: 13 Mar 1776[3].

vii. Lucy Penn, B: 02 Mar 1778[3], M: John Oliver, 07 Apr 1816 in Elbert County, Georgia.

viii. Sarah Jane Penn, B: 06 Sep 1780[3], D: 1856 in Fosterville, Rutherford County, Tennessee, M: Francis Brothers, Abt. 1805 in Virginia.

54. ix. William Penn, B: 10 May 1783[3], D: 1870, M: Abigail Wilson, 05 Aug 1813 in Franklin County, Georgia.

x. Jack Penn, B: 07 Aug 1786[3].

19. Moses Penn Sr.-3(Joseph-2, John-1)[3] was born on 03 Dec 1744 in Caroline County or Spotsylvania County, Virginia[3]. He died on 31 Dec 1795 in Oglethorpe County, Georgia[3]. He married Frances Richardson about 1765 in Amherst County, Virginia.

Notes for Frances Richardson:

Last name may have been Richerson.

Children of Moses Penn Sr. and Frances Richardson are:

55. i. Moses Penn Jr., B: 1782, D: Bef. 22 Mar 1853 in Chambers County, Alabama, M: Perina Bird, 25 Jun 1804 in Greene County, Georgia[3].

56. ii. Elizabeth Penn, B: 1772, D: 1848, M: William Cashwell, Nov 1791 in Amherst County, Virginia.

57. iii. Mary Penn, D: Wilkes County, Georgia, M: William Stewart, Abt. 1785.

iv. Lucy Penn, D: 1827 in Oglethorpe County, Georgia.

58. v. James Richardson Penn, B: Virginia, D: 1845 in Kentucky, M: Mary Major, 05 Dec 1791 in Amherst County, Virginia[3].

vi. Edmond Penn.

vii. Frances Penn.

viii. Richard Penn.

20. Frances Penn-3(Joseph-2, John-1)[3] was born on 30 Jan 1756 in Caroline County or Spotsylvania County, Virginia[3]. She died in 1824. She married John Hunt on 05 Aug 1771 in Granville County, North Carolina[3]. He was born in 1752[3]. He died in 1818[3].

Children of Frances Penn and John Hunt are:

i. Mary Hunt, B: 26 Feb 1773.

ii. Sarah Hunt, B: 13 Feb 1775.

iii. Francis Hunt, B: 1777.

iv. James Hunt, B: 1779.

v. David Hunt, B: 1781.

vi. Elizabeth Hunt, B: 04 Mar 1783.

vii. Patey Hunt, B: 04 Oct 1784.

viii. Thomas Hunt, B: 03 Mar 1787, D: 21 Jan 1829.

59. ix. John Penn Hunt, B: 08 Jul 1789[3], D: 1850[3], M: Sarah Longmore, 1811[3].

x. Mourning Hunt, B: 17 Jan 1792.

xi. Anne Taylor Hunt, B: 27 Jul 1794.
Notes for Anne Taylor Hunt:
Conflicting date of birth of 7/24/1894.

21. Mary Penn-3(Joseph-2, John-1)[3] was born about 1757 in Caroline County or Spotsylvania County, Virginia[3]. She died on 10 Jan 1830 in Wilkes County, Georgia. She married (1) Joel Walker on 21 Feb 1775 in Amherst County, Virginia[3]. She married (2) Joseph J. Morrison on 07 Oct 1796 in Amherst County, Virginia[3].

Child of Mary Penn and Joel Walker is:

i. Thomas Walker.

22. John Penn-3(Moses-2, John-1)[8] was born on 06 May 1740 in Caroline County, Virginia. He died on 14 Sep 1788 in Granville County, North Carolina. He married Susannah Lyne on 28 Jul 1763, daughter of Henry Lyne.

Notes for John Penn:

He is one of the signers of the Declaration of Independence. Moved from Virginia to Granville County, North Carolina about 1774. There is a conflicting date of birth of 5/17/1761. Conflicting year of death of 1787 also, conflicting date of death of 10/26/1809.

Notes for Susannah Lyne:

Name may have been Sarah Lyme.

Children of John Penn and Susannah Lyne are:

60. i. Lucy Penn, B: 1766 in Caroline County, Virginia[8], D: 1830 in Caroline County, Virginia[8], M: John Taylor, 1781 in Caroline County, Virginia[8].

ii. William Penn, B: Aft. 1763.

iii. Richard

Generation 4

23. Francis Lee-4(Frances-3, George-2, John-1)[3] was born between 1750-1755. He married Nancy Penn in Nov 1786, daughter of John Penn and Elizabeth Munford.

Children of Francis Lee and Nancy Penn are:

i. Sophia Lee, M: Seaton M. Penn, 25 Aug 1804 in Amherst County, Virginia[3].

ii. William Lee, B: 11 Jul 1790, D: 17 Jan 1823 in Barren County, Kentucky, M: Elizabeth Penn, 29 Jan 1809 in Amherst County, Virginia[3].

24. Elizabeth Lee-4(Frances-3, George-2, John-1) was born between 1750-1755. She married Samuel Crutcher.

Child of Elizabeth Lee and Samuel Crutcher is:

i. Frances Crutcher.

25. Susanna Lee-4(Frances-3, George-2, John-1)[3] was born about 1755. She died about 1832. She married Richard Harrison Sr..

Children of Susanna Lee and Richard Harrison Sr. are:

i. Benjamin Harrison.

ii. George Harrison.

62. iii. Harriet Harrison, D: 1876.

iv. Nicholas Harrison.

v. Richard Harrison Jr., M: Sophia Lee, 13 Aug 1810 in Amherst County, Virginia[3].

vi. William Harrison.

62. vii. Francis B. Harrison, B: Abt. 1782, D: Abt. 1835, M: Frances Crutcher, 08 Mar 1803.

26. William Lee-4(Frances-3, George-2, John-1) was born after 1755. He died in 1785 in Amherst County, Virginia. He married Susannah Dawson on 03 Sep 1770, daughter of Joseph Dawson.

Children of William Lee and Susannah Dawson are:

i. James Lee.

ii. William Lee.

27. George Penn III-4(George-3, George-2, John-1) was born in Amherst County, Virginia. He died before 01 Mar 1834 in Smith County, Tennessee. He married Permelia Freeland.

Child of George Penn III and Permelia Freeland is:

63. i. William Nelson Penn, B: 12 Oct 1804 in Amherst County, Virginia, D: 18 Aug 1873 in Monroe County, Missouri, M: Sarah Emerine Carter, 12 Oct 1831.

28. Mary Penn-4(George-3, George-2, John-1)[5]. She married James Harrison on 08 Nov 1780[5]. Child of Mary Penn and James Harrison is:

i. John Harrison.

29. Frances Penn-4(George-3, George-2, John-1) was born in 1762. She died on 06 Oct 1831. She married William Burton on 06 Mar 1780 in Amherst County, Virginia.

Child of Frances Penn and William Burton is:

64. i. Frances Burton, B: 1794, D: 1842.

30. George Penn-4(Phillip-3, George-2, John-1) was born about 1763 in Amherst County, Virginia. He died before 22 Aug 1828 in Rutherford County, Tennessee. He married Martha Ferris on 08 Dec 1784 in Henry County, Virginia, daughter of Jacob Ferris and Ruth Haden.

Children of George Penn and Martha Ferris are:

i. Gabriel Penn.

ii. Martha Penn.

iii. Wilson Penn.

iv. William Penn, B: Abt. 1786, D: Abt. 1851 in Smith County, Tennessee, M: Martha Stovall, 25 Dec in Campbell County, Virginia.
Notes for William Penn:
Listed as age 64 in the 1850 Smith County, Tennessee census. No known children.

65. v. Elizabeth Penn, B: Abt. 1788 in Henry County, Virginia, D: Bef. 1814 in Patrick County, Virginia, M: William Banks Jr., 04 Feb 1808 in Patrick County, Virginia.

v. Joseph Penn, B: Bet. 1788-1791, M: Polly Chitwood, Dec 1810 in Patrick County, Virginia.

66. vii. Frances Penn, B: 27 May 1792 in Patrick County, Virginia, D: 16 Jan 1879 in Smith County, Tennessee, M: William Banks Jr., 12 Oct 1814 in Patrick County, Virginia.

67. viii. Ruth Penn, B: Abt. 1794 in Patrick County, Virginia, D: Abt. 1855, M: William Finney, 22 Jul 1823 in Rutherford County, Tennessee.

68. ix. Josiah Penn, B: 1799 in Patrick County, Virginia, D: Abt. 1855 in Humboldt Township, Gibson County, Tennessee, M: Ruth Wallace Broughton, 11 Jun 1825 in Rutherford County, Tennessee.

69. x. Jacob F. Penn, B: 1802 in Patrick County, Virginia, M: Bef. 1829.

70. xi. George Douglas Penn, B: Abt. 1804 in Patrick County, Virginia, M: Telitha Patterson Clay, 15 Oct 1831 in Rutherford County, Tennessee.

71. xii. Luvenia Penn, B: Abt. 1804 in Patrick County, Virginia, D: Abt. 1850.

xiii. Martha Penn, B: Abt. 1805 in Patrick County, Virginia, M: Amos S. Wallis, 11 Jun 1825 in Rutherford County, Tennessee.

31. Wilson Penn-4 (3-Phillip, 2-George, 1-John), born ca 1775, married Sally Chitwood 28 Dec 1798, Patrick County, VA. Died ca. 1834 Casey County, Kentucky.

Children of Wilson Penn and Sally Chitwood are:

i. Phillip Penn – born ca 1797, Patrick County, VA, married Lucinda Tucker, 13 Dec 1829 Casey County, KY, died ca. 1865 Harrison County, IN.

Offspring:

a. Robert Penn – born 1831, married Sarah Clark 7 Aug 1856, Harrison County, IN. Died 20 Jan 1891 Williamson County, TN

1. Lucinda J. Penn – born 21 May 1857, Harrison County, IN, married Robert White, Hamilton, TN 27 Dec 1874, died 21 Jul 1907, Williamson County, TN

2. Sarah E. Penn – born 1859, Harrison County, IN

3. Catherine Penn- born 1861, Harrison County, IN
4. William Wesley Penn – born 30 Dec 1862, Harrison County, IN, married Nellie Elizabeth Crow,15 Aug 1886, Hickman County, TN, died 2 Nov 1935, Hickman County, TN
5. Mary Elisa Penn – born 1866, Harrison County, IN, married John Thomas Hall, Williamson County, TN 30 Dec 1888
6. Martha Ellen Penn – born 1869, Harrison County, IN
7. Frances Isabelle Penn – born 1872, Harrison County, IN
8. Nancy E. Penn – born 1872, Harrison County, IN
9. Susan Ann Penn – born 1875, Harrison County, IN

b. Phoeby Penn born 1832

c. Gabriel Jackson Penn – born 1834, married Elizabeth Jane Ellis 24 Nov 1859, Harrison County, IN; Olly Sullivan 10 Jan 1867 Dubois County, IN; died 2 Apr 1894, Daviess County, IN
1. Phoebe Ann – 11 March 1861, Harrison County, IN, married Crite Sappenfield, two sons, Elmer Sappenfield, James Sappenfield, died Harrison County, IN 1946
2. Daniel Penn – born Sep 1865, Harrison County, IN, married Minerva Jane Tarr, 25 Sep 1896, Orange County, IN, died Orange County, IN 17 Feb 1913; offspring: Harrison Penn, born and died 1901, William Earl Penn, 1903-1934, Nellie Mae Penn Maudlin, 1905-1935.

d. Nelly Penn - born 1836

e. Edward Penn – born 1838

f. Lucinda Penn – born 1841

ii. Edmund Penn – married Nancy J. Freeman 9 Oct 1834

iii. Gabriel Jackson Penn – born 1818, Patrick County, VA, married Cynthia Conder, Casey County, KY, died 1889 Casey County, KY

Offspring:

a. Phebe Penn
b. Molly Penn
c. Virginia Penn
d. Sarah Penn
e. Lucy Jane Penn
f. David Penn
g. Frank Penn
h. Martin Wilson Penn – born 1852, married Isabel May

iv. William Penn – married Frances Penn 14 Jan 1831, Casey County, KY

v. Lucy Penn

vi. Sallie Penn – married Levi Farrell 13 Nov 1832, Casey County, KY

32. James Penn-4(Gabriel-3, George-2, John-1) was born in Virginia. He died in Feb 1823 in New Orleans, Orleans County, Louisiana. He married Margaret Ann Cowan on 20 Feb 1787 in Bedford County, Virginia.

Children of James Penn and Margaret Ann Cowan are:

i. Robert Cowan Penn, B: 19 Feb 1789 in Campbell County, Virginia, D: 02 Jul 1856 in St. Helena, Beford County, Virginia, M: Lucinda Steptoe, 15 Jun 1814 in Bedford County, Virginia.

ii. Elizabeth Penn.

iii. Matilda Penn.

iv. James Penn, B: Abt. 1797, D: Abt. 1823.

v. Gabriel Penn, B: Abt. 1799, D: 18 Jan 1830 in Tuscaloosa, Alabama.

vi. William Penn, B: Abt. 1800, D: 1822 in Alabama.

73. vii. Alfred Penn, B: 1800 in Lynchburg, Virginia, D: 1875, M: Evelyn Carter Bradfute, 02 Sep 1833 in Lynchburg, Virginia.

viii. Margaret Penn.

ix. Julia Penn.

x. John Penn.

xi. Virginia Penn.

33. Sophia M. Penn-4(Gabriel-3, George-2, John-1) was born in 1771. She died on 08 Oct 1844 in Louisville, Kentucky. She married William Sidney Crawford in Nov 1785 in Amherst County, Virginia.

Child of Sophia M. Penn and William Sidney Crawford is:

74. i. Van Tramp Crawford.

34. Nancy C. Penn-4(Gabriel-3, George-2, John-1) was born in 1777. She died about 1822. She married (1) Alexander Brydie in Dec 1795 in Amherst County, Virginia.

Child of Nancy C. Penn and Alexander Brydie is:

75. i. Margaret Brydie, B: Abt. 1796, D: 1888, M: William Hay Dyer, 1814.

35. George Penn-4(Abraham-3, George-2, John-1) was born on 06 Jan 1770. He died on 12 Mar 1828 in Tammany Parish, Madisonville, Louisiana. He married M. A. Gordon on 23 Nov 1795.

Children of George Penn and M. A. Gordon are:

76. i. Alexander Gordon Penn, B: 1799 in Patrick County, Virginia, D: 08 May 1866 in Washington, D.C..

ii. Abram Stovall Penn, B: 1810.

77. iii. Martin Gordon Penn, B: 09 Jun 1805, M: Harriet Tyson Elltott, 02 Apr 1829.

iv. Judith Gordon Penn.

v. Lucinda Stovall Penn.

vi. Martha Ann Penn.

36. Lucinda Penn-4(Abraham-3, George-2, John-1) was born on 03 Sep 1771. She died on 04 Sep 1850 in Patrick County, Virginia. She married Samuel G. Staples on 30 Dec 1790 in Patrick County, Virginia.

Children of Lucinda Penn and Samuel G. Staples are:

i. John C. Staples.

ii. Keziah Staples.

iii. Ruth Penn Staples.

79. iv. Abram P. Staples, B: 09 Mar 1793 in Patrick County, Virginia, M: Mary S. Penn, 23 Oct 1820.

37. Gabriel Penn-4(Abraham-3, George-2, John-1) was born on 14 Nov 1773 in Pittsylvania County, Virginia. He died on 18 Jul 1818 in Patrick County, Virginia. He married Jane Clark on 06 Feb 1797 in Virginia.

Children of Gabriel Penn and Jane Clark are:

79. i. Clark Penn, B: 07 Dec 1797, D: 03 Aug 1858, M: Barbara Ann L. Penn, 21 Jun 1831 in Patrick County, Virginia.

ii. Ruth Penn, B: 11 Feb 1800, M: Samuel Abe Martin, 24 Aug 1827.

iii. Abram Penn, B: 16 Mar 1803, D: 15 Dec 1848, M: Catherine Reid, 26 Feb 1824.

iv. Sarah Penn, B: 11 Dec 1805, D: 06 Apr 1821.

v. Mary Penn, B: 29 Dec 1807, M: Josiah Ferris, 27 Oct 1825.

vi. Greensville Penn, B: 22 Oct 1810, M: Henrietta Maria Cardwell, 18 Oct 1836.

80. vii. Frances R. Penn, B: 31 May 1815, D: 25 Jun 1833.

81. viii. Gabriel Penn.

38. Horatio Penn Sr.-4(Abraham-3, George-2, John-1) was born on 14 Nov 1775 in Pittsylvania County, Virginia. He died in Oct 1838 in St. Charles, Ralls County, Missouri. He married Nancy May Parr on 14 Jul 1807 in Patrick County, Virginia.

Children of Horatio Penn Sr. and Nancy May Parr are:

82. i. Ruth M. Penn, B: 1808 in Virginia, D: 1845 in St. Charles, Ralls County, Missouri, M: Joseph T. Abington, 21 Mar 1827 in Patrick County, Virginia.

83. ii. Keziah S. Penn, B: 1809 in Virginia, M: Hanceford Brown, 18 Jan 1835 in Ralls County, Missouri.

84. iii. Gabriel Penn, B: 22 Nov 1811 in Virginia, D: 18 Nov 1867, M: Lucinda Ann Glasscock, 10 Jan 1839 in Ralls County, Missouri.

iv. Amanda F. Penn, B: 1814 in Virginia, M: Taylor Abington, 14 Jun 1832 in Ralls County, Missouri.
Notes for Amanda F. Penn:
No children.

85. v. John W. Penn, B: 1816 in Virginia, D: 1880 in St. Charles, Ralls County, Missouri, M: Elizabeth S. Major, 11 Sep 1839 in St. Charles County, Missouri.

vi. Edmond P. Penn, B: 1818 in Virginia, D: 04 Dec 1851 in Ralls County, Missouri, M: Malissa Brown, 04 Dec 1851 in Ralls County, Missouri.

86. vii. Horatio Penn Jr., B: 1821 in Virginia, D: 1909 in Ralls County, Missouri, M: Jane Catherine Kelley, 25 May 1851 in Ralls County, Missouri.

viii. Glovina Ann Penn, B: 1823 in Virginia.

ix. Christopher T. Penn, B: 1825.

x. Lucinda M. Penn, B: 1828 in Virginia, M: Jacob B. Penn, 05 Jan 1845 in Ralls County, Missouri.

xi. Thomas J. Penn, B: 1830 in Virginia, M: Marietta Caldwell, 07 Mar 1854 in Ralls County, Missouri.

39. Mary Penn-4(Abraham-3, George-2, John-1) was born on 01 Jul 1777 in Henry County, Virginia. She died in 1849 in Patrick County, Virginia. She married Charles Foster on 08 Sep 1811.

Children of Mary Penn and Charles Foster are:

87. i. Louvenia Penn Foster, B: 13 Jun 1812, D: 15 Apr 1885.

ii. Loucinda Staples Foster, B: 13 Jun 1812.

88. iii. Abram Penn Foster, B: 1813, D: 1891, M: Mary Jane Critz, 19 Dec 1838.

iv. Ruth Stovall Foster, B: 08 May 1815.

v. James Monroe Foster, B: 1817.

vi. Keziah Redd Foster, B: 07 Aug 1819.

vii. Martha Staples Foster, B: 07 Aug 1819.

40. Greensville Penn-4(Abraham-3, George-2, John-1) was born on 16 May 1779 in Henry County, Virginia. He died on 20 Jun 1844 in Patrick County, Virginia. He married (1) Anna Leath before 1811.

Notes for Anna Leath:

She was from Manchester, Virginia.

Children of Greensville Penn and Anna Leath are:

i. Mary Penn.

ii. George Penn.

iii. Edmund Penn.

Notes for Edmund Penn:

Was living in South Carolina in 1832.

90. iv. Gabriel Penn, B: 1814.

91. v. Peter Phillip Penn, B: 1811.

Children of Greensville Penn and Martha Reed are:

i. William Penn.

Notes for William Penn:

Died in infancy.

ii. Sophia Penn.

iii. Catherine Lucinda Penn.

iv. Ann Marie Penn.

v. Elizabeth Penn.

41. Thomas Penn-4(Abraham-3, George-2, John-1) was born on 15 Jun 1781 in Henry County, Virginia. He died on 29 Mar 1858 in Popular Grove, Patrick County, Virginia. He married (1) Martha Frances Leath on 18 Nov 1805 in Patrick County, Virginia. She died on 28 Aug 1816. He married (2) Mary Christian Kennerly on 25 Dec 1818 in Patrick County, Virginia. She died in 1857.

Notes for Thomas Penn:

Conflicting date of birth of 7/15/1781.

Children of Thomas Penn and Martha Frances Leath are:

i. Peter Leath Penn, B: 31 Aug 1806, D: 22 May 1835 in Taladega County, Alabama.

ii. Columbus F. Penn, B: 01 Nov 1808, D: Fayette County, Texas.

91. iii. Andrew Jackson Penn, B: 27 Mar 1811 in Popular Grove, Patrick County, Virginia, D: 27 Mar 1877 in Locust Grove, Patrick County, Virginia, M: Martha Kennerly, 02 Oct 1832.

Children of Thomas Penn and Mary Christian Kennerly are:

i. Martha Ann Catherine Penn, B: 09 Aug 1820 in Patrick County, Virginia, D: Nov 1897, M: John N. Zentmeyer, 15 Sep 1847.

92. ii. George Washington Penn, B: 16 Oct 1822 in Patrick County, Virginia, D: 17 Aug 1867.

iii. LaFayette Penn, B: 09 Nov 1824 in Patrick County, Virginia, D: 13 Nov 1829 in Patrick County, Virginia.

iv. Eliza Penn, B: 14 Dec 1826 in Patrick County, Virginia, D: 01 Jan 1900, M: Samuel W. Hairston, 26 Oct 1848 in Patrick County, Virginia.

v. Sarah Ruth Penn, B: 09 Sep 1829 in Patrick County, Virginia, D: 1898, M: Randall Duke Hay, 12 Jun 1857.

vi. Joseph Abram Goodman Penn, B: 10 Feb 1832 in Patrick County, Virginia, M: Ruth Stoval Shelton, 06 Dec 1866.

93. vii. Lucinda Susan Penn, B: 13 Oct 1834 in Patrick County, Virginia, M: James Abram Penn, 23 Sep 1857.

viii. Thomas Greensville Penn, B: 15 Jan 1838 in Patrick County, Virginia, D: 21 Jun 1887.
Notes for Thomas Greensville Penn:
Never married.

94. ix. William Alexander Penn, B: 07 Jul 1840, D: 21 Jun 1887, M: Marie Louise Bagby, 10 Aug 1865.

x. John S. Penn, B: 04 Dec 1842, D: 27 Oct 1861 in Lewisburg, Virginia.
Notes for John S. Penn:
Died of typhoid fever while serving for the Confederacy during the Civil War.

42. Abram Penn-4(Abraham-3, George-2, John-1) was born on 14 Mar 1783 in Henry County, Virginia. He died before 1850 in Tennessee. He married Sally Kreitz in Patrick County, Virginia.

Child of Abram Penn and Sally Kreitz is:

95. i. William H. Penn Sr., B: 1810, D: Aft. 1885, M: Mary Ann Pollack, 15 Mar 1831.

43. James Francis Penn-4(Abraham-3, George-2, John-1) was born on 31 Jan 1785 in Henry County, Virginia. He died in 1849 in Patrick County, Virginia. He married (1) Catherine Leath on 10 May 1808 in Virginia. He married (2) Mary Shelton on 10 Nov 1818 in Henry County, Virginia.

Notes for Catherine Leath:
She was from Manchester, Virginia.

Children of James Francis Penn and Catherine Leath are:

i. Thomas Jefferson Penn.

ii. Luvenia Penn, B: 1812.

iii. Ruth Baker Penn.

96. iv. Barbara Ann L. Penn, B: 01 Apr 1809, D: 30 Jun 1837, M: Clark Penn, 21 Jun 1831 in Patrick County, Virginia.

Children of James Francis Penn and Mary Shelton are:

97. i. Catherine Leath Penn, B: 16 Jan 1821, D: 04 Mar 1914, M: Harrison Carter France, 09 Oct 1842.

ii. William Shelton Penn.

98. iii. James Abram Penn, M: Lucinda Susan Penn, 23 Sep 1857.

44. Edmond Penn-4(Abraham-3, George-2, John-1) was born on 08 Jan 1789 in Henry County, Virginia. He died on 11 Aug 1860 in Kentucky. He married Mary Clark Ferris on 11 Jun 1816 in Patrick County, Virginia, daughter of Josiah Farris and Mary Stovall.

Children of Edmond Penn and Mary Clark Ferris are:

99. i. William Abraham Clark Penn, B: 07 May 1818 in Murfreesboro, Rutherford County, Tennessee, M: Levenia Kelton, 07 Jul 1841 in Gibson County, Tennessee.

100. ii. Josiah Ferris Penn, B: 11 Sep 1819 in Murfreesboro, Rutherford County, Tennessee, M: Mirah M. Sneed, 26 Nov 1840 in Rutherford County, Tennessee.

101. iii. Sarah Elizabeth Penn, B: 16 Sep 1823 in Murfreesboro, Rutherford County, Tennessee, M: Benjamin Franklin Harris, 20 Mar 1844 in Gibson County, Tennessee.

102. iv. Mary Ruth Penn, B: 25 Nov 1827 in Murfreesboro, Rutherford County, Tennessee.

103. v. George Stovall Penn, B: 19 Feb 1830 in Murfreesboro, Rutherford County, Tennessee, D: Weatherford, Texas, M: Eliza Ellen Conner, 15 Feb 1854 in Gibson County, Tennessee.

104. vi. Martha Luvenia Penn, B: 26 Apr 1832 in Murfreesboro, Rutherford County, Tennessee, M: Benjamin Franklin Harris, 24 Jan 1859 in Gibson County, Tennessee.

105.vii. Gabriel Thomas Penn, B: 07 Jan 1836 in Murfreesboro, Rutherford County, Tennessee.

45. Phillip Penn-4(Abraham-3, George-2, John-1) was born on 05 Mar 1792 in Patrick County, Virginia. He died in Tennessee. He married Louise Briscoe.

Notes for Louise Briscoe:

She was from Bedford County, Virginia. Child of Phillip Penn and Louise Briscoe is:

106. i. Charity Warren Penn, B: 1825, D: 1899, M: Hendley S. Jenkins, 23 Oct 1844.

46. Nancy Penn-4(John-3, Joseph-2, John-1)[3]. She married Francis Lee in Nov 1786, son of Ambrose Lee and Frances Penn. He was born between 1750-1755.

Children of Nancy Penn and Francis Lee are:

i. Sophia Lee, M: Seaton M. Penn, 25 Aug 1804 in Amherst County, Virginia[3].

ii. William Lee, B: 11 Jul 1790, D: 17 Jan 1823 in Barren County, Kentucky, M: Elizabeth Penn, 29 Jan 1809 in Amherst County, Virginia[3].

47. Joseph Penn-4(John-3, Joseph-2, John-1)[1, 2] was born on 22 Nov 1757 in Spotsylvania County, Virginia[1, 2, 6]. He died in 1792 in Amherst County, Virginia[1, 2]. He married Frances Burrus on 04 Dec 1780 in Amherst County, Virginia[1, 2, 3], daughter of Charles Burrus Sr. and Sarah Woolfolk. She was born on 03 Sep 1763 in Albemarle County, Virginia[1, 2]. She died in 1792 in Amherst County, Virginia[1, 2, 3].

Notes for Joseph Penn:

Conflicting birth year of 1759 (this from Barbar Baughan).

Joseph Penn's date of birth comes from the Journal of William Edmunds. There is an Administrator's Bond in Amherst County, Virginia dated 15 Oct. 1792 where Fanny Penn (widow) and Joseph Burrus were appointed administrators of the estate of Joseph Penn, deceased with Charles Burrus and Benjamin Stone securities.

It is not known if Joseph actually fought in the Revolutionary War. There is a 2 April 1782 Amherst County, Virginia Court Order Book entry where Joseph Penn and John Penn and many others made a claim for property impressed or taken for public service in support of the Revolutionary War. I believe that this qualifies Joseph Penn for DAR and SAR entry.

Notes for Frances Burrus:

The Douglas Register has a birth date for Fanny Buress, daughter of Charles Buress and Sarah Woodfork of 3 Sept. 1763, and a baptism date of 23 Dec. 1763. William Douglas recorded the following in his register of "Deaths and Funerals": "Dec 23 1763 Capt. Childers funeral, Sermon in Albemarle on Ecc:12.7" which is the source of information used to place Frances' (probable) birth in Albemarle County, Virginia.

Regarding her date of death, she survived her husband. There is an Administrator's Bond for the estate of Joseph Penn, deceased, dated 15 Oct. 1792 in which Joseph Burrus and Fanny Penn are appointed as co administrators of the estate and were obligated, among other things to do an inventory of the estate. The inventory of the estate was dated 19 June 1797 and only mentioned Joseph Burrus as the administrator, suggesting that Fanny had previously died.

Children of Joseph Penn and Frances Burrus are:

i. Charles Burrus Penn, B: Amherst County, Virginia, D: Abt. 1833.

Notes for Charles Burrus Penn:

Possibly a judge in Botetourt County, Virginia in 1822.

ii. Joseph Penn, B: Amherst County, Virginia, D: 19 Apr 1840.

iii. Seaton M. Penn, D: Jul 1808 in Amherst County, Virginia, M: Sophia Lee, 25 Aug 1804 in Amherst County, Virginia[3].

107. iv. Sarah Penn, B: Abt. 1781 in Amherst County, Virginia, M: Robert Holloway, 18 Nov 1797 in Amherst County, Virginia[3].

v. Elizabeth Penn, B: Abt. 1786 in Amherst County, Virginia, D: 07 May 1864 in Barren County, Kentucky, M: William Lee, 29 Jan 1809 in Amherst County, Virginia[3].

108. vi. Mary Ann Penn, B: 11 Feb 1790 in Amherst County, Virginia[1, 2, 9], D: 03 Mar 1846 in Barren County, Kentucky[1, 2, 9], M: William Edmunds, 30 Mar 1805 in Amherst County, Virginia[1, 2, 3].

48. Alexander Penn-4(John-3, Joseph-2, John-1)[3]. He died on 15 Nov 1813. He married Nancy Watts on 11 Oct 1805 in Amherst County, Virginia[3].

Children of Alexander Penn and Nancy Watts are:

i. Edward Penn.

110. ii. Charles A. Penn, B: Abt. 1810 in Nelson County, Virginia, D: 1860 in Amherst County, Virginia[3], M: Mary Coleman, 15 Jun 1838 in Amherst County, Virginia[3].

49. Amy Gatewood-4(Catherine-3, Joseph-2, John-1) was born on 12 Jan 1757 in Essex County, Virginia. She died on 28 Dec 1826 in Elbert County, Georgia. She married John Upshaw Sr. on 07 Mar 1776 in Amherst County, Virginia, son of Forest Upshaw and Ann Hunt.

Children of Amy Gatewood and John Upshaw Sr. are:

110. i. John Upshaw Jr., B: 24 Dec 1776, D: 1818.

111. ii. Sarah Upshaw, B: 31 Jan 1779 in Amherst County, Virginia, D: Abt. 1833 in Elbert County, Georgia, M: Benjamin Thornton Sr., 12 Jun 1796.

iii. Nancy Ann Upshaw, B: 02 Mar 1781.

iv. Catherine Upshaw, B: 12 Jan 1783.

v. Leroy Upshaw, B: 26 May 1785.

vi. James Upshaw, B: 24 Sep 1789.

vii. Thomas Upshaw, B: 19 Oct 1793.

viii. George Upshaw, B: 05 Jan 1797.

ix. Middleton C. Upshaw, B: 17 Jun 1799.

50. Mary Gatewood-4(Catherine-3, Joseph-2, John-1) was born about 1760. She died before 1809 in Elbert County, Georgia. She married Benjamin Higginbotham Jr., son of Benjamin Higginbotham Sr..

Children of Mary Gatewood and Benjamin Higginbotham Jr. are:

i. Sarah Higginbotham.

ii. Ann Higginbotham.

iii. Elizabeth Higginbotham.

iv. Benjamin Higginbotham III.

v. Peter Higginbotham.

vi. Larkin Higginbotham.

51. Mary Penn-4(Phillip-3, Joseph-2, John-1)[3] was born on 22 Mar 1766[3]. She married Absolam Stinchcomb on 24 Dec 1785 in Amherst County, Virginia[3], son of John Stinchcomb and Catherine.

Children of Mary Penn and Absolam Stinchcomb are:

112. i. Mary C. Stinchcomb, B: 05 Jul 1806 in Elbert County, Georgia, D: 24 Mar 1889 in Elbert County, Georgia, M: Joseph Sewell, 01 Nov 1827 in Elbert County, Georgia.

ii. Alexander Stinchcomb.

iii. Arron Stinchcomb.

iv. Levi Stinchcomb.

113. v. Nathaniel Stinchcomb, B: 1799 in Georgia, M: Susannah Clements, Elijah Similin.

vi. Phillip Stinchcomb.

vii. Lucy Stinchcomb.

viii. Caty Stinchcomb.

52. Joseph Roscoe Penn-4(Phillip-3, Joseph-2, John-1)[3] was born on 30 Jul 1768 in Virginia[3]. He died on 27 Dec 1848 in St. Clair County, Illinois[3]. He married (1) Sally King on 22 Apr 1790 in Bedford County, Virginia[3].

Notes for Joseph Roscoe Penn:

Moved from Georgia to Illinois in 1811-1812.

Children of Joseph Roscoe Penn and Sally King are:

114. i. Susanna Penn, B: 12 Aug 1791.

ii. Phillip Penn, B: 16 Jul 1792, D: Nov 1850 in St. Clari County, Illinois.

iii. William Penn, B: 19 Nov 1796 in Elbert County, Georgia, D: 08 Apr 1851 in Ridge Prairie, St. Clari County, Illinois.

115. iv. Joseph Penn, B: 06 Jan 1798 in Elbert County, Georgia, D: 25 Nov 1840 in Carlinville, Macoupin County, Illinois, M: Candis Barton, 08 Oct 1817 in St. Clair County, Illinois.

116. v. Sarah Penn, B: 15 May 1800 in Elbert County, Georgia, D: 11 May 1882 in Paragonah, Iron County, Utah, M: John Barton, 1817 in St. Clair County, Illinois.

117. vi. John Anderson Penn, B: 16 Mar 1804 in Murray County, Georgia, D: 01 Dec 1871 in Pana, Christian County, Illinois, M: Nancy Anderson, 08 Jun 1825 in Bourbon County, Kentucky.

vii. Elizabeth Penn, B: 02 Apr 1806 in Elbert County, Georgia, D: Bef. 1853.

viii. Julia Penn, B: 19 Jul 1808 in Franklin County, Georgia, D: 01 Oct 1819.

53. John Penn-4(Phillip-3, Joseph-2, John-1)[3] was born on 10 Nov 1772[3]. He died about 1828 in Elbert County, Georgia. He married Mary.

Children of John Penn and Mary are:

118. i. Sarah Jane Penn, B: Abt. 1808 in Elbert County, Georgia, D: Aft. 1850 in Madison County, Georgia, M: William W. Smith, 20 May 1831 in Elbert County, Georgia.

ii. Winney Penn, M: Thomas A. Smith, 15 Sep 1833 in Elbert County, Georgia.

iii. Elizabeth Penn.

iv. Martha Penn.

v. John Penn.

vi. Mary Penn.

vii. Fanny Penn, B: 14 Nov 1815, M: William Mason, Elbert County, Georgia.

viii. Lucinda Penn, M: William H. Threlkeld, 07 Oct 1840 in Elbert County, Georgia.

54. William Penn-4(Phillip-3, Joseph-2, John-1)[3] was born on 10 May 1783[3]. He died in 1870. He married Abigail Wilson on 05 Aug 1813 in Franklin County, Georgia.

Child of William Penn and Abigail Wilson is:

119. i. John Wilson Penn, B: 1820, D: 1877.

55. Moses Penn Jr.-4(Moses-3, Joseph-2, John-1)[3] was born in 1782. He died before 22 Mar 1853 in Chambers County, Alabama. He married Perina Bird on 25 Jun 1804 in Greene County, Georgia[3].

Children of Moses Penn Jr. and Perina Bird are:

120. i. Thomas Lee Penn, B: 14 Nov 1807, D: 20 May 1874, M: Elizabeth White, 16 Jun 1831.

121. ii. Emeline Penn, B: 1813 in Oglethorpe County, Georgia, D: Bef. 02 Nov 1876 in Schley County, Georgia, M: Simpson Edge, 25 Jun 1831.

56. Elizabeth Penn-4(Moses-3, Joseph-2, John-1) was born in 1772. She died in 1848. She married William Cashwell in Nov 1791 in Amherst County, Virginia.

Child of Elizabeth Penn and William Cashwell is:

122. i. Judith Cashwell.

57. Mary Penn-4(Moses-3, Joseph-2, John-1)[3]. She died in Wilkes County, Georgia. She married William Stewart about 1785.

Children of Mary Penn and William Stewart are:

123. i. Thomas Stewart, B: 30 Sep 1786, D: 14 Jun 1871, M: Nancy Jane Russell, 1812.

iv. James Stewart, B: 10 Jun 1793, D: 03 Feb 1870.

v. Mary Stewart, B: 1807 in Oglethorpe County, Georgia, D: 18 Dec 1878.

124. iv. William Blanton Stewart.

58. James Richardson Penn-4(Moses-3, Joseph-2, John-1)[3, 10] was born in Virginia. He died in 1845 in Kentucky. He married Mary Major on 05 Dec 1791 in Amherst County, Virginia[3], daughter of Harwood Major and Lucy Watson.

Notes for James Richardson Penn:

Last known to be in Campbell County, Kentucky in 1803. His middle name was either Richardson or Richeson.

Children of James Richardson Penn and Mary Major are:

i. Edmond Penn.

ii. Frances Penn, M: James Greenwell, 14 Dec 1822 in Green County, Kentucky.

Notes for Frances Penn:

Her paternity is still open to question.

iii. George Penn.

iv. John Penn.

v. Lucy Penn, M: Joseph Farmer, 21 May 1822 in Green County, Kentucky.

Notes for Lucy Penn:

Her paternity is still open to question.

vi. Mary Jane Penn, M: Samuel Shively, 12 Feb 1828 in Green County, Kentucky.
Notes for Mary Jane Penn:
Her paternity is still open to question.

126.vii. Richardson Penn, B: 1793 in Bedford County, Virginia, D: 1868 in Montgomery County, Missouri, M: Lucinda DeWitt, 1813 in Campbell County, Virginia.

127.viii. Harwood Major Penn, B: 1794 in Bedford County, Virginia, D: 1880 in Cass County, Nebraska.

128. ix. Moses Penn, B: 06 Mar 1796 in Bedford County, Virginia, D: 1878 in Virginia, M: Edna Penina White, 19 Oct 1824 in Bedford County, Virginia.

129. x. Thomas Major Penn, B: 11 Jun 1798, D: Taylor County, Kentucky, M: Lou Ann Spurling, Kentucky.

130. xi. James R. Penn, B: 22 Feb 1810 in Bedford County, Virginia, D: Missouri, M: Mary Jane Shively, 31 Oct 1831 in Campbellsville, Green County, Kentucky.

131.xii. William Penn, B: 13 Apr 1816 in Bedford County, Virginia, D: 14 Sep 1868 in Hydesburg, Marion County, Missouri, M: Nancy Shively, 13 Apr 1838.

59. John Penn Hunt-4(Frances-3, Joseph-2, John-1)[3] was born on 08 Jul 1789[3]. He died in 1850[3]. He married Sarah Longmore in 1811[3].

Children of John Penn Hunt and Sarah Longmore are:

i. Hannah Britt Hunt, B: 23 Dec 1812, D: 18 Apr 1890.

ii. Joseph Penn Hunt, B: 14 Jul 1814, D: 08 Jun 1880.

iii. George Washington Hunt, B: 10 Dec 1816, D: 27 Jun 1876.

iv. J. W. Hunt, B: 12 Mar 1819.

v. Albert Jackson Hunt, B: 12 Nov 1820.

vi. Frances C. Hunt, B: 08 Feb 1825.

vii. Robert Longmire Hunt, B: 24 Jul 1827, D: 01 Apr 1883.

viii. David Alexander Hunt, B: 10 Jan 1831, D: 12 Dec 1891.

ix. James Thomas Hunt, B: 16 Jun 1833, D: 04 Nov 1879.

x. Mary Elizabeth Hunt, B: 28 Jul 1836, D: Abt. 1836.

60. Lucy Penn-4(John-3, Moses-2, John-1) was born in 1766 in Caroline County, Virginia[8]. She died in 1830 in Caroline County, Virginia[8]. She married John Taylor in 1781 in Caroline County, Virginia[8], son of James Taylor and Anne Pollard. He was born on 19 Dec 1753 in Caroline County, Virginia[8]. He died on 21 Aug 1824 in Caroline County, Virginia[8].

Children of Lucy Penn and John Taylor are:

i. Lucy Taylor, B: Aft. 1798.

ii. William Penn Taylor.

iii. George Taylor.

iv. Edwin Taylor.

132. v. John Taylor Jr., B: 07 Sep 1784 in Caroline County, Virginia[8], D: 08 Aug 1853 in Caroline County, Virginia[8], M: Lucy Woodford, Bef. 1821.

vi. Edmund Pendleton Taylor.

132.vii. Henry Taylor, B: 1800, D: 1845.

viii. Randolph Taylor.

GENERATION 5

61. Harriet Harrison-5(Susanna-4, Frances-3, George-2, John-1). She died in 1876. She married William France, son of Peter Frans and Susannah Carter.

Children of Harriet Harrison and William France are:

133. i. Susan Lee France, B: 20 Jun 1813, D: 18 Jan 1892.

134. ii. Harrison Carter France, B: 1818, D: 1896, M: Catherine Leath Penn, 09 Oct 1842.

62. Francis B. Harrison-5(Susanna-4, Frances-3, George-2, John-1) was born about 1782. He died about 1835. He married Frances Crutcher on 08 Mar 1803.

Child of Francis B. Harrison and Frances Crutcher is:

i. Francis M. Harrison, B: 18 Jun 1826, D: 09 Mar 1908, M: Nancy Mildred Collins, 02 Feb 1848.

63. William Nelson Penn-5(George-4, George-3, George-2, John-1) was born on 12 Oct 1804 in Amherst County, Virginia. He died on 18 Aug 1873 in Monroe County, Missouri. He married Sarah Emerine Carter on 12 Oct 1831.

Child of William Nelson Penn and Sarah Emerine Carter is:

i. Catherine Rowena Penn, B: 14 Jun 1841, D: 1918, M: Theodore Brace, 12 Oct 1858.

64. Frances Burton-5(Frances-4, George-3, George-2, John-1) was born in 1794. She died in 1842. She married Josiah Turpin.

Child of Frances Burton and Josiah Turpin is:

i. Callowhill Turpin, B: 1818, D: 1882.

65. Elizabeth Penn-5(George-4, Phillip-3, George-2, John-1) was born about 1788 in Henry County, Virginia. She died before 1814 in Patrick County, Virginia. She married William Banks Jr. on 04 Feb 1808 in Patrick County, Virginia, son of William Banks Sr..

Children of Elizabeth Penn and William Banks Jr. are:

i. George F. Banks, B: 1809 in Patrick County, Virginia, D: Aft. Feb 1861, M: Mariah W. Sims, 01 Jan 1833 in Rutherford County, Tennessee.

ii. Elijah S. Banks, B: 03 Jan 1810 in Patrick County, Virginia, D: 22 Jul 1860 in Gibson County, Tennessee, M: Ermenilda Chambers, 30 Dec 1830 in Smith County, Tennessee.

iii. Joseph P. Banks, B: Abt. 1811 in Patrick County, Virginia, D: Bef. Nov 1833 in Smith County, Tennessee.
Notes for Joseph P. Banks:
Never married.

66. Frances Penn-5(George-4, Phillip-3, George-2, John-1) was born on 27 May 1792 in Patrick County, Virginia. She died on 16 Jan 1879 in Smith County, Tennessee. She married William Banks Jr. on 12 Oct 1814 in Patrick County, Virginia, son of William Banks Sr..

Children of Frances Penn and William Banks Jr. are:

i. Frances Elizabeth Banks, B: 1818 in Smith County, Tennessee, D: Bef. 1881 in Smith County, Tennessee, M: William S. Bradley, Abt. 1840 in Smith County, Tennessee.

ii. William T. Banks, B: Abt. 1819 in Smith County, Tennessee, D: 1891 in Gibson County, Tennessee, M: Mary A., Abt. 1844.

iii. Martha A. Banks, B: Abt. 1821 in Smith County, Tennessee, D: Aft. 1880.

iv. Luvenia Ruth Banks, B: Abt. 1822 in Smith County, Tennessee, D: Abt. 1844 in Smith County, Tennessee.
Notes for Luvenia Ruth Banks:
Never married.

67. Ruth Penn-5(George-4, Phillip-3, George-2, John-1) was born about 1794 in Patrick County, Virginia. She died about 1855. She married William Finney on 22 Jul 1823 in Rutherford County, Tennessee.

Children of Ruth Penn and William Finney are:

i. George Penn Finney.

ii. Martha Finney.

68. Josiah Penn-5(George-4, Phillip-3, George-2, John-1) was born in 1799 in Patrick County, Virginia. He died about 1855 in Humboldt Township, Gibson County, Tennessee. He married Ruth Wallace Broughton on 11 Jun 1825 in Rutherford County, Tennessee.

Children of Josiah Penn and Ruth Wallace Broughton are:

i. Elizabeth Penn.

ii. William Clinton Penn, B: 24 Jul 1828 in Rutherford County, Tennessee, D: Aft. 1885 in Gibson County, Tennessee, M: Texie Boyce, 01 Oct 1862 in Gibson County, tenness.

iii. Martha Watkins Penn, B: 1831 in Rutherford County, Tennessee.
Notes for Martha Watkins Penn:
Never married.

iv. George Penn, B: 1833 in Rutherford County, Tennessee.
Notes for George Penn:
Never married.

v. James Watkins Penn, B: 31 Aug 1836 in Humboldt Township, Gibson County, Tennessee, D: 1895 in Humboldt Township, Gibson County, Tennessee, M: Cordilia Hemens Stilwell, 17 May 1860 in Humboldt Township, Gibson County, Tennessee.

vi. Winchester Josiah Penn, B: 1839 in Humboldt Township, Gibson County, Tennessee.

vii. Lavinia Penn, B: 1842 in Humboldt Township, Gibson County, Tennessee.

viii. America Penn, B: 1845 in Humboldt Township, Gibson County, Tennessee, D: Bef. 1860 in Humboldt Township, Gibson County, Tennessee.

69. Jacob F. Penn-5(George-4, Phillip-3, George-2, John-1) was born in 1802 in Patrick County, Virginia. He married before 1829. He married (2) Margrett Odle on 02 May 1838 in Gibson County, Tennessee.

i. William Penn, B: Abt. 1829, M: Eliza E. Bryant, 12 Apr 1854 in Gibson County, Tennessee.

ii. Pinkney Penn, B: Abt. 1832, M: Frances O. Alexander, 30 Aug 1851 in Gibson County, Tennessee.

iii. Josiah Penn, B: Abt. 1835.

Children of Jacob F. Penn and Margrett Odle are:

i. Mary Penn, B: Abt. 1839.

ii. Thankful Penn, B: Abt. 1840.

iii. James Penn, B: Abt. 1842.

iv. Melissa Penn, B: Abt. 1843.

v. Lavinia Penn, B: Abt. 1846.

vi. Frances Penn, B: Abt. 1848.

70. George Douglas Penn-5(George-4, Phillip-3, George-2, John-1) was born about 1804 in Patrick County, Virginia. He married Telitha Patterson Clay on 15 Oct 1831 in Rutherford County, Tennessee.

Child of George Douglas Penn and Telitha Patterson Clay is:

i. Evander Penn, B: 02 Aug 1832, D: Apr 1895 in Eureka Springs, Arkansas.

71. Luvenia Penn-5(George-4, Phillip-3, George-2, John-1) was born about 1804 in Patrick County, Virginia. She died about 1850. She married (1) Joseph Magruder Watkins. She married (2) Theophilus Sharpe before 1830.

Children of Luvenia Penn and Joseph Magruder Watkins are:

i. Thomas Watkins.

ii. John Watkins.

iii. Martha Watkins.

iv. Mary Elizabeth Watkins.

Child of Luvenia Penn and Theophilus Sharpe is:

i. George Sharpe, B: 1830, D: 1859.

72. Robert Cowan Penn-5(James-4, Gabriel-3, George-2, John-1) was born on 19 Feb 1789 in Campbell County, Virginia. He died on 02 Jul 1856 in St. Helena, Beford County, Virginia. He married Lucinda Steptoe on 15 Jun 1814 in Bedford County, Virginia.

Children of Robert Cowan Penn and Lucinda Steptoe are:

i. James Steptoe Penn, B: 20 Mar 1817, D: 09 Nov 1854 in Bedford County, Virginia.

ii. Frances Louise Penn, B: 21 Jan 1818, M: David Rodes, 12 May 1846 in St. Helena, Bedford County, Virginia.

iii. LaFayette Penn, B: 06 Aug 1820, D: 29 Apr 1840 in Fincastle, Virginia.

iv. Elizabeth Johnson Penn, B: 09 Oct 1823, M: Hezekian Jordan, 07 Nov 1850.

v. Margaret Penn, B: 03 Apr 1828, D: 19 Aug 1828 in St. Helena, Beford County, Virginia.

73. Alfred Penn-5(James-4, Gabriel-3, George-2, John-1) was born in 1800 in Lynchburg, Virginia. He died in 1875. He married Evelyn Carter Bradfute on 02 Sep 1833 in Lynchburg, Virginia.

Children of Alfred Penn and Evelyn Carter Bradfute are:

i. Davidson Bradfute Penn, B: 13 May 1836 in Lynchburg, Virginia, D: 15 Nov 1902 in New Orleans, Louisiana.

ii. Bertha Beverley Penn, B: 1838, M: William Butler Krumbhaar, 25 Apr 1867 in New Orleans, Louisiana.

74. Van Tramp Crawford-5(Sophia M.-4, Gabriel-3, George-2, John-1). He married Margaret M. Dunn.

Child of Van Tramp Crawford and Margaret M. Dunn is:

i. Julia Octavia Crawford.

75. Margaret Brydie-5(Nancy C.-4, Gabriel-3, George-2, John-1) was born about 1796. She died in 1888. She married William Hay Dyer in 1814.

Children of Margaret Brydie and William Hay Dyer are:

i. Alexander Brydie Dyer, B: 1815, D: 1874.

ii. Ann Evelyn Dyer, B: 1817, D: 1874, M: Samuel Grant Mason, 1835.

76. Alexander Gordon Penn-5(George-4, Abraham-3, George-2, John-1) was born in 1799 in Patrick County, Virginia. He died on 08 May 1866 in Washington, D.C..

Notes for Alexander Gordon Penn:

Last known to have lived in New Orleans, Louisiana. He died while traveling in Washington, D.C.

i. Sarah Delphine Davidson Penn.

77. Martin Gordon Penn-5(George-4, Abraham-3, George-2, John-1) was born on 09 Jun 1805. He married Harriet Tyson Elltott on 02 Apr 1829.

Child of Martin Gordon Penn and Harriet Tyson Elltott is:

i. George Henry Penn Sr., B: 25 Jan 1830, M: Lucinda Elizabeth Martee, Bef. 1858.

78. Abram P. Staples-5(Lucinda-4, Abraham-3, George-2, John-1) was born on 09 Mar 1793 in Patrick County, Virginia. He married Mary S. Penn on 23 Oct 1820, daughter of Granville Penn.

Child of Abram P. Staples and Mary S. Penn is:

i. Waller R. Staples, B: 24 Feb 1826.

79. Clark Penn-5(Gabriel-4, Abraham-3, George-2, John-1) was born on 07 Dec 1797. He died on 03 Aug 1858. He married (1) Barbara Ann L. Penn on 21 Jun 1831 in Patrick County, Virginia, daughter of James Francis Penn and Catherine Leath. She was born on 01 Apr 1809. She died on 30 Jun 1837. He married (2) Mary M. Harris on 24 Apr 1826. He married (3) Susannah Kennerly on 08 Oct 1848.

Children of Clark Penn and Barbara Ann L. Penn are:

i. Abram Penn, B: 08 Apr 1832, D: 30 Apr 1832.

ii. Sarah Catherine Penn, B: 08 Apr 1832, D: 15 May 1865, M: George Wade Hylton, 07 Oct 1858 in Patrick County, Virginia.

iii. Gabriel J. Penn, B: 27 Nov 1836, D: 28 Mar 1905, M: Susan Elizabeth Penn, 07 Oct 1857.

80. Frances R. Penn-5(Gabriel-4, Abraham-3, George-2, John-1) was born on 31 May 1815. She died on 25 Jun 1833. She married Peter Phillip Penn, son of Greensville Penn and Anna Leath. He was born in 1811.

Child of Frances R. Penn and Peter Phillip Penn is:

i. Francis Penn, D: 13 Jul 1833.

81. Gabriel Penn-5(Gabriel-4, Abraham-3, George-2, John-1).

i. John Penn, B: 03 Jul 1837 in Patrick County, Virginia, D: 27 Sep 1895.

82. Ruth M. Penn-5(Horatio-4, Abraham-3, George-2, John-1) was born in 1808 in Virginia. She died in 1845 in St. Charles, Ralls County, Missouri. She married Joseph T. Abington on 21 Mar 1827 in Patrick County, Virginia.

Children of Ruth M. Penn and Joseph T. Abington are:

i. Kesiah Ann Abington, B: 1827, D: 1865.

ii. Catherine E. Abington, B: 1830.

iii. Oliver Perry Abington, B: 1831.

iv. Fanny Abington, B: 1833.

v. George M. Abington, B: 1837.

vi. William P. Abington, B: 1839.

vii. Amanda P. Abington, B: 1842.

83. Keziah S. Penn-5(Horatio-4, Abraham-3, George-2, John-1) was born in 1809 in Virginia. She married Hanceford Brown on 18 Jan 1835 in Ralls County, Missouri.

Children of Keziah S. Penn and Hanceford Brown are:

i. William P. Brown, B: 1836.

ii. Josephus H. Brown, B: 1838.

iii. Ruth A. Brown, B: 1840.

iv. Mary J. Brown, B: 1841.

v. Frances M. Brown, B: 1843.

vi. Lucinda S. Brown, B: 1845.

84. Gabriel Penn-5(Horatio-4, Abraham-3, George-2, John-1) was born on 22 Nov 1811 in Virginia. He died on 18 Nov 1867. He married Lucinda Ann Glasscock on 10 Jan 1839 in Ralls County, Missouri. She died on 05 Jun 1880.

Children of Gabriel Penn and Lucinda Ann Glasscock are:

i. Peter Penn, B: 03 Nov 1839, D: 15 Feb 1843.

ii. Nancy G. Penn, B: 13 Oct 1840, D: 15 Oct 1844.
Notes for Nancy G. Penn:
Conflicting month of death of November.

iii. William H. Penn, B: 08 Jun 1842, M: Emma Evans, 08 Jan 1868.

iv. Kiziah F. Penn, B: 04 Mar 1845, D: 15 Oct 1887.

v. Mary Elizabeth Penn, B: 22 Jul 1847, D: Brookhaven, Mississippi, M: Isaac Cope, Bef. 1865.

vi. John E. Penn, B: 03 Sep 1849, D: 1924 in Sacramento, California.

vii. Gabriel Penn, B: 18 Nov 1851, D: 15 Oct 1867.

viii. Charles H. Penn, B: 24 Nov 1855, D: 1934, M: Sallie E. Lewis, 18 Jun 1881.

ix. Penn, B: 31 Aug 1858, D: 26 Feb 1859 in Clinton, Mississippi.

85. John W. Penn-5(Horatio-4, Abraham-3, George-2, John-1) was born in 1816 in Virginia. He died in 1880 in St. Charles, Ralls County, Missouri. He married Elizabeth S. Major on 11 Sep 1839 in St. Charles County, Missouri.

Children of John W. Penn and Elizabeth S. Major are:

i. Horatio G. Penn, B: 14 Jan 1841 in St. Charles County, Missouri.
Notes for Horatio G. Penn:
Conflicting date of birth of 6/14/1841.

ii. Nancy M. Penn, B: 1842, M: Robert A. Spain, 1865.

iii. Tobitha Penn, B: 1844.

iv. Lucinda M. Penn, B: 1846.

v. May C. Penn, B: 1847.

vi. James G. Penn, B: 1850.

vii. William E. Penn, B: 1850.

86. Horatio Penn Jr.-5(Horatio-4, Abraham-3, George-2, John-1) was born in 1821 in Virginia. He died in 1909 in Ralls County, Missouri. He married Jane Catherine Kelley on 25 May 1851 in Ralls County, Missouri.

Children of Horatio Penn Jr. and Jane Catherine Kelley are:

i. Mary M Penn, B: 1853.

ii. Robert G. Penn, B: 1856, D: 1933.

iii. Penn, B: 1859.

87. Louvenia Penn Foster-5(Mary-4, Abraham-3, George-2, John-1) was born on 13 Jun 1812. She died on 15 Apr 1885. She married Charles Ross.

Children of Louvenia Penn Foster and Charles Ross are:

i. Charles Foster Ross.

ii. James Ross.
Notes for James Ross:
Died in the Civil War.

iii. George G. Ross, D: 1929.

iv. Tennie Ross, B: 1843, D: 1902.

v. Martha Ross, B: 30 Sep 1849, D: 31 Jan 1913, M: John Abe Nolen, 02 Feb 1871.

vi. William L. Ross, B: 1850, D: 1910.

88. Abram Penn Foster-5(Mary-4, Abraham-3, George-2, John-1) was born in 1813. He died in 1891. He married Mary Jane Critz on 19 Dec 1838.

Child of Abram Penn Foster and Mary Jane Critz is:

i. J. Edmond Foster, B: 1858, D: 1928.

89. Gabriel Penn-5(Greensville-4, Abraham-3, George-2, John-1) [11] was born in 1814. He married Susan Lee France, daughter of William France and Harriet Harrison. She was born on 20 Jun 1813. She died on 18 Jan 1892.

Children of Gabriel Penn and Susan Lee France are:

i. William Leath Penn, B: 29 Jul 1834[11].

ii. Edward Penn, B: 03 Jul 1837[11].

90. Peter Phillip Penn-5(Greensville-4, Abraham-3, George-2, John-1) was born in 1811. He married Frances R. Penn, daughter of Gabriel Penn and Jane Clark. She was born on 31 May 1815. She died on 25 Jun 1833.

Child of Peter Phillip Penn and Frances R. Penn is:

i. Francis Penn, D: 13 Jul 1833.

91. Andrew Jackson Penn-5(Thomas-4, Abraham-3, George-2, John-1) was born on 27 Mar 1811 in Popular Grove, Patrick County, Virginia. He died on 27 Mar 1877 in Locust Grove, Patrick County, Virginia. He married Martha Kennerly on 02 Oct 1832.

Children of Andrew Jackson Penn and Martha Kennerly are:

i. Thomas Jackson Penn, B: 25 Sep 1833 in Patrick County, Virginia.

ii. Peter Leath Penn, B: 08 Dec 1835 in Patrick County, Virginia, D: 26 Mar 1901.

iii. James Christopher Penn, B: 04 Dec 1838 in Patrick County, Virginia.

iv. Abram C. Penn, B: 01 Jul 1842.

v. Samuel Alexander Penn, B: 05 Apr 1844.
Notes for Samuel Alexander Penn:
Never married.

vi. Martha Frances Penn, B: 21 Mar 1842, M: Patrick Lewis/ Louis Fgeorge, 04 Oct 1865.

vii. Louis George Penn, B: 17 Mar 1848.

viii. Sarah Jane Penn, B: 19 May 1852.

ix. Robert Rives Penn, B: 15 Jul 1853 in Patrick County, Virginia, D: Callaway, Virginia.

x. Martin Tupper Penn, B: 24 Nov 1854.

xi. Susan Elizabeth Penn, B: 04 Dec 1837 in Patrick County, Virginia, D: 31 May 1919 in Waxahachie, Ellis County, texas, M: Gabriel J. Penn, 07 Oct 1857.

92. George Washington Penn-5(Thomas-4, Abraham-3, George-2, John-1) was born on 16 Oct 1822 in Patrick County, Virginia. He died on 17 Aug 1867. He married Mary Ann Penn.

Notes for Mary Ann Penn:

Mary Ann Penn is supposed to be George Washington Penn's 1st cousin by way of her father is Edmund Penn.

Children of George Washington Penn and Mary Ann Penn are:

i. Edmund Penn, B: 03 Apr 1852.

Notes for Edmund Penn:

Edmund's birth date is subject to some criticism because his parents Mary Ann Penn and George Washington Penn were supposedly married on July 30, 1854 and it is believed that you just didn't do "those" things in the 1800's.

ii. Mary Ann Penn, B: 16 Apr 1854.

iii. Bella Penn, B: 26 Nov 1857, D: Jun 1963.

Notes for Bella Penn:

Bella's death date is open to some criticism. I have seen the death date as June 1863 instead of June 1963, it is a difference of 100 years. I suppose one could argue that it is rare that people would live 106 year, BUT it does happen. Personally, I am taking the 1963 until I have proof to the contrary.

93. Lucinda Susan Penn-5(Thomas-4, Abraham-3, George-2, John-1) was born on 13 Oct 1834 in Patrick County, Virginia. She married James Abram Penn on 23 Sep 1857, son of James Francis Penn and Mary Shelton.

Children of Lucinda Susan Penn and James Abram Penn are:

i. Thomas Penn, B: 16 Jul 1858.

ii. James Penn, B: 06 Jan 1860.

iii. Joseph Penn, B: 23 Nov 1861.

iv. Mary C. Penn, B: 11 Sep 1863.

v. Penn, B: 16 Apr 1868, D: Jun 1868.

94. William Alexander Penn-5(Thomas-4, Abraham-3, George-2, John-1) was born on 07 Jul 1840. He died on 21 Jun 1887. He married Marie Louise Bagby on 10 Aug 1865.

Children of William Alexander Penn and Marie Louise Bagby are:

i. Mary Elizabeth Penn, B: 20 Aug 1866 in Popular Grove, Patrick County, Virginia, M: John Foster Edd, 01 Dec 1886.

ii. Thomas Bennett Penn, B: 25 Mar 1868 in Red Bend, Virginia.

iii. Martha Susan Penn, B: 13 Aug 1870, D: 11 Feb 1926, M: William Moore Tatum, 13 Dec 1890.

iv. Ellen Maxwell Penn, B: 20 Oct 1872.

95. William H. Penn Sr.-5(Abram-4, Abraham-3, George-2, John-1) was born in 1810. He died after 1885. He married Mary Ann Pollack on 15 Mar 1831.

Child of William H. Penn Sr. and Mary Ann Pollack is:

i. William H. Penn Jr., B: 1832, D: Aft. 1885, M: Sarah E. Wyatt, 24 Jan 1856.

96. Barbara Ann L. Penn-5(James Francis-4, Abraham-3, George-2, John-1) was born on 01 Apr 1809. She died on 30 Jun 1837. She married Clark Penn on 21 Jun 1831 in Patrick County, Virginia, son of Gabriel Penn and Jane Clark. He was born on 07 Dec 1797. He died on 03 Aug 1858.

Children of Barbara Ann L. Penn and Clark Penn are:

i. Abram Penn, B: 08 Apr 1832, D: 30 Apr 1832.

ii. Sarah Catherine Penn, B: 08 Apr 1832, D: 15 May 1865, M: George Wade Hylton, 07 Oct 1858 in Patrick County, Virginia.

iii. Gabriel J. Penn, B: 27 Nov 1836, D: 28 Mar 1905, M: Susan Elizabeth Penn, 07 Oct 1857.

97. Catherine Leath Penn-5(James Francis-4, Abraham-3, George-2, John-1) was born on 16 Jan 1821. She died on 04 Mar 1914. She married Harrison Carter France on 09 Oct 1842, son of William France and Harriet Harrison. He was born in 1818. He died in 1896.

Children of Catherine Leath Penn and Harrison Carter France are:

i. Annie Redd France.

ii. Susan Barbara France, B: 1843, D: 04 Jul 1927.

iii. James Penn France.

iv. Catherine France.

v. Peter Shelton France.

vi. William Starling France.

98. James Abram Penn-5(James Francis-4, Abraham-3, George-2, John-1). He married Lucinda Susan Penn on 23 Sep 1857, daughter of Thomas Penn and Mary Christian Kennerly. She was born on 13 Oct 1834 in Patrick County, Virginia.

Children of James Abram Penn and Lucinda Susan Penn are:

i. Thomas Penn, B: 16 Jul 1858.

ii. James Penn, B: 06 Jan 1860.

iii. Joseph Penn, B: 23 Nov 1861.

iv. Mary C. Penn, B: 11 Sep 1863.

v. Penn, B: 16 Apr 1868, D: Jun 1868.

99. William Abraham Clark Penn-5(Edmond-4, Abraham-3, George-2, John-1) was born on 07 May 1818 in Murfreesboro, Rutherford County, Tennessee. He married (1) Levenia Kelton on 07 Jul 1841 in Gibson County, Tennessee. He married (2) Gillia Ann Rigsbee on 10 Mar 1858 in Gibson County, Tennessee.

Children of William Abraham Clark Penn and Levenia Kelton are:

i. Martha Penn.

ii. Elizabeth Penn.

iii. Robert Penn.

iv. Lucinda Penn.

v. Emma Penn.

vi. Flavius Josephus Penn.

Child of William Abraham Clark Penn and Gillia Ann Rigsbee is:

i. W. T. Penn.

100. Josiah Ferris Penn-5(Edmond-4, Abraham-3, George-2, John-1)[12] was born on 11 Sep 1819 in Murfreesboro, Rutherford County, Tennessee. He married (1) Mirah M. Sneed on 26 Nov 1840 in Rutherford County, Tennessee. He married (2) Frances Ann Wade on 07 Nov 1850 in Gibson County, Tennessee.

Children of Josiah Ferris Penn and Mirah M. Sneed are:

i. William Penn, B: 1841 in Gibson County, Tennessee.

ii. Mary Ann Penn, B: 1843 in Gibson County, Tennessee.

iii. Adilaide Penn, B: 1844 in Gibson County, Tennessee.

iv. Sarah Penn, B: 1846.

v. James Penn, B: 1847 in Gibson County, Tennessee.

vi. George Penn, B: 1849.

Children of Josiah Ferris Penn and Frances Ann Wade are:

i. Mariah Penn.

ii. Eliza Penn.

iii. Idella Penn.

iv. Jodie Perry Penn.

v. Lelia Penn.

101. Sarah Elizabeth Penn-5(Edmond-4, Abraham-3, George-2, John-1) was born on 16 Sep 1823 in Murfreesboro, Rutherford County, Tennessee. She married Benjamin Franklin Harris on 20 Mar 1844 in Gibson County, Tennessee.

Child of Sarah Elizabeth Penn and Benjamin Franklin Harris is:

i. Hannibal Harris, B: Abt. 1845.

102. Mary Ruth Penn-5(Edmond-4, Abraham-3, George-2, John-1) was born on 25 Nov 1827 in Murfreesboro, Rutherford County, Tennessee. She married William Harvey.

Children of Mary Ruth Penn and William Harvey are:

i. Richard Harvey.

ii. George Harvey.

iii. Mattie Harvey.

iv. Anna Harvey.

v. Elizabeth Harvey.

103. George Stovall Penn-5(Edmond-4, Abraham-3, George-2, John-1) was born on 19 Feb 1830 in Murfreesboro, Rutherford County, Tennessee. He died in Weatherford, Texas. He married Eliza Ellen Conner on 15 Feb 1854 in Gibson County, Tennessee.

Children of George Stovall Penn and Eliza Ellen Conner are:

i. Lewis Edmund Penn, B: 1860 in Cadiz, Kentucky.

ii. John Thomas Penn.

iii. Charles Conner Penn.

iv. George Penn.

v. Lillian Lee Penn.

vi. Oscar Penn.

vii. Mary Lewis Penn.

104. Martha Luvenia Penn-5(Edmond-4, Abraham-3, George-2, John-1) was born on 26 Apr 1832 in Murfreesboro, Rutherford County, Tennessee. She married Benjamin Franklin Harris on 24 Jan 1859 in Gibson County, Tennessee.

Children of Martha Luvenia Penn and Benjamin Franklin Harris are:

i. Thomas Harris.

ii. Benjamin Harris.

iii. William Harris.

iv. May Harris.

v. Delia Harris.

105. Gabriel Thomas Penn-5(Edmond-4, Abraham-3, George-2, John-1) was born on 07 Jan 1836 in Murfreesboro, Rutherford County, Tennessee. He married Mary Elizabeth Mitchell.

Children of Gabriel Thomas Penn and Mary Elizabeth Mitchell are:

i. Martha Laura Penn.

ii. James Edmond Penn.

iii. Anna Ruth Penn – *she married Robert Warren; three offspring: Robert Penn Warren, born 1905, Mary C. Warren, born 1909, William T. Warren, born 1912*

iv. Mary M. Penn.

v. Sarah Thomas Penn.

vi. Bessie George Penn.

vii. Daisy Penn.

106. Charity Warren Penn-5(Phillip-4, Abraham-3, George-2, John-1) was born in 1825. She died in 1899. She married Hendley S. Jenkins on 23 Oct 1844.

Child of Charity Warren Penn and Hendley S. Jenkins is:

i. Harriet Elizabeth Jenkins, B: 1848, D: 1914, M: William P. Hulbert, 05 Oct 1869.

107. Sarah Penn-5(Joseph-4, John-3, Joseph-2, John-1)[3] was born about 1781 in Amherst County, Virginia. She married Robert Holloway on 18 Nov 1797 in Amherst County, Virginia[3].

Children of Sarah Penn and Robert Holloway are:

i. George Seaton Holloway.

ii. Elizabeth Catherine Holloway.

108. Mary Ann Penn-5(Joseph-4, John-3, Joseph-2, John-1)[1, 2, 3] was born on 11 Feb 1790 in Amherst County, Virginia[1, 2, 9]. She died on 03 Mar 1846 in Barren County, Kentucky[1, 2, 9]. She married William Edmunds on 30 Mar 1805 in Amherst County, Virginia[1, 2, 3], son of James Edmunds Sr. and Sarah Lavender. He was born on 16 Oct 1776 in Amherst County, Virginia[1, 2, 9]. He died on 21 Jun 1863 in Barren County, Kentucky[1, 2, 9].

Notes for Mary Ann Penn:

Her date of birth and names of parents and place of birth are recorded in the William Edmunds bible.

Her Father's date of birth and the names and dates of birth and marriage for his father's parents are included in the William Edmunds Journal.

Notes for William Edmunds:

He likely lived in the part of Amherst County, Virginia which was broken off to form Nelson County, Virginia in 1807 until his move to Barren County, Virginia in about 1810.

He wrote his Will on 22 May 1862 while a resident of Barren County, Kentucky. It was proved in Court on 27 June 1863. The entire Will is written in his own handwriting. It mentions his daughter, Sally R. Snoddy and her children William A. Snoddy and Robert A. Snoddy, Charles Penn Edmunds, Martha Ann, Elizabeth L., James Terrence, William Henry, his daughter-in law, A. Edmunds (wife of William Henry, and their children Crittenden and William), Caroline Winston, Edmund Alexander (he got the homestead).

He has a bible with an 1835 copyright in which he has vital statistics entered for his parents, his siblings, himself, his wife and his children. The initial entries were made on 12/27/1839. Thereafter, the entries were presumable made as they occurred.

Children of Mary Ann Penn and William Edmunds are:

135. i. Sally Penn Edmunds, B: 05 Jan 1806, D: 18 Sep 1828, M: Carey A. Snoddy Sr., 05 Sep 1820.

ii. William Gatt Edmunds, B: 05 Jan 1808, D: 23 Aug 1808.

136. iii. Mary Jane Edmunds, B: 31 Oct 1809, D: 22 Jun 1832, M: James B. Sterrett, 12 Oct 1824.

137. iv. Charles Penn Edmunds, B: 24 Dec 1811 in Barren County, Kentucky[1, 2], D: 22 Mar 1883 in Glasgow, Barren County, Kentucky[1, 2], M: Elizabeth T. Eubank, 24 Nov 1829 in Barren County, Kentucky[1, 2].

138. v. Martha Ann Edmunds, B: 07 Dec 1813, D: 23 Jun 1868, M: Haiden T. Curd, 24 Feb 1830.

139. vi. Elizabeth Lee Edmunds, B: 02 Nov 1815, D: Jan 1883 in Bonham, Texas, M: William Crawford Whitsett, 15 Dec 1836.

140. vii. James Terrance Edmunds, B: 14 Jan 1818, D: 21 Jan 1895, M: Catherine M. Foster, 17 Aug 1837.

viii. Joseph Penn Edmunds, B: 03 Apr 1820, D: 27 Aug 1847 in Lexington, Kentucky.

ix. Infant Edmunds, B: 05 Jan 1822, D: 05 Jan 1822.

141. x. William Henry Edmunds, B: 17 Jun 1823 in Barren County, Kentucky, D: 24 Nov 1900 in Barren County, Kentucky, M: Amanda Moss, 19 Aug 1847.

142. xi. Caroline Winston Edmunds, B: 26 May 1825, D: 08 May 1890 in Montgomery, Alabama, M: John Mulkey Barton, 04 May 1843.

143. xii. Sarah Lavender Edmunds, B: 14 Aug 1829, D: 03 Oct 1853, M: Hanson Trigg Lewis, 17 Mar 1847.

144. xiii. Frances Burrus Edmunds, B: 07 Dec 1831, D: 02 Sep 1917 in Barren County, Kentucky, M: James Forbis Barton, 07 Dec 1847.

145.xiv. Edmund Alexander Edmunds, B: 12 Jun 1827 in Kentucky, D: 22 Apr 1906, M: Henrietta Shepherd Lewis, 08 Sep 1853.

109. Charles A. Penn-5(Alexander-4, John-3, Joseph-2, John-1)[3] was born about 1810 in Nelson County, Virginia. He died in 1860 in Amherst County, Virginia[3]. He married Mary Coleman on 15 Jun 1838 in Amherst County, Virginia[3].

Children of Charles A. Penn and Mary Coleman are:

i. Maria W. Penn, B: Abt. 1841.

ii. Millie A. Penn, B: Abt. 1843, M: J. N. Taliferro, 04 May 1870.

iii. Elizabeth Daniel Penn, B: 1845, M: Henry M. Loving Jr., 10 Dec 1867 in Amherst County, Virginia.

iv. Susan S. Penn, B: 1852, M: Samuel W. Brockman, 03 Feb 1882.

v. Edward A. Penn.

110. John Upshaw Jr.-5(Amy-4, Catherine-3, Joseph-2, John-1) was born on 24 Dec 1776. He died in 1818. He married Rebecca Cook, daughter of Benjamin Cook and Effy.

Children of John Upshaw Jr. and Rebecca Cook are:

i. Middleton Cook Upshaw.

ii. Elizabeth Upshaw.

111. Sarah Upshaw-5(Amy-4, Catherine-3, Joseph-2, John-1)[13] was born on 31 Jan 1779 in Amherst County, Virginia. She died about 1833 in Elbert County, Georgia. She married Benjamin Thornton Sr. on 12 Jun 1796, son of Dozier Thornton and Lucy Hill.

Children of Sarah Upshaw and Benjamin Thornton Sr. are:

i. Reuben Thornton, B: 1797, D: 30 Aug 1855, M: Elizabeth Lane Jackson, 18 Jun 1837.

ii. Thomas Thornton, B: 1798.

iii. Priscilla Thornton, B: 1800, M: Sion Hunt, 31 Jul 1823 in Elbert County, Georgia.

iv. Benjamin Thornton Jr., B: 15 Aug 1801 in Elbert County, Georgia, D: Aft. 1852, M: Nancy Payne, 16 Sep 1819.

v. Elizabeth Thornton, B: 25 Oct 1802 in Elbert County, Georgia, D: 1854, M: John Dickerson, 29 Dec 1812 in Elbert County, Georgia[13].

vi. John Thornton, B: 1803.

vii. Polly Thornton, B: 01 Aug 1807.

viii. Daniel Thornton, B: 11 Nov 1811.

ix. Mary Thornton, B: 1812.

x. Dozier Thornton, B: 1813.

xi. Sarah Thornton, B: 1814.

112. Mary C. Stinchcomb-5(Mary-4, Phillip-3, Joseph-2, John-1) was born on 05 Jul 1806 in Elbert County, Georgia. She died on 24 Mar 1889 in Elbert County, Georgia. She married Joseph Sewell on 1 Nov 1827 in Elbert County, Georgia, son of James Sewell and Margaret Harris.

Children of Mary C. Stinchcomb and Joseph Sewell are:

i. Mary Margaret Sewell, B: 1828, D: Aft. 15 Mar 1875, M: William T. Norman, Nov 1844 in Elbert County, Georgia.

ii. Sarah Sewell, B: 1829 in Elbert County, Georgia, D: Aft. 15 Mar 1832, M: Thomas Clinton Ham(m), 20 Dec 1849 in Elbert County, Georgia.

iii. James Victor Sewell, B: 05 Jul 1832 in Elbert County, Georgia, D: 09 Jan 1880 in Elbert County, Georgia, M: Edna Ann Ham(m), 01 Nov 1855 in Elbert County, Georgia.

iv. Cornellia H. Sewell, B: 1835 in Elbert County, Georgia, D: Aft. 15 Mar 1875, M: John P. Howell, 02 Sep 1856 in Elbert County, Georgia.

147. v. Olivia C. Sewell, B: 03 Oct 1843 in Elbert County, Georgia, D: 13 Oct 1886 in Elbert County, Georgia, M: Mallory J. Thornton Sr., 07 Nov 1865 in Elbert County, Georgia.

vi. Susan Rebecca Sewell, B: 19 Jan 1847 in Elbert County, Georgia, D: 19 Jan 1931 in Augusta, Georgia, M: William Hartwell Dickerson, 14 Jan 1869[13].

113. Nathaniel Stinchcomb-5(Mary-4, Phillip-3, Joseph-2, John-1) was born in 1799 in Georgia. He married Susannah Clements in Elijah Similin.

Child of Nathaniel Stinchcomb and Susannah Clements is:

i. Elijah Similin Stinchcomb, B: 1854 in Georgia.

114. Susanna Penn-5(Joseph Roscoe-4, Phillip-3, Joseph-2, John-1) [3] was born on 12 Aug 1791. She married Phillip Smith.

Child of Susanna Penn and Phillip Smith is:

i. John Smith, B: 03 Mar 1814 in St. Clair County, Illinois, D: 23 Feb 1883 in Tablerock, Fulton County, Illinois.

115. Joseph Penn-5(Joseph Roscoe-4, Phillip-3, Joseph-2, John-1)[3] was born on 06 Jan 1798 in Elbert County, Georgia. He died on 25 Nov 1840 in Carlinville, Macoupin County, Illinois. He married Candis Barton on 08 Oct 1817 in St. Clair County, Illinois.

Children of Joseph Penn and Candis Barton are:

i. Sarah Penn.

ii. John Penn.

iii. Mary Penn.

iv. Emsley Penn.

v. Banjamin H. Penn.

116. Sarah Penn-5(Joseph Roscoe-4, Phillip-3, Joseph-2, John-1)[3] was born on 15 May 1800 in Elbert County, Georgia. She died on 11 May 1882 in Paragonah, Iron County, Utah. She married John Barton in 1817 in St. Clair County, Illinois.

Children of Sarah Penn and John Barton are:

i. Elizabeth Barton, B: 20 Dec 1818 in St. Clair County, Illinois, D: 27 Oct 1823 in St. Clair County, Illinois.

ii. William Barton, B: 30 Jan 1821 in Illinois, D: Oct 1902 in Paragonah, Iron County, Utah, M: Esther West, 26 Feb 1845 in Nauvoo, Illinois.

iii. John Westley Barton, B: 19 Jan 1823, D: 14 Oct 1841.

iv. Matilda Jane Barton, B: 30 Jun 1825 in Illinois, D: 22 Jun 1908 in St. Clair County, Illinois, M: Joseph Domeny, 05 Dec 1844 in Illinois.

v. Julia King Barton, B: Dec 1828 in Illinois, D: 22 Jun 1859 in Council Bluffs, Iowa, M: William Gedney, 28 May 1846.

vi. Joseph Penn Barton, B: 11 May 1831 in Illinois, D: 15 Sep 1912 in Utah, M: Elizabeth Anderson, 21 May 1854 in Utah.

vii. Sarah Penn Barton, B: 12 Aug 1833 in Illinois, D: 12 Aug 1836 in Illinois.

viii. Eliza Ann Barton, B: 24 Feb 1836 in Illinois, D: 19 Apr 1839 in Illinois.

ix. Stephen Smith Barton, B: 03 Jan 1839 in Illinois, D: 18 Nov 1914 in Paragonah, Iron County, Utah, M: Jane Evans, 05 Feb 1857 in Utah.

x. John Samuel Barton, B: 29 Jul 1839 in Illinois, D: 06 Dec 1913 in Paragonah, Iron County, Utah, M: Eliza Jane Gingell, 06 Nov 1861 in Utah.

117. John Anderson Penn-5(Joseph Roscoe-4, Phillip-3, Joseph-2, John-1)[3] was born on 16 Mar 1804 in Murray County, Georgia. He died on 01 Dec 1871 in Pana, Christian County, Illinois. He married (1) Nancy Anderson on 08 Jun 1825 in Bourbon County, Kentucky. He married (2) Sarah E. Crow on 19 Apr 1867.

Children of John Anderson Penn and Nancy Anderson are:

i. Joseph Rollins Penn, B: 21 Apr 1826 in Lebanon, St. Clair County, Illinois, D: 04 Sep 1899 in Weatland, Dallas County, Texas, M: Nancy Shoup, 09 Mar 1848 in Sangamon County, Illinois.

ii. William Anderson Penn, B: 13 Aug 1828 in St. Clair County, Illinois, D: 1862 in Pea Ridge, Arkansas, M: Sasrah Elizabeth Greenwalt, 06 May 1852 in Sangamon County, Illinois.
Notes for William Anderson Penn:
Killed while fighting for the Confederacy.

iii. John Westley Penn, B: 19 Jun 1833 in St. Clair County, Illinois, D: 23 Jun 1888 in Dallas County, Texas, M: Lucinda Moore, 12 May 1859 in Coffin County, Texas.

iv. Robert Gilmore Penn, B: 02 Oct 1835 in St. Clair County, Illinois, D: 13 Dec 1911 in Atlus, Jackson County, Oklahoma, M: Elizabeth Susan Littrell, 25 Jul 1872 in Dallas County, Texas.

v. Rebecca Jane Penn, B: 03 Nov 1838, D: 23 Jan 1842.

vi. Mary Jane Penn, B: 09 Mar 1842 in Sangamon County, Illinois, D: 10 Sep 1911 in Dallas County, Texas, M: Napoleon Bonaparte Anderson, 07 Apr 1859.

vii. Martha Ann Penn, B: 11 Apr 1845, D: 16 Mar 1879 in Dallas County, Texas.

viii. George Washington Penn, B: 12 Sep 1849 in Sangamon County, Illinois, D: 30 Oct 1878 in Dallas County, Texas, M: Alice Virginia Record, 19 Jan 1874 in Dallas County, Texas.

ix. James Henry Penn, B: 05 Feb 1851, D: 02 Jul 1856.

Child of John Anderson Penn and Sarah E. Crow is:

i. Emily G. Penn, B: Aft. 1867.

118. Sarah Jane Penn-5(John-4, Phillip-3, Joseph-2, John-1) was born about 1808 in Elbert County, Georgia. She died after 1850 in Madison County, Georgia. She married William W. Smith on 20 May 1831 in Elbert County, Georgia.

Child of Sarah Jane Penn and William W. Smith is:

i. John Tom Smith, B: 14 Nov 1833 in Georgia, D: 16 Nov 1901 in Georgia.

119. John Wilson Penn-5(William-4, Phillip-3, Joseph-2, John-1) was born in 1820. He died in 1877. He married Nancy Lidell Cleghorn.

Child of John Wilson Penn and Nancy Lidell Cleghorn is:

i. James Cicero Penn, B: 1864, D: 1922.

120. Thomas Lee Penn-5(Moses-4, Moses-3, Joseph-2, John-1) was born on 14 Nov 1807. He died on 20 May 1874. He married Elizabeth White on 16 Jun 1831.

Children of Thomas Lee Penn and Elizabeth White are:

i. Josephine Penn.

ii. Mary Ann Penn.

iii. Eunice Penn.

iv. Lizzie Lee Penn.

v. Eliza Penn, B: 14 Dec 1826 in Patrick County, Virginia, D: 01 Jan 1900, M: Samuel W. Hairston, 26 Oct 1848 in Patrick County, Virginia.

121. Emeline Penn-5(Moses-4, Moses-3, Joseph-2, John-1)[14] was born in 1813 in Oglethorpe County, Georgia. She died before 02 Nov 1876 in Schley County, Georgia. She married Simpson Edge on 25 Jun 1831.

Children of Emeline Penn and Simpson Edge are:

i. Josephine Edge, B: 23 Oct 1834 in Monroe County, georgia, D: 29 Mar 1913 in Ellaville, Schley County, Georgia, M: William Wallace English, 20 Dec 1849 in Georgia.

ii. John Simpson Edge, B: Abt. 1850 in Macon, Georgia[14], M: Ella Jean Hudson, 12 Oct 1873 in Ellaville, Schley (formerly Marion) County, Georgia[14].

122. Judith Cashwell-5(Elizabeth-4, Moses-3, Joseph-2, John-1). She married Joel Bethel.

Child of Judith Cashwell and Joel Bethel is:

i. William Joel Bethel, B: 1835, D: 1906.

123. Thomas Stewart-5(Mary-4, Moses-3, Joseph-2, John-1) was born on 30 Sep 1786. He died on 14 Jun 1871. He married Nancy Jane Russell in 1812.

Children of Thomas Stewart and Nancy Jane Russell are:

i. Mathilda Stewart, B: 1814, D: 1910, M: Absaslom Ogletree, 1830.

ii. Mary Ann Stewart, B: 1816, D: 1894, M: Turner Barnes Dixon, 1832.

iii. Martha F. Stewart, B: 1820, D: 1875, M: William J. Head, 1840.

iv. Eliza Stewart, B: 1829, D: 1886, M: James Glenn Phinazaa, 1849.

v. Amanda Melvina Stewart, B: 1832.

124. William Blanton Stewart-5(Mary-4, Moses-3, Joseph-2, John-1). He married Regina Maria Dyson.

Child of William Blanton Stewart and Regina Maria Dyson is:

i. Jennie Stewart.

125. Richardson Penn-5(James Richardson-4, Moses-3, Joseph-2, John-1)[3] was born in 1793 in Bedford County, Virginia. He died in 1868 in Montgomery County, Missouri. He married Lucinda DeWitt in 1813 in Campbell County, Virginia.

Child of Richardson Penn and Lucinda DeWitt is:

i. Mary Penn, B: 1818, D: 1890, M: William S. Nelson, 1837.

126. Harwood Major Penn-5(James Richardson-4, Moses-3, Joseph-2, John-1)[3, 15] was born in 1794 in Bedford County, Virginia. He died in 1880 in Cass County, Nebraska. He married Amelia A. Daggs.

Children of Harwood Major Penn and Amelia A. Daggs are:

i. Lucy M. Penn, B: 16 Mar 1838 in Lewis County, Missouri (now Memphis, Scotland County, Missouri)[15], M: Emanuel Samuel Twilegar, 14 Sep 1854 in Memphis, Scotland County, Missouri[15].

ii. Angeline Penn.

iii. Frances Penn.

iv. Jane M. Penn.

v. Margaret Penn.
Notes for Margaret Penn:
Died at age 18.

vi. Mary Ann Penn.

vii. William H. H. Penn.

viii. Ruel Zachariah Penn.

127. Moses Penn-5(James Richardson-4, Moses-3, Joseph-2, John-1)[3] was born on 06 Mar 1796 in Bedford County, Virginia. He died in 1878 in Virginia. He married Edna Penina White on 19 Oct 1824 in Bedford County, Virginia, daughter of Jacob White and Hannah Spiers.

Notes for Edna Penina White:
Alternate spelling of first name is Edney.

Children of Moses Penn and Edna Penina White are:

i. Paul Silas Penn, B: 17 Dec 1829 in Bedford County, Virginia, D: 20 Jul 1884 in Bedford County, Virginia.

ii. James Jacob Penn, B: 22 May 1834.

iii. Edney Penn.

128. Thomas Major Penn-5(James Richardson-4, Moses-3, Joseph-2, John-1)[3] was born on 11 Jun 1798. He died in Taylor County, Kentucky. He married Lou Ann Spurling in Kentucky.

Children of Thomas Major Penn and Lou Ann Spurling are:

i. Martha Ann Penn, B: Taylor County, Kentucky.

ii. Edmund Penn, D: Taylor County, Kentucky, M: Frances Mann, 16 Feb 1859 in Taylor County, Kentucky[16].

iii. Mary Ann Penn.

iv. Anna Liza Penn.

v. Sarah Elizabeth Penn.

vi. Sanford Penn.

vii. John Penn, M: Laura Ann Raley, 18 Mar 1858 in Taylor County, Kentucky[17].

129. James R. Penn-5(James Richardson-4, Moses-3, Joseph-2, John-1)[3, 18] was born on 22 Feb 1810 in Bedford County, Virginia. He died in Missouri. He married (1) Mary Jane Shively on 31 Oct 1831 in Campbellsville, Green County, Kentucky. He married (2) Sally Gregory Bayne on 06 Jul 1862.

Children of James R. Penn and Mary Jane Shively are:

iv. John Westley Penn.

v. Edward M. Penn, B: 1844, D: 1913 in Broken Arrow, Oklahoma.

vi. James Penn, B: 08 Dec 1848 in Green County, Kentucky.

vii. Frances Penn, M: James Greenwell, 14 Dec 1822 in Green County, Kentucky.
Notes for Frances Penn:
Her paternity is still open to question.

viii. Mary Jane Penn, M: Samuel Shively, 12 Feb 1828 in Green County, Kentucky.
Notes for Mary Jane Penn:
Her paternity is still open to question.

130. William Penn-5(James Richardson-4, Moses-3, Joseph-2, John-1)[3] was born on 13 Apr 1816 in Bedford County, Virginia. He died on 14 Sep 1868 in Hydesburg, Marion County, Missouri. He married Nancy Shively on 13 Apr 1838.

Children of William Penn and Nancy Shively are:

i. John Penn.

ii. James Penn.

iii. Mary Penn.

iv. Sally Penn.

131. John Taylor Jr.-5(Lucy-4, John-3, Moses-2, John-1)[8] was born on 07 Sep 1784 in Caroline County, Virginia[8]. He died on 08 Aug 1853 in Caroline County, Virginia[8]. He married (1) Lucy Woodford before 1821. He married (2) Marion Gordon in Statford, Virginia[8]. She was born in 1810[8]. She died on 08 Nov 1843 in Caroline County, Virginia[8].

Children of John Taylor Jr. and Lucy Woodford are:

i. Lucy Penn Taylor, M: Bazil Gordon, 05 Mar 1829 in Caroline County, Virginia.

ii. Edmund Pendleton Taylor, B: 1821, D: 1875.

Child of John Taylor Jr. and Marion Gordon is:

149. i. James Taylor, B: 05 Jun 1841 in Caroline County, Virginia[8], D: 19 Dec 1917 in Washington, D.C.[8], M: Susan Murray Gray, 04 Jun 1889 in Washington, D.C.[8].

132. Henry Taylor-5(Lucy-4, John-3, Moses-2, John-1) was born in 1800. He died in 1845. He married Julia /Dunlap Leiper.

Children of Henry Taylor and Julia /Dunlap Leiper are:

i. Henry Taylor, B: 1827, D: 1914.

ii. Lucy Penn Taylor, B: 1831, D: 1913.

iii. John Taylor.

iv. Leiper Taylor.

v. William Penn Taylor.

vi. Julia Leiper Taylor.

vii. Edmund Pendleton Taylor.

viii. Thomas Leiper Taylor.

Generation 6

133. Susan Lee France-6(Harriet-5, Susanna-4, Frances-3, George-2, John-1)[11] was born on 20 Jun 1813. She died on 18 Jan 1892. She married Gabriel Penn, son of Greensville Penn and Anna Leath. He was born in 1814.

Children of Susan Lee France and Gabriel Penn are:

i. William Leath Penn, B: 29 Jul 1834[11].

ii. Edward Penn, B: 03 Jul 1837[11].

134. Harrison Carter France-6(Harriet-5, Susanna-4, Frances-3, George-2, John-1) was born in 1818. He died in 1896. He married Catherine Leath Penn on 09 Oct 1842, daughter of James Francis Penn and Mary Shelton. She was born on 16 Jan 1821. She died on 04 Mar 1914.

Children of Harrison Carter France and Catherine Leath Penn are:

i. Annie Redd France.

ii. Susan Barbara France, B: 1843, D: 04 Jul 1927.

iii. James Penn France.

iv. Catherine France.

v. Peter Shelton France.

vi. William Starling France.

135. Sally Penn Edmunds-6(Mary Ann-5, Joseph-4, John-3, Joseph-2, John-1) was born on 05 Jan 1806. She died on 18 Sep 1828. She married Carey A. Snoddy Sr. on 05 Sep 1820.

Children of Sally Penn Edmunds and Carey A. Snoddy Sr. are:

150. i. Mary Ann Snoddy, B: 28 Jul 1821, M: Franklin Overstreet, 28 Jan 1842.

ii. William E. Snoddy, B: 26 Aug 1823.

iii. Robert C. Snoddy, B: 17 Dec 1825.

iv. Carey A. Snoddy Jr., B: 11 Jul 1828, D: 11 Jul 1858.

136. Mary Jane Edmunds-6(Mary Ann-5, Joseph-4, John-3, Joseph-2, John-1) was born on 31 Oct 1809. She died on 22 Jun 1832. She married (1) James B. Sterrett on 12 Oct 1824. She married (2) Thomas Feeland on 25 Jan 1831. She married (3) Thomas Feland on 26 Jan 1831.

Child of Mary Jane Edmunds and James B. Sterrett is:

i. Mary Elizabeth Sterrett, D: 24 Nov 1828.

Child of Mary Jane Edmunds and Thomas Feland is:

i. William Thomas Feland, B: 31 Oct 1831, D: 06 Feb 1852.
Notes for William Thomas Feland:
Conflicting year of death of 1859.

137. Charles Penn Edmunds-6(Mary Ann-5, Joseph-4, John-3, Joseph-2, John-1)[1, 2] was born on 24 Dec 1811 in Barren County, Kentucky[1, 2]. He died on 22 Mar 1883 in Glasgow, Barren County, Kentucky[1, 2]. He married Elizabeth T. Eubank on 24 Nov 1829 in Barren County, Kentucky[1, 2], daughter of Joseph E. Eubank Sr. and Elizabeth Glenn White. She was born on 19 Jan 1811 in Glasgow, Barren County, Kentucky. She died on 24 Nov 1881 in Glasgow, Barren County, Kentucky[1, 2].
Notes for Elizabeth T. Eubank:
A conflicting date of birth is 1/17/1811

Children of Charles Penn Edmunds and Elizabeth T. Eubank are:

151. i. James Christopher Edmunds, B: 22 Sep 1830 in Kentucky, D: 28 Aug 1908, M: Evaline Elizabeth Holman, 20 Mar 1855.

152. ii. Mary Jane Edmunds, B: 08 Jul 1832, D: 13 Nov 1903, M: Richard F. Bethel, 30 Nov 1848.

153. iii. Catherine Eubank Edmunds, B: 21 Aug 1834 in Glasgow, Barren County, Kentucky[1, 2, 9], D: 10 Jan 1916 in Bowling Green, Warren County, Kentucky[1, 2, 9, 19], M: Nathan Perry Allen, 23 Oct 1855 in Glasgow, Barren County, Kentucky[1, 2, 20].

154. iv. Charles Henry Edmunds Sr., B: 15 Apr 1837, D: 28 Jul 1878, M: Jennie Jordan, 31 May 1870.

155. v. Elizabeth Frances Edmunds, B: 13 Oct 1841, D: 1882, M: Franklin H. Barton, 08 Jan 1867.

vi. Lucy Ellen Edmunds, B: 13 Oct 1841, D: 07 Nov 1841.

vii. Caroline Barton Edmunds, B: 04 Dec 1843, D: 23 Jul 1858.

viii. Edmonia Thomas Edmunds, B: 08 Jan 1846, D: 08 Jul 1853.

Notes for Edmonia Thomas Edmunds:

Conflicting date of death of 8/8/1859.

156. ix. William Persifer Smith Edmunds, B: 15 Apr 1848, D: 13 Oct 1925, M: Julia A. Bobo, 05 Oct 1876.

157. x. John Curd Edmunds, B: 05 Aug 1853, D: 13 Oct 1909, M: Sally A. Waller, 21 Feb 1878.

158. xi. Laura Wilson Edmunds, B: 28 Jul 1857 in Barren County, Kentucky, D: 12 Mar 1929 in Barren County, Kentucky, M: Frank M. Willis, 21 Feb 1878 in Barren County, Kentucky.

159. xii. Martha Ann Edmunds, B: 23 Jun 1839, D: 09 Apr 1916, M: Sidney Holman, 24 Dec 1861.

xiii. Haiden Lewis Edmunds, B: 07 Jan 1851, D: 16 Aug 1869.

138. Martha Ann Edmunds-6(Mary Ann-5, Joseph-4, John-3, Joseph-2, John-1) was born on 07 Dec 1813. She died on 23 Jun 1868. She married Haiden T. Curd on 24 Feb 1830. He died on 24 Feb 1859.

Children of Martha Ann Edmunds and Haiden T. Curd are:

i. John T. Curd, B: 01 Mar 1831, D: 05 Apr 1841.

ii. William E. Curd, B: 22 Apr 1833.

iii. Mary F. Curd, B: 24 Feb 1835.

iv. Lucy James Curd, B: 04 Apr 1838, D: Apr 1838.

v. Daniel Curd, B: 14 Dec 1839, D: 24 Mar 1841.

vi. Martha Ann Curd, B: 23 Jul 1843.

139. Elizabeth Lee Edmunds-6(Mary Ann-5, Joseph-4, John-3, Joseph-2, John-1) was born on 02 Nov 1815. She died in Jan 1883 in Bonham, Texas. She married William Crawford Whitsett on 15 Dec 1836, son of William Whitsett Jr..

Children of Elizabeth Lee Edmunds and William Crawford Whitsett are:

160. i. William Edmund Whitsett, B: 13 Nov 1837 in Glasgow, Barren County, Kentucky, D: 1938 in Sallisaw, Sequoyah County, Oklahoma.

ii. Joseph Whitsett, B: 09 Jul 1839, D: 14 Nov 1839.

iii. Mary Jane Whitsett, B: 19 Mar 1841, D: 04 Aug 1859 in Texas, M: James M. Collins, 04 Aug 1859 in Texas.

iv. Elizabeth Henry Whitsett, B: 25 Mar 1843.

v. James Whitsett, B: May 1845, D: 01 Jan 1862 in Fayetteville, Arkansas.

vi. Joseph Haiden Whitsett, B: 18 Sep 1847, D: 1951, M: Betty Stone, 13 Mar 1873.

vii. W. C. Whitsett, B: Jan 1852, D: Jan 1882.

140. James Terrance Edmunds-6(Mary Ann-5, Joseph-4, John-3, Joseph-2, John-1) was born on 14 Jan 1818. He died on 21 Jan 1895. He married (1) Catherine M. Foster on 17 Aug 1837. He married (2) Martha Gaither Carr on 14 Jan 1862.

Children of James Terrance Edmunds and Catherine M. Foster are:

i. William Edmunds.

ii. Honery Edmunds.

141. William Henry Edmunds-6(Mary Ann-5, Joseph-4, John-3, Joseph-2, John-1) was born on 17 Jun 1823 in Barren County, Kentucky. He died on 24 Nov 1900 in Barren County, Kentucky. He married (1) Amanda Moss on 19 Aug 1847. He married (2) Sammi Alice Crain about 1875.

Children of William Henry Edmunds and Amanda Moss are:

161. i. Crittenden Moss Edmunds, B: 08 Apr 1849 in Glasgow, Barren County, Kentucky, M: Sarah F. Dishman, 01 May 1872 in Barren County, Kentucky.

ii. William Edmunds, B: 1850.
Notes for William Edmunds:
He was last living in Chicago, Illinois.

iii. Henry Edmunds, B: 22 May 1851, D: 02 Apr 1854.

Children of William Henry Edmunds and Sammi Alice Crain are:

162. i. Lallie Lucille Edmunds.

ii. Mary Ann Edmunds, D: 1974.
Notes for Mary Ann Edmunds:
She was the first woman lawyer of Barren County, Kentucky but she did not practice law. She taught school at Eastern Kentucky College/University.

163. iii. Carrie Belle Edmunds, B: 1878.

164. iv. Chase Edmunds, B: 1879.

v. James Edmunds, B: 14 Nov 1881, D: 28 Aug 1908.
Notes for James Edmunds:
Never married.

165. vi. Bryant Ralston Edmunds, B: 10 Mar 1887, D: 12 May 1966, M: Pearl Soper, 05 Oct 1938.

142. Caroline Winston Edmunds-6(Mary Ann-5, Joseph-4, John-3, Joseph-2, John-1) was born on 26 May 1825. She died on 08 May 1890 in Montgomery, Alabama. She married John Mulkey Barton on 04 May 1843.

Children of Caroline Winston Edmunds and John Mulkey Barton are:

166. i. James Edmunds Barton, B: 30 Mar 1844 in Barren County, Kentucky, D: Mar 1918 in Memphis, Shelby County, Tennessee, M: Sammie Summerville, 22 Jul 1875.

167. ii. Caroline Barton, B: 30 Jul 1851 in Barren County, Kentucky, M: B. James Dunn, 18 Dec 1873.

iii. Annie Curd Barton, B: Abt. 1854 in Barren County, Kentucky, D: 19 Jan 1878 in Nashville, Davidson County, Tennessee.

168. iv. Martha Curd Barton, B: 04 Feb 1857 in Logan County, Kentucky, D: 14 Jul 1882 in Montgomery, Alabama, M: Morgan Smith Gilmer, 30 Nov 1874 in Montgomery, Alabama.

169. v. Elizabeth H. Barton, B: 22 Oct 1858 in Logan County, Kentucky, D: 01 Feb 1929 in Louisville, Kentucky, M: C. F. Cantwell, 07 Nov 1878.

170. vi. Clarissa Barton, B: 18 Oct 1860 in Logan County, Kentucky, D: 1926 in Florida, M: Ralph C. Mason, 23 Oct 1877 in Montgomery, Alabama.

vii. Ella Barton, B: Bet. 1861-1864 in Logan County, Kentucky.

viii. Henrietta Barton, B: 13 Jan 1863 in Logan County, Kentucky, D: 04 Jun 1865 in Logan County, Kentucky.

ix. Helen Barton, B: 29 Apr 1865 in Logan County, Kentucky, D: 18 Dec 1933 in Montgomery, Alabama, M: Morgan Smith Gilmer, 10 Sep 1883.

x. Jonnie Barton, B: 26 Mar 1869 in Logan County, Kentucky, D: Jun 1903 in Dallas, Dallas County, Texas, M: Henry J. Whipple, 18 Aug 1888.

171. xi. Alice Forbes Barton, B: 23 Jul 1846 in Barren County, Kentucky, D: 20 Jan 1920 in Montgomery, Alabama, M: Frank Gilmer Browder, 22 Nov 1867.

172.xii. Sarah Frances Barton, B: 27 Nov 1848 in Barren County, Kentucky, D: 12 Jun 1922 in Montgomery, Alabama, M: Leroy H. Fogleman, 11 Feb 1868.

173.xiii. Carrio Barton.

143. Sarah Lavender Edmunds-6(Mary Ann-5, Joseph-4, John-3, Joseph-2, John-1) was born on 14 Aug 1829. She died on 03 Oct 1853. She married Hanson Trigg Lewis on 17 Mar 1847.

Children of Sarah Lavender Edmunds and Hanson Trigg Lewis are:

i. North Lewis, B: 10 Jul 1848.

ii. South Lewis, B: 03 Apr 1853.

iii. Thomas W. Lewis, B: Bet. 1849-1852, M: Jane Page, 09 Sep.

iv. Jane Lewis, B: Bef. 03 Oct 1853, D: 11 Dec 1867.

144. Frances Burrus Edmunds-6(Mary Ann-5, Joseph-4, John-3, Joseph-2, John-1) was born on 07 Dec 1831. She died on 02 Sep 1917 in Barren County, Kentucky. She married (1) James Forbis Barton on 7 Dec 1847. He died on 11 Oct 1873. She married (2) James T. Barton Sr. on 04 May 1843. He died on 11 Oct 1873. She married (3) Andrew Monroe Hardin on 31 Oct 1877 in Memphis, Shelby County, Tennessee.

Children of Frances Burrus Edmunds and James Forbis Barton are:

174. i. James Terrence Barton, B: 20 Jul 1850 in Tipton County, Tennessee, D: 08 Jan 1925 in Memphis, Shelby County, Tennessee, M: Vara Hoblitzell, 11 Dec 1888 in Baltimore, Maryland.

ii. Henry Franklin Barton, B: 05 Dec 1857, D: Jan 1886.

175. iii. Lee Barton Sr., B: 26 Sep 1863, D: Sep 1930.

iv. John Fogleman Barton, B: 08 Dec 1861, D: 11 Sep 1884.

176. v. Charles Penn Barton, B: 06 Sep 1852 in Barren County, Kentucky, D: 03 Jan 1911, M: Susan Elizabeth Holt, 08 Sep 1874 in Barren County, Kentucky.

vi. Richard T. Barton, B: 19 Jul 1854, D: 19 Jul 1857.

177.vii. Robert White Barton Sr., B: 17 Mar 1860, D: 20 Dec 1939 in Los Angeles, California.

178.viii. William Edmunds Barton Sr., B: 16 Dec 1848 in Tipson County, Tennessee, D: 11 Sep 1936 in Searcy, Arkansas.

Children of Frances Burrus Edmunds and James T. Barton Sr. are:

178. i. William Edmunds Barton Sr., B: 16 Dec 1848 in Tipson County, Tennessee, D: 11 Sep 1936 in Searcy, Arkansas.

ii. James T. Barton Jr., B: 20 Apr 1850.

176. iii. Charles Penn Barton, B: 06 Sep 1852 in Barren County, Kentucky, D: 03 Jan 1911, M: Susan Elizabeth Holt, 08 Sep 1874 in Barren County, Kentucky.

iv. Richard T. Barton, B: 19 Jul 1854, D: 19 Jul 1857.

v. Harry F. Barton, B: 05 Dec 1857, D: Jan 1886.

177. vi. Robert White Barton Sr., B: 17 Mar 1860, D: 20 Dec 1939 in Los Angeles, California.

vii. John Fogleman Barton, B: 08 Dec 1861, D: 11 Sep 1884.

175.viii. Lee Barton Sr., B: 26 Sep 1863, D: Sep 1930.

145. Edmund Alexander Edmunds-6(Mary Ann-5, Joseph-4, John-3, Joseph-2, John-1) was born on 12 Jun 1827 in Kentucky. He died on 22 Apr 1906. He married (1) Henrietta Shepherd Lewis on 08 Sep 1853. He married (2) Junie F. Bowls on 26 Jan 1899 in Gallatin, Tennessee.

Children of Edmund Alexander Edmunds and Henrietta Shepherd Lewis are:

i. William Thomas Edmunds, B: 26 Sep 1856, D: 29 May 1879, M: Ada T. Davidson, 21 May 1879.

179. ii. Mary Jane Edmunds, B: 29 May 1858, D: 09 Dec 1908, M: Preston L. Ford, 27 Nov 1879.

iii. Infant Edmunds, B: 25 Jun 1860, D: 28 Jun 1860.

iv. Haiden Curd Edmunds, B: 21 May 1864, D: Jul 1926, M: Jennie B. Gibbs, 12 Dec 1889.

v. Henry Lewis Edmunds, B: 21 May 1864, D: 07 Aug 1944, M: Maggie Howard, 24 Dec 1890.

vi. Annie Elizabeth Edmunds, B: 08 Mar 1866, D: 15 Sep 1877.

vii. Edmund Roger Edmunds, B: 13 Aug 1868, D: Nov 1915.

viii. Charles Page Edmunds, B: 09 Oct 1870, D: 09 Mar 1927.

ix. Charles Penn Edmunds, B: 09 Oct 1870, D: 22 Feb 1927.

x. Carrie Frances Barton Edmunds, B: 25 Sep 1872, M: Joe D. Studebaker, 01 Mar 1900.

Child of Edmund Alexander Edmunds and Junie F. Bowls is:

180. i. Mary Diana Edmunds, B: 28 Sep 1902, D: 06 Jan 1918.

146. Elizabeth Thornton-6(Sarah-5, Amy-4, Catherine-3, Joseph-2, John-1)[13] was born on 25 Oct 1802 in Elbert County, Georgia. She died in 1854. She married John Dickerson on 29 Dec 1812 in Elbert County, Georgia[13]. He was born on 20 Nov 1784 in Hanover County, Virginia[13]. He died about 1862 in Elbert County, Georgia[13].

Notes for Elizabeth Thornton:

Her birth date and marriage date are in question. Dennis Ward shows her birth date Abt. 1790 in North Carolina. Death Abt. 1854.

Children of Elizabeth Thornton and John Dickerson are:

i. Mary Ann Dickerson, B: Abt. 1822 in Elbert County, Georgia[13], D: 04 Apr 1899 in Madison County, Georgia[13], M: William W. Tyner, 22 Jul 1845 in Elbert County, Georgia[13, 21].

ii. William Hartwell Dickerson, B: 25 Dec 1839 in Elbert County, Georgia[13], D: 22 Mar 1920 in Augusta, Georgia[13], M: Susan Rebecca Sewell, 14 Jan 1869[13].

147. Olivia C. Sewell-6(Mary C.-5, Mary-4, Phillip-3, Joseph-2, John-1) was born on 03 Oct 1843 in Elbert County, Georgia. She died on 13 Oct 1886 in Elbert County, Georgia. She married Mallory J. Thornton Sr. on 07 Nov 1865 in Elbert County, Georgia.

Child of Olivia C. Sewell and Mallory J. Thornton Sr. is:

i. Mallory J. Thornton Jr..

148. George Washington Penn-6(James R.-5, James Richardson-4, Moses-3, Joseph-2, John-1)[18] was born on 14 Nov 1839 in Campbell, Taylor County, Kentucky[18]. He died on 26 Jan 1898 in St. Charles County, Missouri[18]. He married Mary A. Reynolds on 02 Apr 1861 in Calloway County, Missouri[18]. She was born on 29 Nov 1839 in Callaway County, Missouri[18]. She died on 17 Oct 1907 in St. Louis, Missouri[18].

Children of George Washington Penn and Mary A. Reynolds are:

i. Howard S. Penn.

ii. George S. Penn.

iii. James Penn.
Notes for James Penn:
Committed suicide after he was caught embezzling money.

iv. Andrew Penn.
Notes for Andrew Penn:
Died at age 19.

v. Nancy Chapell Penn.

149. James Taylor-6(John-5, Lucy-4, John-3, Moses-2, John-1)[8] was born on 05 Jun 1841 in Caroline County, Virginia[8]. He died on 19 Dec 1917 in Washington, D.C.[8]. He married Susan Murray Gray on 4 Jun 1889 in Washington, D.C.[8]. She was born on 19 Feb 1857 in Janesville, Wisconsin[8]. She died on 03 Nov 1905 in Washington, D.C.[8].

Child of James Taylor and Susan Murray Gray is:

181. i. Marion Gordon Taylor, B: 04 Feb 1892 in Washington, D.C.[8], M: Clayton Lyman Drew, 20 Jan 1912 in Washington, D.C.[8].

Generation 7

150. Mary Ann Snoddy-7(Sally Penn-6, Mary Ann-5, Joseph-4, John-3, Joseph-2, John-1) was born on 28 Jul 1821. She married Franklin Overstreet on 28 Jan 1842.

Children of Mary Ann Snoddy and Franklin Overstreet are:

i. Sally Snoody Overstreet, B: 09 Nov 1842, D: 08 Apr 1844.

ii. James Cary Overstreet, B: 28 Apr 1844, D: 24 Jun 1865.

151. James Christopher Edmunds-7(Charles Penn-6, Mary Ann-5, Joseph-4, John-3, Joseph-2, John-1) was born on 22 Sep 1830 in Kentucky. He died on 28 Aug 1908. He married Evaline Elizabeth Holman on 20 Mar 1855, daughter of Joseph Henry Holman and Nancy Davis Settle. She died on 26 Jan 1929.

Children of James Christopher Edmunds and Evaline Elizabeth Holman are:

182. i. William Franklin Edmunds, B: 10 Feb 1856, D: 22 May 1926, M: Mary Bell King, 1876.

183. ii. Bennie R. Edmunds, B: 17 Jun 1865, D: 22 Jun 1953 in Barren County, Kentucky, M: Eva W. Carter, 01 Feb 1893.

184. iii. Lizzie Dora Edmunds, B: 17 Oct 1869, D: 15 May 1960, M: John Page Lewis, 17 Nov 1887.

152. Mary Jane Edmunds-7(Charles Penn-6, Mary Ann-5, Joseph-4, John-3, Joseph-2, John-1) was born on 08 Jul 1832. She died on 13 Nov 1903. She married Richard F. Bethel on 30 Nov 1848.

Children of Mary Jane Edmunds and Richard F. Bethel are:

i. John William Bethel, B: 04 Oct 1849, D: 07 Dec 1869.

ii. Alice Davis Bethel, B: 19 Feb 1851, M: Moss Barrick, 1873.

iii. Ann Elizabeth Bethel, B: 05 May 1853, D: 17 Dec 1882.

iv. Mary Ellen Bethel, B: 05 May 1853, D: Abt. 27 Feb 1854.

v. Kate Thomas Bethel, B: 30 May 1855, D: 29 Aug 1859.

vi. Ella Frances Bethel, B: 10 May 1857, M: John Boles, 01 Mar 1880.

vii. Nannie E. Bethel, B: 15 May 1861.

viii. Norris E. Bethel, B: 15 May 1861.

ix. Charles R. Bethel, B: 22 Jun 1863.

153. Catherine Eubank Edmunds-7(Charles Penn-6, Mary Ann-5, Joseph-4, John-3, Joseph-2, John-1)[1, 2, 9, 20] was born on 21 Aug 1834 in Glasgow, Barren County, Kentucky[1, 2, 9]. She died on 10 Jan 1916 in Bowling Green, Warren County, Kentucky[1, 2, 9, 19]. She married Nathan Perry Allen on 23 Oct 1855 in Glasgow, Barren County, Kentucky[1, 2, 20], son of Nathan Allen and Sarah Gleaves. He was born on 30 Apr 1830 in Cumberland County, Kentucky[1, 2, 20, 22, 23, 24, 25, 26, 27, 28, 29, 30, 31]. He died on 15 Feb 1909 in Bowling Green, Warren County, Kentucky[1, 2, 20, 22, 23, 24, 25, 26, 27, 28, 29, 30, 31].

Notes for Catherine Eubank Edmunds:

Her date of birth and marriage are recorded in the William Edmunds bible.

Her death certificate says that she was born in 1835.

Notes for Nathan Perry Allen:

Documentation of facts:

1. Nathan Perry Allen bible.
2. Nathan Allen bible.
3. Various newspaper articles on family ancestry written by Nathan Perry Allen.
4. Obituary of Nathan Perry Allen.
5. Warren County, Kentucky census records for 1840, 1850, 1860, 1870, 1880 and 1900.

Children of Catherine Eubank Edmunds and Nathan Perry Allen are:

i. Charles Nathan Allen, B: 10 Oct 1856[20], D: 29 Nov 1882 in Smiths Grove, Warren County, Kentucky[20], M: Lucy Belle Drane, 08 Dec 1881[20].

185. ii. James Crittendon Allen, B: 10 Apr 1858[20], D: 10 Jun 1936 in Garden City, Finney County, Kansas, M: Anna M. Barrick, 16 Sep 1885[20].

186. iii. William Edmunds Gleaves Allen, B: 20 Dec 1859 in Madison County, Kentucky[1, 2, 20], D: 09 Sep 1931 in Loveland, Larimer County, Colorado[1, 2], M: Eleanora Amanda Cates, 07 Feb 1884 in Glasgow, Barren County, Kentucky[1, 2, 20].

iv. Sarah Elizabeth Allen, B: 07 Jun 1861[20], D: 19 Oct 1863[20].

187. v. Mary Emeline Allen, B: 06 Oct 1862[20], D: 03 Sep 1911 in Clovis, Curry County, New Mexico[20], M: William Elihu Davis, 13 Jan 1885[20].

vi. Edmonia Allen, B: 15 Oct 1864[20], D: 01 Dec 1949, M: George W. McIntire, 15 Feb 1887 in Warren County, Kentucky[20].

188. vii. Katherine Edmunds Allen, B: 07 Dec 1866[20], D: 24 Oct 1918 in Bowling Green, Warren County, Kentucky[20], M: Gustavus Allen Fogleman Sr., 17 Dec 1896[20].

189. viii. Hiram Perry Allen, B: 28 Jan 1869[20], D: 09 Mar 1948 in Luling, Caldwell County, Texas, M: Elizabeth Stagner, 15 Jan 1896 in Luling, Caldwell County, Texas[20].

190. ix. Frank Barton Allen, B: 19 Feb 1871[20], D: 24 Jan 1951 in Hobart, Lake County, Indiana, M: Annie Easterling, 28 Jul 1908[20].

x. George Richard Allen, B: 24 Mar 1873[20], D: 28 Sep 1890 in Garden City, Finney County, Kansas[20].

191. xi. Ora Laura Allen, B: 12 Apr 1875[20], D: 24 Jun 1961 in Bowling Green, Warren County, Kentucky, M: Roy G. Blakeman, 25 May 1899[20].

154. Charles Henry Edmunds Sr.-7(Charles Penn-6, Mary Ann-5, Joseph-4, John-3, Joseph-2, John-1) was born on 15 Apr 1837. He died on 28 Jul 1878. He married Jennie Jordan on 31 May 1870.

Children of Charles Henry Edmunds Sr. and Jennie Jordan are:

i. Charles Henry Edmunds Jr..

ii. Louis Jordan Edmunds, B: 24 Sep 1871, D: 1923.

193. iii. Callie Eubank Edmunds, B: 08 Nov 1872.

iv. Jennie S. Edmunds, B: 14 May 1874.

v. Kate Settle Edmunds, B: 16 Oct 1875.

vi. Jerry S. Edmunds, B: 14 May 1874.

155. Elizabeth Frances Edmunds-7(Charles Penn-6, Mary Ann-5, Joseph-4, John-3, Joseph-2, John-1) was born on 13 Oct 1841. She died in 1882. She married Franklin H. Barton on 08 Jan 1867.

Children of Elizabeth Frances Edmunds and Franklin H. Barton are:

193. i. Mary Thomas Barton, B: 05 Mar 1868, D: 06 Feb 1890, M: Gustavus Adolphus Fogleman, 25 Jul 1889.

ii. Charles Edmunds Barton, B: 01 Jan 1870, D: 19 Sep 1874.

iii. James Christopher Barton, B: 26 Apr 1871, D: 21 Aug 1872.

194. iv. Louis Hardin Barton, B: 10 Jan 1873, D: 27 Sep 1959, M: Mary Smith, 14 Apr 1897 in Marion, Arkansas.

195. v. Charles Grigsby Barton Sr., B: 07 Feb 1875, D: 17 Nov 1939, M: Musie Foster, 1899.

vi. Perry Allen Barton, B: 11 Jul 1877, D: 15 Apr 1963.

vii. Robert Edmunds Barton, B: 18 May 1879, D: 31 May 1880.

196.viii. Richard Bethel Barton Sr., B: 01 Jun 1881, D: 12 Jul 1948, M: Hardin Cheek, 1909.

156. William Persifer Smith Edmunds-7(Charles Penn-6, Mary Ann-5, Joseph-4, John-3, Joseph-2, John-1) was born on 15 Apr 1848. He died on 13 Oct 1925. He married Julia A. Bobo on 05 Oct 1876.

Notes for Julia A. Bobo:

She was from Celina, Tennessee.

Children of William Persifer Smith Edmunds and Julia A. Bobo are:

197. i. Allen Edmunds.

ii. Bessie Edmunds.

iii. Charles P. Edmunds.

iv. Florence B. Edmunds.

v. Lacy Edmunds.

vi. Virgil B. Edmunds, B: 25 Jul 1877, D: 02 Jan 1892.

vii. Elizabeth R. Edmunds, B: 10 Apr 1881, D: 01 Feb 1948 in Glasgow, Barren County, Kentucky, M: Curtis Jones, 25 Oct 1900.

viii. William Bobo Edmunds, B: 22 Aug 1901, D: 16 Apr 1932.

Notes for William Bobo Edmunds:

Hung himself.

157. John Curd Edmunds-7(Charles Penn-6, Mary Ann-5, Joseph-4, John-3, Joseph-2, John-1) was born on 05 Aug 1853. He died on 13 Oct 1909. He married Sally A. Waller on 21 Feb 1878.

Children of John Curd Edmunds and Sally A. Waller are:

i. Walter Rogers Edmunds, B: 30 Jul 1880.

Notes for Walter Rogers Edmunds:

Never married.

198. ii. James Buford Edmunds, B: 04 May 1883.

199. iii. Leonard Matthews Edmunds, B: 22 Feb 1886, D: 10 Nov 1951, M: Maud Emerson, 25 Dec 1915.

iv. Mary Agnes Edmunds, B: 20 Sep 1887.

200. v. Flora Laura Edmunds, B: 03 Nov 1890.

158. Laura Wilson Edmunds-7(Charles Penn-6, Mary Ann-5, Joseph-4, John-3, Joseph-2, John-1) was born on 28 Jul 1857 in Barren County, Kentucky. She died on 12 Mar 1929 in Barren County, Kentucky. She married Frank M. Willis on 21 Feb 1878 in Barren County, Kentucky.

Children of Laura Wilson Edmunds and Frank M. Willis are:

i. Annie Willis.

ii. Frank S. Willis, D: 1899.

202. iii. Jessie Willis.

203. iv. Kate Willis.

204. v. Minnie Lee Willis, B: 10 Aug 1879, D: 17 May 1900, M: George Duvall, 27 Dec 1896.

vi. Lula Willis, B: 1887, D: 1890.

204. vii. Mayme Willis, B: 30 Nov 1890 in Barren County, Kentucky, D: 22 Sep 1913 in Barren County, Kentucky, M: William Thomas Lewis, 1911.

205. viii. Pattie Willis.

159. Martha Ann Edmunds-7(Charles Penn-6, Mary Ann-5, Joseph-4, John-3, Joseph-2, John-1) was born on 23 Jun 1839. She died on 09 Apr 1916. She married Sidney Holman on 24 Dec 1861.

Children of Martha Ann Edmunds and Sidney Holman are:

i. James Clarence Holman, B: 28 Sep 1862.

207. ii. Henry Malcom Holman, B: 17 Dec 1864, D: 22 Dec 1918.

iii. William Haiden Holman, B: 20 May 1869.

207. iv. Paul Wilson Holman Sr., B: Apr 1873.

v. Haid Holman, B: Bet. 1874-1882.

vi. Lizzie Kate Holman, B: 08 Dec 1882.

160. William Edmund Whitsett-7(Elizabeth Lee-6, Mary Ann-5, Joseph-4, John-3, Joseph-2, John-1) was born on 13 Nov 1837 in Glasgow, Barren County, Kentucky. He died in 1938 in Sallisaw, Sequoyah County, Oklahoma.

Notes for William Edmund Whitsett:

Wounded, Shiloh, Tn, 4/6/1862- Right Knee, seriously Military Induction 10/14 /1861 Bonham, Fannin Co. Tx

Title: Served 11/3/1837-4/15/1901 Confederate Service Pvt. Company H 9th Texas Infantry

208. i. Charles Bell Whitsett.

161. Crittenden Moss Edmunds-7(William Henry-6, Mary Ann-5, Joseph-4, John-3, Joseph-2, John-1) was born on 08 Apr 1849 in Glasgow, Barren County, Kentucky. He married (1) Sarah F. Dishman on 1 May 1872 in Barren County, Kentucky.

Child of Crittenden Moss Edmunds and Sarah F. Dishman is:

i. Ernest Chauncy Edmunds.

i. Chauncey Edmunds.

162. Lallie Lucille Edmunds-7(William Henry-6, Mary Ann-5, Joseph-4, John-3, Joseph-2, John-1). She married (1) Garrett Lykens.

Children of Lallie Lucille Edmunds and Garrett Lykens are:

i. Henry Lykens.

ii. Alice Rose Lykens.

iii. Anita Lykens.

iv. James B. Lykens.

v. Owen Curtis Lykens.

vi. Geneve Lykens.

163. Carrie Belle Edmunds-7(William Henry-6, Mary Ann-5, Joseph-4, John-3, Joseph-2, John-1) was born in 1878. She married Garland Page.

Children of Carrie Belle Edmunds and Garland Page are:

i. Mary Page.

ii. Thomas Page.

iii. Will Hackney Page.

iv. Porter Page.

164. Chase Edmunds-7(William Henry-6, Mary Ann-5, Joseph-4, John-3, Joseph-2, John-1) was born in 1879. He married Lula Mae Emerson.

Children of Chase Edmunds and Lula Mae Emerson are:

i. Nellie Mae Edmunds.

ii. Evelyn Elizabeth Edmunds, B: 18 Nov 1914.

iii. Alice Agnes Edmunds, B: 02 Dec 1917.

iv. Lucy Ann Edmunds, B: 06 Jul 1923.

165. Bryant Ralston Edmunds-7(William Henry-6, Mary Ann-5, Joseph-4, John-3, Joseph-2, John-1) was born on 10 Mar 1887. He died on 12 May 1966. He married (1) Pearl Soper on 05 Oct 1938. He married (2) Edith Payne in 1910.

Notes for Bryant Ralston Edmunds:

Has 2 children.

Children of Bryant Ralston Edmunds and Edith Payne are:

i. Ralston Payne Edmunds, B: 21 Dec 1911.

Notes for Ralston Payne Edmunds:

Attended University of California at Berkeley. Was living in Tulsa, Oklahoma on 10/22/1941.

ii. William Henry Edmunds, B: 18 May 1914, M: Helene Stephenson, 22 Feb 1941.

166. James Edmunds Barton-7(Caroline Winston-6, Mary Ann-5, Joseph-4, John-3, Joseph-2, John-1) was born on 30 Mar 1844 in Barren County, Kentucky. He died in Mar 1918 in Memphis, Shelby County, Tennessee. He married Sammie Summerville on 22 Jul 1875.

Notes for Sammie Summerville:

She was from Mason Depot, Tennessee.

Children of James Edmunds Barton and Sammie Summerville are:

i. Mary Barton.

ii. Richard Barton.

iii. Alice Barton.

iv. Susie Barton.

v. Paul Barton.

vi. Nell Barton.
Notes for Nell Barton:
No children.

vii. Robert Barton.
Notes for Robert Barton:
No children.

167. Caroline Barton-7(Caroline Winston-6, Mary Ann-5, Joseph-4, John-3, Joseph-2, John-1) was born on 30 Jul 1851 in Barren County, Kentucky. She married B. James Dunn on 18 Dec 1873.

Children of Caroline Barton and B. James Dunn are:

i. James Lee Dunn.

ii. William Dunn.

iii. Ralph Dunn.

168. Martha Curd Barton-7(Caroline Winston-6, Mary Ann-5, Joseph-4, John-3, Joseph-2, John-1) was born on 04 Feb 1857 in Logan County, Kentucky. She died on 14 Jul 1882 in Montgomery, Alabama. She married Morgan Smith Gilmer on 30 Nov 1874 in Montgomery, Alabama.

Child of Martha Curd Barton and Morgan Smith Gilmer is:

i. Pattie Gilmer.

169. Elizabeth H. Barton-7(Caroline Winston-6, Mary Ann-5, Joseph-4, John-3, Joseph-2, John-1) was born on 22 Oct 1858 in Logan County, Kentucky. She died on 01 Feb 1929 in Louisville, Kentucky. She married C. F. Cantwell on 07 Nov 1878.

Children of Elizabeth H. Barton and C. F. Cantwell are:

i. Ernest Cantwell.

ii. Otto Cantwell.

iii. Haiden Cantwell.

iv. Sydney Cantwell.

v. Albert Cantwell.

vi. Harold Cantwell.

vii. Ben Cantwell.

170. Clarissa Barton-7(Caroline Winston-6, Mary Ann-5, Joseph-4, John-3, Joseph-2, John-1) was born on 18 Oct 1860 in Logan County, Kentucky. She died in 1926 in Florida. She married (1) Ralph C. Mason on 23 Oct 1877 in Montgomery, Alabama. She married (2) Wakeland about 1925 in Los Angeles, California.

Notes for Ralph C. Mason:

Is from Snowden, Alabama.

Children of Clarissa Barton and Ralph C. Mason are:

i. Josie Mason.

ii. Helen Mason.

iii. James Mason.

209. iv. Clara Barton Mason, B: 07 May 1893, D: 07 Oct 1966 in Birmingham, Alabama, M: Herbert Spence Sutton Sr., Possibly in Birmingham Alabama.

v. Ralph Mason.

vi. Winston Mason.

171. Alice Forbes Barton-7(Caroline Winston-6, Mary Ann-5, Joseph-4, John-3, Joseph-2, John-1) was born on 23 Jul 1846 in Barren County, Kentucky. She died on 20 Jan 1920 in Montgomery, Alabama. She married Frank Gilmer Browder on 22 Nov 1867.

Children of Alice Forbes Barton and Frank Gilmer Browder are:

i. Mayme Browder.

210. ii. Morgan Browder.

iii. Alice Forbes Browder.

iv. Carrie Lewis Browder.

211. v. Frank Browder Sr..

vi. George Montgomery Browder.

vii. James Browder.

viii. Robert Browder.
Notes for Robert Browder:
No children.

172. Sarah Frances Barton-7(Caroline Winston-6, Mary Ann-5, Joseph-4, John-3, Joseph-2, John-1) was born on 27 Nov 1848 in Barren County, Kentucky. She died on 12 Jun 1922 in Montgomery, Alabama. She married (1) Leroy H. Fogleman on 11 Feb 1868. She married (2) John N. Browder on 30 Jul 1890.

Children of Sarah Frances Barton and Leroy H. Fogleman are:

i. Fanny Bee Fogleman.

ii. Alice Elizabeth Fogleman.

iii. Carrie Lee Fogleman.

iv. John L. Fogleman.

v. Sarah Hall Fogleman.

173. Carrio Barton-7(Caroline Winston-6, Mary Ann-5, Joseph-4, John-3, Joseph-2, John-1). She married James Dunn.

Children of Carrio Barton and James Dunn are:

i. James Lee Dunn.

ii. Ralph Dunn.

iii. William Dunn.

174. James Terrence Barton-7(Frances Burrus-6, Mary Ann-5, Joseph-4, John-3, Joseph-2, John-1) was born on 20 Jul 1850 in Tipton County, Tennessee. He died on 08 Jan 1925 in Memphis, Shelby County, Tennessee. He married (1) Vara Hoblitzell on 11

Dec 1888 in Baltimore, Maryland. He married (2) Lizzie Bordon Hardin before 1880.

Children of James Terrence Barton and Vara Hoblitzell are:

- i. Taylor Embrey Barton, B: 19 Jan 1890, D: 13 Dec 1891.
- ii. Henrietta H. Barton, B: 23 Mar 1891, D: 19 Dec 1891.
- iii. Lottie Barton, B: 21 Jun 1892, D: Aug 1894.
- iv. William Hoblitzell Barton, B: 15 Jul 1894.
- 213. v. Terrence Miller Barton, B: 12 Aug 1895, D: 24 May.
- vi. John Frederick Barton, B: 11 Oct 1896, D: 1916.
- vii. Charles Lyman Barton, B: 15 Dec 1897, D: 22 Jan 1918.
- viii. Frances Edmunds Barton, B: 05 May 1899.
- ix. Oliver H. Barton, B: 02 Jan 1902.
- x. Forbis M. Barton, B: 07 Jul 1904.

Child of James Terrence Barton and Lizzie Bordon Hardin is:

- i. James Andrew Barton, B: 04 Oct 1880 in Clarksdale, Arkansas, D: 21 Aug 1956 in Memphis, Shelby County, Tennessee.

175. Lee Barton Sr.-7(Frances Burrus-6, Mary Ann-5, Joseph-4, John-3, Joseph-2, John-1)[32] was born on 26 Sep 1863. He died in Sep 1930. He married Mary Elizabeth Beard. She was born in 1867.

Child of Lee Barton Sr. and Mary Elizabeth Beard is:

- i. Lee Barton Jr., B: 11 Jun 1899, D: 27 Jan 1950.

176. Charles Penn Barton-7(Frances Burrus-6, Mary Ann-5, Joseph-4, John-3, Joseph-2, John-1) was born on 06 Sep 1852 in Barren County, Kentucky. He died on 03 Jan 1911. He married Susan Elizabeth Holt on 08 Sep 1874 in Barren County, Kentucky.

Notes for Charles Penn Barton:

Conflicting birth month of August.

Children of Charles Penn Barton and Susan Elizabeth Holt are:

213. i. Frances Mary Barton, B: 02 Nov 1875, D: 09 Jan 1922.

214. ii. Love Wilkins Barton, B: 02 May 1878 in Memphis, Shelby County, Tennessee.

215. iii. Birdie Holt Barton, B: 26 Mar 1882 in Searcy, Arkansas, D: Jul 1972, M: Thomas Henry Moore Sr., 28 Jan 1908.

177. Robert White Barton Sr.-7(Frances Burrus-6, Mary Ann-5, Joseph-4, John-3, Joseph-2, John-1) was born on 17 Mar 1860. He died on 20 Dec 1939 in Los Angeles, California. He married (1) Cora. He married (2) Mary Garland in Baltimore, Maryland.

Children of Robert White Barton Sr. and Mary Garland are:

i. Phoebe Housen Barton, B: 1886, D: 1892.

ii. Frances Edmunds Barton, B: 1888, D: 1892.

iii. Mary Garland Barton, B: 27 Nov 1892 in Marion, Arkansas, M: C. W. Jones, Bef. 1916 in Carson City, Neveda.

iv. Robert White Barton Jr., B: 12 Feb 1897 in Marion, Arkansas, M: Juanita Hite, 14 Mar 1920.

178. William Edmunds Barton Sr.-7(Frances Burrus-6, Mary Ann-5, Joseph-4, John-3, Joseph-2, John-1) was born on 16 Dec 1848 in Tipson County, Tennessee. He died on 11 Sep 1936 in Searcy, Arkansas.

i. Flavel Wilkins Barton, B: 07 Dec 1876, D: 21 Dec 1950 in Searcy, Arkansas.

ii. William Edmunds Barton Jr., B: 08 Aug 1879, D: 02 May 1949 in Jamestown, Kentucky, M: Meta Nelson, 1919 in Dermont, Arkansas.

179. Mary Jane Edmunds-7(Edmund Alexander-6, Mary Ann-5, Joseph-4, John-3, Joseph-2, John-1) was born on 29 May 1858. She died on 09 Dec 1908. She married Preston L. Ford on 27 Nov 1879.

Children of Mary Jane Edmunds and Preston L. Ford are:

i. Litie Ford.

ii. Leslie Ford.

180. Mary Diana Edmunds-7(Edmund Alexander-6, Mary Ann-5, Joseph-4, John-3, Joseph-2, John-1) was born on 28 Sep 1902. She died on 06 Jan 1918. She married A. Earl Lawrence.

Child of Mary Diana Edmunds and A. Earl Lawrence is:

i. Edwin Lawrence.

181. Marion Gordon Taylor-7(James-6, John-5, Lucy-4, John-3, Moses-2, John-1)[8] was born on 04 Feb 1892 in Washington, D.C.[8]. She married Clayton Lyman Drew on 20 Jan 1912 in Washington, D.C.[8]. He was born on 10 Dec 1890 in Ansonia, Connecticut[8]. He died on 23 Aug 1967 in Vacaville, California[8].

Child of Marion Gordon Taylor and Clayton Lyman Drew is:

219. i. Dorris Lyman Drew, B: 13 Apr 1914 in Washington, D.C.[8], M: Walter Moulden Eiker, 24 Jun 1937 in Washington, D.C.[8].

Generation 8

182. William Franklin Edmunds-8(James Christopher-7, Charles Penn-6, Mary Ann-5, Joseph-4, John-3, Joseph-2, John-1) was born on 10 Feb 1856. He died on 22 May 1926. He married (1) Mary Bell King in 1876.

Children of William Franklin Edmunds and Mary Bell King are:

217. i. Clara Edmunds.

ii. Alice Edmunds.

iii. Roger Edmunds.

183. Bennie R. Edmunds-8(James Christopher-7, Charles Penn-6, Mary Ann-5, Joseph-4, John-3, Joseph-2, John-1) was born on 17 Jun 1865. He died on 22 Jun 1953 in Barren County, Kentucky. He married (1) Eva W. Carter on 01 Feb 1893. She died in 1946.

He married (2) Minnie McGlocklin on 17 Nov 1887.

Children of Bennie R. Edmunds and Eva W. Carter are:

i. Jessie Edmunds.

ii. Ray Edmunds.

iii. Clarence Edmunds.

184. Lizzie Dora Edmunds-8(James Christopher-7, Charles Penn-6, Mary Ann-5, Joseph-4, John-3, Joseph-2, John-1) was born on 17 Oct 1869. She died on 15 May 1960. She married John Page Lewis on 17 Nov 1887. He was born on 20 May 1864.

Children of Lizzie Dora Edmunds and John Page Lewis are:

218. i. Minnie May Lewis, B: 23 Oct 1888, M: Charlie Furlong, 13 Nov 1905.

219. ii. Chris E. Lewis, B: 04 May 1891[33], D: Feb 1967 in Glasgow, Barren County, Kentucky[33], M: Jessie May Everett, 27 Dec 1916.

220. iii. Joe H. Lewis, B: 07 Feb 1893, M: Ruby Duval, 27 Oct 1913.

221. iv. Anna Laura Lewis, B: 25 Dec 1896, M: Ray Landrum, 20 Dec 1916.

v. Porter Lewis, B: 24 Aug 1899, M: Helen Louise Pryor, 19 Jun 1924.

vi. Pattie Elizabeth Lewis, B: 06 Jan 1909, M: Dwight Sidders, 31 Oct 1926.

185. James Crittendon Allen-8(Catherine Eubank-7, Charles Penn-6, Mary Ann-5, Joseph-4, John-3, Joseph-2, John-1)[20] was born on 10 Apr 1858[20]. He died on 10 Jun 1936 in Garden City, Finney County, Kansas. He married Anna M. Barrick on 16 Sep 1885[20].

Children of James Crittendon Allen and Anna M. Barrick are:

i. Ottis B. Allen.

ii. Samuel Perry Allen, D: 1927[20].

iii. Mary Katherine Allen, M: Charles Curry, 28 Aug 1926[20].

186. William Edmunds Gleaves Allen-8(Catherine Eubank-7, Charles Penn-6, Mary Ann-5, Joseph-4, John-3, Joseph-2, John-1)[1, 2, 20] was born on 20 Dec 1859 in Madison County, Kentucky[1, 2, 20]. He died on 09 Sep 1931 in Loveland, Larimer County, Colorado[1, 2]. He married (1) Eleanora Amanda Cates on 07 Feb 1884 in Glasgow, Barren County, Kentucky[1, 2, 20], daughter of William G. W. Cates and L. Sally Willis. She was born on 31 Jul 1860 in Glasgow, Barren County, Kentucky[1, 2]. She died on 11 Feb 1897 in Canyon City, Colorado[1, 2]. He married (2) Elizabeth Depp on 20 Feb 1902[20]. He married (3) Ibbie Beard on 10 Feb 1906 in Canyon City, Fremont County, Colorado[20].

Notes for William Edmunds Gleaves Allen:

He served in the US Army for the Civil War between 8/11/1864 to 6/13/1865. He was discharged at Benton Barracks.

His parents are believed to have been living in Smiths Grove, Warren County, Kentucky at the time of his birth, however, the Nathan Perry Allen bible records give Madison County, Kentucky at the place of birth.

He served in the U.S. Army for the Civil War between 8/11/1864 to 6/13/1865. He was discharged at Benton Barracks.

He is buried in Smiths Grove, Warren County, Kentucky

Documentation of facts:

1. Family vital statistics entered in Nathan Perry Allen bible
2. Family vital statistics entered in Nathan Allen bible
3. Marriage Certificate to Nora Cates
4. Death Certificate (informant was Ibbie Beard Allen (second wife)
5. Warren County, Kentucky census records for 1860, 1870 and 1880.

Notes for Eleanora Amanda Cates:

There is a conflicting date of birth of 7/31/1861 mentioned in Sallie Willis Cates Declaration in connection with her widow's

Civil War Pension Application based on William G. W. Cates' service. The date of death is either 2/7/1897 or 2/11/1897 or 2/12/1897. The Nathan Allen bible says 2/12/1897.There is a conflicting date of birth of 7/31/1861 mentioned in Sallie Willis Cates Declaration in connection with her widow's Civil War Pension Application based on William G. W. Cates' service. The date of death is either 2/7/1897, 2/11/1897, or 2/12/1897. the Nathan Allen bible says 2/12/1897.

Children of William Edmunds Gleaves Allen and Eleanora Amanda Cates are:

222. i. Charles Burtle Allen, B: 20 Nov 1887 in Dermott, Stevens County, Kansas[1, 2, 20], D: 15 May 1960 in Dodge City, Ford, Kansas, USA[1, 2], M: Carolina Merk, 28 Oct 1908 in Dodge City, Ford, Kansas, USA[1, 2, 20].

ii. Sallie Allen, B: 09 Jan 1885, D: 30 Jan 1885.

223. iii. Horace Cates Allen Sr., B: 11 Nov 1889[20, 34], D: Mar 1968 in Duncan, Stephens County, Oklahoma[34], M: Ima Nichols, 1916 in Oklahoma City, Canadian County, Oklahoma.

iv. Roy C. Allen, B: 10 Nov 1894, D: 28 Sep 1898 in Canon City, Fremont County, Colorado.

Child of William Edmunds Gleaves Allen and Elizabeth Depp is:

i. Depp Edmund Allen, B: 30 Mar 1903 in Bowling Green, Warren County, Kentucky, D: Jun[35], M: Lillie Cox, 19 Sep 1920 in Barren County, Kentucky.

187. Mary Emeline Allen-8(Catherine Eubank-7, Charles Penn-6, Mary Ann-5, Joseph-4, John-3, Joseph-2, John-1)[20] was born on 06 Oct 1862[20]. She died on 03 Sep 1911 in Clovis, Curry County, New Mexico[20]. She married William Elihu Davis on 13 Jan 1885[20].

Children of Mary Emeline Allen and William Elihu Davis are:

i. Claud C. Davis.

ii. Edwin Davis.

225. iii. Helen Davis.

vi. Eula Davis.

vii. Nina Davis.

225. vi. Mable Davis.

vii. Corinne Davis.

188. Katherine Edmunds Allen-8(Catherine Eubank-7, Charles Penn-6, Mary Ann-5, Joseph-4, John-3, Joseph-2, John-1)[20] was born on 07 Dec 1866[20]. She died on 24 Oct 1918 in Bowling Green, Warren County, Kentucky[20]. She married (1) Gustavus Allen Fogleman Sr. on 17 Dec 1896[20].

Child of Katherine Edmunds Allen and Gustavus Allen Fogleman Sr. is:

226. i. Gustavus Allen Fogleman Jr., B: 11 Nov 1897[20].

Child of Katherine Edmunds Allen and Jon Franklin is:

i. Frances Franklin.

189. Hiram Perry Allen-8(Catherine Eubank-7, Charles Penn-6, Mary Ann-5, Joseph-4, John-3, Joseph-2, John-1)[20] was born on 28 Jan 1869[20]. He died on 09 Mar 1948 in Luling, Caldwell County, Texas. He married Elizabeth Stagner on 15 Jan 1896 in Luling, Caldwell County, Texas[20].

Children of Hiram Perry Allen and Elizabeth Stagner are:

i. Allen.

ii. Perry Allen.

iii. George Allen.

228. iv. Katherine Allen.

v. Elizabeth Allen.

190. Frank Barton Allen-8(Catherine Eubank-7, Charles Penn-6, Mary Ann-5, Joseph-4, John-3, Joseph-2, John-1)[20, 36] was born on 19 Feb 1871[20]. He died on 24 Jan 1951 in Hobart,

Lake County, Indiana. He married Annie Easterling on 28 Jul 1908[20].

Children of Frank Barton Allen and Annie Easterling are:

i. Frank Hardee Allen, B: 12 Aug 1908 in Pachta, Mississippi, M: Anne Kathryl Fuhr, 16 Mar 1924.

ii. Edna Katherine Allen, B: 1909, M: Bernard Anderson, 31 Aug 1935.

229. iii. Easterling McIntire Allen, B: 06 Feb 1911 in Chinsia, Oklahoma, M: Mary Sawdor, 17 Oct 1936.

iv. Wilson Bryan Allen, B: 21 Dec 1912 in Duncan, Oklahoma, M: Grace E. Kirtland, 04 Jul 1940 in Freeport, Illinois.

191. Ora Laura Allen-8(Catherine Eubank-7, Charles Penn-6, Mary Ann-5, Joseph-4, John-3, Joseph-2, John-1)[20] was born on 12 Apr 1875[20]. She died on 24 Jun 1961 in Bowling Green, Warren County, Kentucky. She married Roy G. Blakeman on 25 May 1899[20].

Children of Ora Laura Allen and Roy G. Blakeman are:

i. Gus Blakeman.

ii. Earl Colder Blakeman, B: 04 Mar 1900[20], D: 13 Jun 1901[20].

iii. Roger Marion Blakeman, B: 05 Dec 1902[20].

192. Callie Eubank Edmunds-8(Charles Henry-7, Charles Penn-6, Mary Ann-5, Joseph-4, John-3, Joseph-2, John-1) was born on 08 Nov 1872. She married George Carter.

Children of Callie Eubank Edmunds and George Carter are:

i. Edith Verna Carter.

ii. Lewis Penn Carter.

iii. William James Carter.

iv. Charles Henry Carter.

v. Edmund Taylor Carter.

vi. Lester Vearl Carter.

vii. Jerry Perry Carter.

viii. Myrtle Verina Carter.

ix. George Marion Carter.

x. Harvey Norman Carter.

xi. Sterling Robert Carter.

193. Mary Thomas Barton-8(Elizabeth Frances-7, Charles Penn-6, Mary Ann-5, Joseph-4, John-3, Joseph-2, John-1) was born on 05 Mar 1868. She died on 06 Feb 1890. She married Gustavus Adolphus Fogleman on 25 Jul 1889.

Child of Mary Thomas Barton and Gustavus Adolphus Fogleman is:

229. i John Franklin Fogleman.

194. Louis Hardin Barton-8(Elizabeth Frances-7, Charles Penn-6, Mary Ann-5, Joseph-4, John-3, Joseph-2, John-1) was born on 10 Jan 1873. He died on 27 Sep 1959. He married Mary Smith on 14 Apr 1897 in Marion, Arkansas.

Children of Louis Hardin Barton and Mary Smith are:

i. Martha Barton.

ii. Louise Barton.

195. Charles Grigsby Barton Sr.-8(Elizabeth Frances-7, Charles Penn-6, Mary Ann-5, Joseph-4, John-3, Joseph-2, John-1) was born on 07 Feb 1875. He died on 17 Nov 1939. He married Musie Foster in 1899.

Child of Charles Grigsby Barton Sr. and Musie Foster is:

i. Charles Grisby Barton Jr..

196. Richard Bethel Barton Sr.-8(Elizabeth Frances-7, Charles Penn-6, Mary Ann-5, Joseph-4, John-3, Joseph-2, John-1) was born on 01 Jun 1881. He died on 12 Jul 1948. He married Hardin Cheek in 1909.

Child of Richard Bethel Barton Sr. and Hardin Cheek is:

i. Richard Bethel Barton Jr..

197. Allen Edmunds-8(William Persifer Smith-7, Charles Penn-6, Mary Ann-5, Joseph-4, John-3, Joseph-2, John-1). He married Vasta Hanes.

Child of Allen Edmunds and Vasta Hanes is:

i. Julia Edmunds.

198. James Buford Edmunds-8(John Curd-7, Charles Penn-6, Mary Ann-5, Joseph-4, John-3, Joseph-2, John-1) was born on 04 May 1883. He married (1) Kate Willis, daughter of Frank M. Willis and Laura Wilson Edmunds.

Children of James Buford Edmunds and Kate Willis are:

i. Lewis Edmunds.

ii. John Curd Edmunds.

iii. Laura Agnes Edmunds.

iv. Wilton Matthews Edmunds.

v. Katherine Edmunds.

vi. Dorothy Edmunds.

vii. Musie Edmunds, B: May 1925.

viii. Martha Ann Edmunds, B: 1926.

199. Leonard Matthews Edmunds-8(John Curd-7, Charles Penn-6, Mary Ann-5, Joseph-4, John-3, Joseph-2, John-1) was born on 22 Feb 1886. He died on 10 Nov 1951. He married Maud Emerson on 25 Dec 1915.

Children of Leonard Matthews Edmunds and Maud Emerson are:

i. Sallie Bird Edmunds.

ii. Waltor Edmunds.

iii. Flora May Edmunds.

iv. Judson Edmunds.

v. Charles William Edmunds.

vi. John Ellis Edmunds.

vii. Ada Mildred Edmunds, B: 1925.

viii. Betsy Jean Edmunds, B: 08 Nov 1926.

200. Flora Laura Edmunds-8(John Curd-7, Charles Penn-6, Mary Ann-5, Joseph-4, John-3, Joseph-2, John-1) was born on 03 Nov 1890. She married (1) George Washington Pounds.

Notes for Flora Laura Edmunds:

There is a question as to the first name here. It is either Nora, Mora, or Flora. Child of Flora Laura Edmunds and George Washington Pounds is:

i. George Pounds.

201. Jessie Willis-8(Laura Wilson-7, Charles Penn-6, Mary Ann-5, Joseph-4, John-3, Joseph-2, John-1). She married Leonard Hildreth.

Children of Jessie Willis and Leonard Hildreth are:

i. Hugh Hildreth.

ii. Frances Cee Hildreth.

202. Kate Willis-8(Laura Wilson-7, Charles Penn-6, Mary Ann-5, Joseph-4, John-3, Joseph-2, John-1). She married James Buford Edmunds, son of John Curd Edmunds and Sally A. Waller. He was born on 04 May 1883.

Children of Kate Willis and James Buford Edmunds are:

i. Lewis Edmunds.

ii. John Curd Edmunds.

iii. Laura Agnes Edmunds.

iv. Wilton Matthews Edmunds.

v. Katherine Edmunds.

vi. Dorothy Edmunds.

vii. Musie Edmunds, B: May 1925.

viii. Martha Ann Edmunds, B: 1926.

203. Minnie Lee Willis-8(Laura Wilson-7, Charles Penn-6, Mary Ann-5, Joseph-4, John-3, Joseph-2, John-1) was born on 10 Aug 1879. She died on 17 May 1900. She married George Duvall on 27 Dec 1896.

Child of Minnie Lee Willis and George Duvall is:

i. Garnet Duvall, B: Aft. 1896.

204. Mayme Willis-8(Laura Wilson-7, Charles Penn-6, Mary Ann-5, Joseph-4, John-3, Joseph-2, John-1) was born on 30 Nov 1890 in Barren County, Kentucky. She died on 22 Sep 1913 in Barren County, Kentucky. She married William Thomas Lewis in 1911.

Child of Mayme Willis and William Thomas Lewis is:

i. Frankie Lewis, B: Aft. 1911.

205. Pattie Willis-8(Laura Wilson-7, Charles Penn-6, Mary Ann-5, Joseph-4, John-3, Joseph-2, John-1). She married Claude Amos.

Children of Pattie Willis and Claude Amos are:

i. Frank Amos.

ii. Charles Amos.

iii. Louise Amos.

206. Henry Malcom Holman-8(Martha Ann-7, Charles Penn-6, Mary Ann-5, Joseph-4, John-3, Joseph-2, John-1) was born on 17 Dec 1864. He died on 22 Dec 1918. He married (1) Sally Anderson.

Children of Henry Malcom Holman and Sally Anderson are:

i. Malcom Holman.

ii. Ernest Holman.

iii. Mary Holman.

Children of Henry Malcom Holman and Millie Anderson are:

i. Travis Holman.

ii. Guy Holman.

iii. Gwendolyn Holman.

iv. Harry Holman.

v. Mildred Holman.

207. Paul Wilson Holman Sr.-8(Martha Ann-7, Charles Penn-6, Mary Ann-5, Joseph-4, John-3, Joseph-2, John-1) was born in Apr 1873. He married (1) Annie Dickenson.

Children of Paul Wilson Holman Sr. and Annie Dickenson are:

i. Elizabeth Holman.

ii. Paul Wilson Holman Jr..

iii. Sidney Holman.

208. Charles Bell Whitsett-8(William Edmund-7, Elizabeth Lee-6, Mary Ann-5, Joseph-4, John-3, Joseph-2, John-1).

i. Charles Brimmer Whitsett.

209. Clara Barton Mason-8(Clarissa-7, Caroline Winston-6, Mary Ann-5, Joseph-4, John-3, Joseph-2, John-1) was born on 07 May 1893. She died on 07 Oct 1966 in Birmingham, Alabama. She married Herbert Spence Sutton Sr. in Possibly in Birmingham Alabama.

Child of Clara Barton Mason and Herbert Spence Sutton Sr. is:

i. Herbert Spence Sutton Jr..

210. Morgan Browder-8(Alice Forbes-7, Caroline Winston-6, Mary Ann-5, Joseph-4, John-3, Joseph-2, John-1). He married Margaret Waldon.

Child of Morgan Browder and Margaret Waldon is:

i. Margaret Browder.

211. Frank Browder Sr.-8(Alice Forbes-7, Caroline Winston-6, Mary Ann-5, Joseph-4, John-3, Joseph-2, John-1). He married Julia Gordon.

Child of Frank Browder Sr. and Julia Gordon is:

i. Frank Browder Jr..

212. Terrence Miller Barton-8(James Terrence-7, Frances Burrus-6, Mary Ann-5, Joseph-4, John-3, Joseph-2, John-1)[37] was born

on 12 Aug 1895. He died on 24 May. He married Clara Belle Carey. She died about 1992.

Notes for Terrence Miller Barton:

He married July 24, 1917.

He is said to have served with general Pershing. It is also said that he was in the Calvary that went after Poncho Villa and he later fought in WWI and WWII.

Child of Terrence Miller Barton and Clara Belle Carey is:

230. i. Terrence Miller Barton II, B: 18 Jan 1929 in Houston, Texas[37], D: 1976[37].

213. Frances Mary Barton-8(Charles Penn-7, Frances Burrus-6, Mary Ann-5, Joseph-4, John-3, Joseph-2, John-1) was born on 02 Nov 1875. She died on 09 Jan 1922. She married Joel Thomas Bybee Sr.

Child of Frances Mary Barton and Joel Thomas Bybee Sr. is:

i. Joel Thomas Bybee Jr..

214. Love Wilkins Barton-8(Charles Penn-7, Frances Burrus-6, Mary Ann-5, Joseph-4, John-3, Joseph-2, John-1) was born on 02 May 1878 in Memphis, Shelby County, Tennessee. She married Leonidas Fudge Etter Sr..

Child of Love Wilkins Barton and Leonidas Fudge Etter Sr. is:

i. Leonidas Fudge Etter Jr..

215. Birdie Holt Barton-8(Charles Penn-7, Frances Burrus-6, Mary Ann-5, Joseph-4, John-3, Joseph-2, John-1) was born on 26 Mar 1882 in Searcy, Arkansas. She died in Jul 1972. She married Thomas Henry Moore Sr. on 28 Jan 1908.

Child of Birdie Holt Barton and Thomas Henry Moore Sr. is:

i. Thomas Henry Moore Jr..

216. Dorris Lyman Drew-8(Marion Gordon-7, James-6, John-5, Lucy-4, John-3, Moses-2, John-1)[8, 38] was born on 13 Apr 1914 in Washington, D.C.[8]. She married Walter Moulden Eiker on 24 Jun 1937 in Washington, D.C.[8]. He was born on 22 May 1913 in Washington, D.C.[8].

Children of Dorris Lyman Drew and Walter Moulden Eiker are:

i. Charles Clayton Eiker.

ii. Marion Louise Eiker.

iii. Walter Moulden Eiker Jr..

231. iv. Drew Eiker, B: 30 Dec 1949[8], M: Cathy Ann Vernon, 30 Aug 1980 in Guilford Court House, Battlefield, North Carolina[8].

Generation 9

217. Clara Edmunds-9(William Franklin-8, James Christopher-7, Charles Penn-6, Mary Ann-5, Joseph-4, John-3, Joseph-2, John-1). She married Tom Mobley.

Child of Clara Edmunds and Tom Mobley is:

i. Pauline Mobley.

218. Minnie May Lewis-9(Lizzie Dora-8, James Christopher-7, Charles Penn-6, Mary Ann-5, Joseph-4, John-3, Joseph-2, John-1) was born on 23 Oct 1888. She married Charlie Furlong on 13 Nov 1905.

Children of Minnie May Lewis and Charlie Furlong are:

232. i. Lizzie Kate Furlong, B: 05 Oct 1906, M: Einar Settle, 03 Jul 1926.

ii. Leslie Lee Furlong, B: 24 Sep 1909.

iii. Anna May Furlong, B: 12 Nov 1912.

iv. Chris Thomas Furlong, B: 05 Nov 1915[39], D: Jul 1977[39].

v. Lera Ethel Furlong, B: 05 Feb 1920.

vi. Porter Horace Furlong, B: 12 Feb 1922.

219. Chris E. Lewis-9(Lizzie Dora-8, James Christopher-7, Charles Penn-6, Mary Ann-5, Joseph-4, John-3, Joseph-2, John-1)[33] was born on 04 May 1891[33]. He died in Feb 1967 in Glasgow, Barren County, Kentucky[33]. He married Jessie May Everett on 27 Dec 1916.

Children of Chris E. Lewis and Jessie May Everett are:

i. Bernice Lee Lewis, B: 06 Jan 1920.

ii. Dora Morgan Lewis, B: 12 Sep 1921.

220. Joe H. Lewis-9(Lizzie Dora-8, James Christopher-7, Charles Penn-6, Mary Ann-5, Joseph-4, John-3, Joseph-2, John-1) was born on 07 Feb 1893. He married Ruby Duval on 27 Oct 1913.

Children of Joe H. Lewis and Ruby Duval are:

i. Virginia Helen Lewis, B: 02 Aug 1920.

ii. Clifton Richard Lewis, B: 11 Aug 1923[40], D: 27 Sep 1989 in Glasgow, Barren County, Kentucky[40].

221. Anna Laura Lewis-9(Lizzie Dora-8, James Christopher-7, Charles Penn-6, Mary Ann-5, Joseph-4, John-3, Joseph-2, John-1) was born on 25 Dec 1896. She married Ray Landrum on 20 Dec 1916.

Children of Anna Laura Lewis and Ray Landrum are:

i. Beatrice Landrum, B: 13 Oct 1917.

ii. Yancy Porter Landrum, B: 28 Mar 1921.

iii. Glen Allen Landrum, B: 19 Apr 1926.

222. Charles Burtle Allen-9(William Edmunds Gleaves-8, Catherine Eubank-7, Charles Penn-6, Mary Ann-5, Joseph-4, John-3, Joseph-2, John-1)[1, 2, 20] was born on 20 Nov 1887 in Dermott, Stevens County, Kansas[1, 2, 20]. He died on 15 May 1960 in Dodge City, Ford, Kansas, USA[1, 2]. He married Carolina Merk on 28 Oct 1908 in Dodge City, Ford, Kansas, USA[1, 2, 20], daughter of John Merk and Wilhelmine Ewy. She was born on 19 Dec 1885 in Dodge City, Ford, Kansas, USA[1, 2, 20, 35]. She died on 13 Feb 1976 in Dodge City, Ford, Kansas, USA[1, 2, 35].

Notes for Charles Burtle Allen:

Documentation of facts:

1. Application for Delayed Certificate of Birth signed by Mrs. Lena Allen on 2/16/1942.

2. Delayed Birth Certificate of Donald Eugene Allen issued 2/2?/1942.

3. Marriage Record signed by Claud Z. Spiers, Baptist Minister on 10/28/1908.

4. Death Certificate signed 5/16/1960

Notes for Carolina Merk:

Documentation of facts:

1. Marriage Record signed by Claude Z. Spiers, Baptist Minister on 10/28/1908.

Children of Charles Burtle Allen and Carolina Merk are:

233. i. Horrace John Allen, B: 18 Aug 1909 in Howell, Kansas[20, 41].

234. ii. Lester William Allen, B: 11 Jul 1911 in Howell, Kansas[20, 41].

235. iii. Edna Vera Allen, B: 24 Dec 1913 in Dodge City, Ford, Kansas, USA[20], M: Charles Andrew Reynolds, 06 Sep 1942 in Bellflower, Los Angeles County, California[42].

236. iv. Pauline Mable Allen, B: 24 Oct 1916 in Howell, Kansas[20], M: Stephen John Irsik Sr., 27 Jan 1946 in Ingalls, Kansas[43].

v. Donald Eugene Allen, B: 18 Sep 1918[20].

237. vi. Eldred Maxine Allen, B: 28 Dec 1922[20].

223. Horace Cates Allen Sr.-9(William Edmunds Gleaves-8, Catherine Eubank-7, Charles Penn-6, Mary Ann-5, Joseph-4, John-3, Joseph-2, John-1)[20, 34] was born on 11 Nov 1889[20, 34]. He died in Mar 1968 in Duncan, Stephens County, Oklahoma[34]. He married Ima Nichols in 1916 in Oklahoma City, Canadian County, Oklahoma.

Children of Horace Cates Allen Sr. and Ima Nichols are:

i. Horace Cates Allen Jr..

ii. Joan Allen, B: 1925.

224. Helen Davis-9(Mary Emeline-8, Catherine Eubank-7, Charles Penn-6, Mary Ann-5, Joseph-4, John-3, Joseph-2, John-1)[20]. She married Merritt Martindale.

Children of Helen Davis and Merritt Martindale are:

i. John Martindale.

ii. Margaret Martindale.

iii. Rosamond Martindale.

225. Mable Davis-9(Mary Emeline-8, Catherine Eubank-7, Charles Penn-6, Mary Ann-5, Joseph-4, John-3, Joseph-2, John-1)[20]. She married George Stierer.

Children of Mable Davis and George Stierer are:

i. Infant Stierer.

ii. Robert Allen Stierer.

226. Gustavus Allen Fogleman Jr.-9(Katherine Edmunds-8, Catherine Eubank-7, Charles Penn-6, Mary Ann-5, Joseph-4, John-3, Joseph-2, John-1)[20] was born on 11 Nov 1897[20]. He married (1) Mamie Duddy.

Children of Gustavus Allen Fogleman Jr. and Mamie Duddy are:

i. Katherine Jane Allen Fogleman, B: Bef. 1923.

ii. Gustavus Allen Fogleman III, B: Nov 1923[20].

Child of Gustavus Allen Fogleman Jr. and Jen Frankland is:

i. Frances Fogleman.

227. Katherine Allen-9(Hiram Perry-8, Catherine Eubank-7, Charles Penn-6, Mary Ann-5, Joseph-4, John-3, Joseph-2, John-1)[20]. She married Gordon Baker.

Child of Katherine Allen and Gordon Baker is:

i. Gordon Allen Baker.

228. Easterling McIntire Allen-9(Frank Barton-8, Catherine Eubank-7, Charles Penn-6, Mary Ann-5, Joseph-4, John-3, Joseph-2, John-1)[20, 36] was born on 06 Feb 1911 in Chinsia, Oklahoma. He married Mary Sawdor on 17 Oct 1936.

Child of Easterling McIntire Allen and Mary Sawdor is:

i. Robert James Allen.

229. John Franklin Fogleman-9(Mary Thomas-8, Elizabeth Frances-7, Charles Penn-6, Mary Ann-5, Joseph-4, John-3, Joseph-2, John-1)[44]. He married Julia McAdams.

Children of John Franklin Fogleman and Julia McAdams are:

i. John Fogleman.

ii. Mamie Olive Fogleman.

iii. Julian Fogleman.

iv. Franklin Fogleman.

230. Terrence Miller Barton II-9(Terrence Miller-8, James Terrence-7, Frances Burrus-6, Mary Ann-5, Joseph-4, John-3, Joseph-2, John-1)[37] was born on 18 Jan 1929 in Houston, Texas[37]. He died in 1976[37].

i. Terrence Miller Barton III.

231. Drew Eiker-9(Dorris Lyman-8, Marion Gordon-7, James-6, John-5, Lucy-4, John-3, Moses-2, John-1)[8, 38] was born on 30 Dec 1949[8]. He married Cathy Ann Vernon on 30 Aug 1980 in Guilford Court House, Battlefield, North Carolina[8]. She was born on 15 Nov 1953 in Greensboro, North Carolina[8].

Children of Drew Eiker and Cathy Ann Vernon are:

i. Shaun Eiker, B: 24 Aug 1981 in Greensboro, North Carolina[8].

ii. Brandon Eiker, B: 30 Mar 1984 in Greensboro, North Carolina[8].

Generation 10

232. Lizzie Kate Furlong-10(Minnie May-9, Lizzie Dora-8, James Christopher-7, Charles Penn-6, Mary Ann-5, Joseph-4, John-3, Joseph-2, John-1) was born on 05 Oct 1906. She married Einar Settle on 03 Jul 1926.

Child of Lizzie Kate Furlong and Einar Settle is:

i. Charles Alfred Settle, B: 24 Feb 1927.

233. Horrace John Allen-10(Charles Burtle-9, William Edmunds Gleaves-8, Catherine Eubank-7, Charles Penn-6, Mary Ann-5, Joseph-4, John-3, Joseph-2, John-1)[20, 41] was born on 18 Aug 1909 in Howell, Kansas[20, 41]. He married Vivian Tucker.

Child of Horrace John Allen and Vivian Tucker is:

i. Jim Allen.

234. Lester William Allen-10(Charles Burtle-9, William Edmunds Gleaves-8, Catherine Eubank-7, Charles Penn-6, Mary Ann-5, Joseph-4, John-3, Joseph-2, John-1)[20, 41] was born on 11 Jul 1911 in Howell, Kansas[20, 41]. He married Katie Lanius.

Children of Lester William Allen and Katie Lanius are:

i. Joy Allen.

ii. Kay Allen, D: 15 Feb 1952.
Notes for Kay Allen:
Kay died while she was on the school playground when she was about 8 years old.

235. Edna Vera Allen-10(Charles Burtle-9, William Edmunds Gleaves-8, Catherine Eubank-7, Charles Penn-6, Mary Ann-5, Joseph-4, John-3, Joseph-2, John-1)[20] was born on 24 Dec 1913 in Dodge City, Ford, Kansas, USA[20]. She married Charles Andrew Reynolds on 06 Sep 1942 in Bellflower, Los Angeles County, California[42], son of Joseph Leroy Reynolds and Sarah Matildah Walker. He was born on 30 May 1915 in Arlington, Reno County, Kansas[45]. He died on 20 Aug 2005 in Kansas Soliers Home, Halsey Hall, Dodge City, Ford County, Kansas[45].
Notes for Charles Andrew Reynolds:

Went to school in Arlington, Kansas. Moved to Dodge City, Kansas in 1938. He worked for Gum Motor Company until he went into the Army. He served with General Patton's 3rd Army as a Tech Sergeant and received 5 Battle Stars and 3 citations. He was a member of the First Presbyterian Church, Dodge City, where he served as an elder and deacon and a member of the session and taught Sunday school for 25 years. He was a member of the

American Legion, VFW Post 1714, RSVP and Masonic Lodge, all of Dodge City, and AARP and NRA.

He was cremated and his ashes were buried.

Children of Edna Vera Allen and Charles Andrew Reynolds are:

238. i. Carol Lynn Reynolds, B: 11 Jun 1943 in Dodge City, Ford, Kansas, USA, D: 21 Mar 2009 in Hays, Ellis County, Kansas, M: David Otis Clough, 11 Jul 1962 in Dodge City, Ford, Kansas, USA.

239. ii. Allen Leroy Reynolds, B: 10 Jul 1948 in Dodge City, Ford County, Kansas.

236. Pauline Mable Allen-10(Charles Burtle-9, William Edmunds Gleaves-8, Catherine Eubank-7, Charles Penn-6, Mary Ann-5, Joseph-4, John-3, Joseph-2, John-1)[20, 46] was born on 24 Oct 1916 in Howell, Kansas[20]. She married Stephen John Irsik Sr. on 27 Jan 1946 in Ingalls, Kansas[43]. He was born on 30 Jul 1915[43]. He died on 08 Jan 1999.

Children of Pauline Mable Allen and Stephen John Irsik Sr. are:

240. i. Stephen John Irsik Jr., B: 01 Nov 1946, M: Kay Bolens, 26 Dec 1967.

241. ii. Michael Garrison Irsik, B: 08 May 1949, M: Debra Schwartz, Dec 1975.

242. iii. Maxson Brent Irsik Sr, B: 15 Sep 1951, M: Donna Mae DeHart, 26 May 1972[43].

243. iv. Robert Allen Irsik, B: 29 Oct 1952, M: Ellen Berger, 13 Nov 1982.

244. v. Ronald Dean Irsik, B: 15 Feb 1955, M: Patricia Tucker, 11 Aug 1985.

237. Eldred Maxine Allen-10(Charles Burtle-9, William Edmunds Gleaves-8, Catherine Eubank-7, Charles Penn-6, Mary Ann-5, Joseph-4, John-3, Joseph-2, John-1)[20] was born on 28 Dec 1922[20]. She married Earl Johnson.

Children of Eldred Maxine Allen and Earl Johnson are:

i. Beverly Ann Johnson.

ii. Charlie Johnson.

iii. Richard Johnson.

Generation 11

238. Carol Lynn Reynolds-11(Edna Vera-10, Charles Burtle-9, William Edmunds Gleaves-8, Catherine Eubank-7, Charles Penn-6, Mary Ann-5, Joseph-4, John-3, Joseph-2, John-1)[42] was born on 11 Jun 1943 in Dodge City, Ford, Kansas, USA. She died on 21 Mar 2009 in Hays, Ellis County, Kansas. She married David Otis Clough on 11 Jul 1962 in Dodge City, Ford, Kansas, USA, son of Otis Lawson Clough and Elizabeth Beatrice Barker. He was born on 01 Jan 1941 in Dodge City, Ford, Kansas, USA. He died on 10 Mar 2015 in Hays, Ellis County, Kansas.

Children of Carol Lynn Reynolds and David Otis Clough are:

245. i. Christina Lynn Clough, B: 13 Oct 1964 in Dodge City, Ford, Kansas, USA, M: Martin Steven Lueth, 04 Aug 1985 in Dodge City, Ford, Kansas, USA.

246. ii. David Andrew Clough, B: 30 Jan 1966 in Dodge City, Ford County, Kansas, M: Gloria Ann Coleman, 22 Apr 1999 in Hays, Ellis County, Kansas.

239. Allen Leroy Reynolds-11(Edna Vera-10, Charles Burtle-9, William Edmunds Gleaves-8, Catherine Eubank-7, Charles Penn-6, Mary Ann-5, Joseph-4, John-3, Joseph-2, John-1)[42] was born on 10 Jul 1948 in Dodge City, Ford County, Kansas. He married Barbara. She was born on 26 Sep 1948 in Kansas City.

Children of Allen Leroy Reynolds and Barbara are:

247. i. Renae Ann Reynolds, B: 22 Nov 1974.

ii. Christopher Andrew Reynolds, B: 12 Sep 1977.

iii. Kimberly Kay Reynolds, B: 21 Aug 1982.

240. Stephen John Irsik Jr.-11(Pauline Mable-10, Charles Burtle-9, William Edmunds Gleaves-8, Catherine Eubank-7, Charles Penn-6, Mary Ann-5, Joseph-4, John-3, Joseph-2, John-1)[43]

was born on 01 Nov 1946. He married Kay Bolens on 26 Dec 1967. She was born on 30 Sep 1945.

Children of Stephen John Irsik Jr. and Kay Bolens are:

248. i. Michele Irsik, B: 19 Nov 1968, M: Timothy James Flax Sr., 12 Jun 1991.

ii. Stephen J. Irsik III, B: 24 Jan 1970.

241. Michael Garrison Irsik-11(Pauline Mable-10, Charles Burtle-9, William Edmunds Gleaves-8, Catherine Eubank-7, Charles Penn-6, Mary Ann-5, Joseph-4, John-3, Joseph-2, John-1)[43] was born on 08 May 1949. He married Debra Schwartz in Dec 1975.

Children of Michael Garrison Irsik and Debra Schwartz are:

i. Andre Nicole Irsik, B: 28 Jan 1981.

ii. John Allen Irsik, B: 28 Feb 1986.

242. Maxson Brent Irsik Sr-11(Pauline Mable-10, Charles Burtle-9, William Edmunds Gleaves-8, Catherine Eubank-7, Charles Penn-6, Mary Ann-5, Joseph-4, John-3, Joseph-2, John-1)[43] was born on 15 Sep 1951. He married (1) Donna Mae DeHart on 26 May 1972[43]. She was born on 12 Feb 1951[43].

Children of Maxson Brent Irsik Sr and Donna Mae DeHart are:

i. Maxson Brent Irsik Jr., B: 14 Nov 1978.

ii. Tessa Mae Irsik, B: 12 Aug 1980.

iii. Maudie Lena Irsik, B: 20 Dec 1984.

243. Robert Allen Irsik-11(Pauline Mable-10, Charles Burtle-9, William Edmunds Gleaves-8, Catherine Eubank-7, Charles Penn-6, Mary Ann-5, Joseph-4, John-3, Joseph-2, John-1)[43] was born on 29 Oct 1952. He married Ellen Berger on 13 Nov 1982. She was born on 31 Jul 1958.

Children of Robert Allen Irsik and Ellen Berger are:

i. Charity Irsik, B: 23 Aug 1983.

ii. Matthew Irsik, B: 13 Aug 1985.

iii. Mary Catherine Irsik, B: 14 Sep 1988.

244. Ronald Dean Irsik-11(Pauline Mable-10, Charles Burtle-9, William Edmunds Gleaves-8, Catherine Eubank-7, Charles Penn-6, Mary Ann-5, Joseph-4, John-3, Joseph-2, John-1)[43] was born on 15 Feb 1955. He married Patricia Tucker on 11 Aug 1985. She was born on 31 Dec 1962.

Children of Ronald Dean Irsik and Patricia Tucker are:

i. Joseph K Irsik, B: 09 Dec 1986.

ii. Jessica Irsik, B: 18 Aug 1989.

Generation 12

245. Christina Lynn Clough-12(Carol Lynn-11, Edna Vera-10, Charles Burtle-9, William Edmunds Gleaves-8, Catherine Eubank-7, Charles Penn-6, Mary Ann-5, Joseph-4, John-3, Joseph-2, John-1)[42] was born on 13 Oct 1964 in Dodge City, Ford, Kansas, USA. She married Martin Steven Lueth on 04 Aug 1985 in Dodge City, Ford, Kansas, USA, son of Martin Harry Lueth and Bertha Martha Bruns. He was born on 11 Aug 1955 in Marion, Marion County, Kansas.

Children of Christina Lynn Clough and Martin Steven Lueth are:

i. Garrett Alexander Lueth, B: 15 Jul 1990 in Hays, Ellis County, Kansas.

ii. Chason Anton Lueth, B: 16 Oct 1993 in Hays, Ellis County, Kansas.

iii. Dorian Ashton Lueth, B: 21 Aug 1998 in Hays, Ellis County, Kansas.

246. David Andrew Clough-12(Carol Lynn-11, Edna Vera-10, Charles Burtle-9, William Edmunds Gleaves-8, Catherine Eubank-7, Charles Penn-6, Mary Ann-5, Joseph-4, John-3, Joseph-2, John-1)[42, 47] was born on 30 Jan 1966 in Dodge City, Ford County, Kansas. He married (1) Gloria Ann Coleman on 22 Apr 1999 in Hays, Ellis County, Kansas, daughter of Arnold Allen Coleman and Doreen Marie Wendler. She was born on 28 Jan 1971 in Orange, Orange County, California. He married (2) Anelia Von

Glebocki on 24 Sep 1988 in Chicago, Cook County, Illinois. She was born on 24 Sep 1970 in Denver, Denver County, Colorado.

Child of David Andrew Clough and Gloria Ann Coleman is:

i. Lawson Everet Clough, B: 02 Aug 2002 in Aurora, Colorado.

Child of David Andrew Clough and Anelia Von Glebocki is:

i. Vincent Michael Clough, B: 15 Nov 1989 in San Diego, California.

247. Renae Ann Reynolds-12(Allen Leroy-11, Edna Vera-10, Charles Burtle-9, William Edmunds Gleaves-8, Catherine Eubank-7, Charles Penn-6, Mary Ann-5, Joseph-4, John-3, Joseph-2, John-1)[42] was born on 22 Nov 1974. She married Anthony Mercado.

Child of Renae Ann Reynolds and Anthony Mercado is:

i. Mercado.

248. Michele Irsik-12(Stephen John-11, Pauline Mable-10, Charles Burtle-9, William Edmunds Gleaves-8, Catherine Eubank-7, Charles Penn-6, Mary Ann-5, Joseph-4, John-3, Joseph-2, John-1) was born on 19 Nov 1968. She married Timothy James Flax Sr. on 12 Jun 1991.

Children of Michele Irsik and Timothy James Flax Sr. are:

i. Katalyn Flax, B: 09 Nov 1993.

ii. Mikaela Flax, B: 18 Oct 1995.

iii. Timothy James Flax Jr., B: 07 Sep 1997.

iv. Joseph Steven Flax, B: 11 Feb 1999.

Sources

1 Robert Allen, 1649900.ftw, Date of Import: Nov 24, 2001.

2 RobertMAllen.ftw, Date of Import: Jul 26, 2001.

3 Barbara Baughan from Patrick County Historical Society in Virginia sent document, Compiled research by Catherine Murphey (1987).

4 Abstract of John Taylor's Bible.

5 Eugene Harris, By an e-mail from EHARRIS1@coumbus.rr.com (Ann Fleming is his 6th great-grandmother), E-mail dated November 23, 2000.

6 Journal, William Edmunds' Journal.

7 Barbara Baughan from Patrick County Historical Society in Virginia sent document, Compiled research by Catherine Murphey (1987), According to the books, "Mitchell Kith and Kin" and "The Mitchell-Pearman Families", Elizabeth married Nimrod Mitchell on 12/25/1766, Granville County North Carolina and died 2/2/1818 Laurens County South Carolina.

8 Shaun Eiker, By an e-mail from hummer6511@hotmail.com, E-mail dated March 18, 2001.

9 Family Bible, William Edmunds' Bible.

10 Kristina Weiss, By an e-mail from kweiss@uswest.net, E-mail dated April 10, 2001.

11 Bynum Tudor, Jr., By an e-mail from BynumTudor@aol.com, E-mail dated November 14, 2002.

12 By an e-mail from virtused@aol.com, E-mail dated March 20, 2002.

13 Dennis Ward, By an e-mail from skdward@earthlink.net, E-mail dated January 26, 2002.

14 By an e-mail from redbirdacres@email.com, E-mail is dated November 26, 2001.

15 Gordon Twilegar in Emmett, Idaho, By an e-mail from TwilegarG@rmci.net, E-mail dated February 24, 2002.

16 Tamera Parkison, By an e-mail from parkison@netnitco.net, E-mail dated March 4, 2002. Licensed to marry in Taylor County, Kentucky - Mg. Bk. 3, pg. 136.

17 Tamera Parkison, By an e-mail from parkison@netnitco.net, E-mail dated March 4, 2002. Licensed to marry in Taylor County, Kentucky - Mg. Bk. 3, pg. 84.

18 Vern, By an e-mail from dante@lemoorenet.com, E-mail dated February 24, 2002.

19 Kentucky Death Index 1911 - present, Name: ALLEN, CATHERINE E Death Date: 10 01 16; Death Place: WARRN Residence: (Blank) Age: 081.

20 Ora Laura (Allen) Blakeman, Ora Blakeman - The Allen Family (It was written in 1929), Gloria A. (Coleman) Clough has it.

21 Marriage Record Book 1836-67, 179. Elbert County.

22 Robert M. Allen - Descendants of Robert Allen, Sr.

23 Family Bible, Nathan Perry Allen's Bible.

24 Family Bible, Nathan Allen's Bible.

25 Obituary, Obituary of Nathan Perry Allen.

26 1840 Warren County, Kentucky Census.

27 1850 Warren County, Kentucky Census.

28 1860 Warren County, Kentucky Census.

29 1870 Warren County, Kentucky Census.

30 1880 Warren County, Kentucky Census.

31 1890 Warren County, Kentucky Census.

32 Janice B. Palmer, By an e-mail from jbpalmer22@cox.net.

33 Federal Government, SSDI (Social Security Death Index), Chris Lewis SSN 404-03-4614 Born 4 May 1891 Died Feb 1967 Residence: 42141 Glasgow, Barren, Kentucky Last Benefit: (Blank) Issued: Kentucky (Before 1951).

34 Federal Government, SSDI (Social Security Death Index), Name: Allen, Horace Born: 11 Nov 1889 Died: Mar 1968 Residence: 73533 Duncan, Oklahoma SSN: 441-03-5583 Issued: Oklahoma Death State: Oklahoma.

35 Personal Memory, Memory of Edna Vera (Allen) Reynolds.

36 Robert James Allen, By an e-mail from Bobzeta@worldnet.att.net, E-mail dated January 1, 2002.

37 Terrence Miller Barton, III, By an e-mail from BartonTM@everett.navy.mil, E-mail dated May 2, 2002.

38 Brandon Eiker, By an e-mail from BDEiker@triad.rr.com, E-mail dated 2/26/2008.

39 Federal Government, SSDI (Social Security Death Index), Chris Furlong SSN 404-24-3229 Born 4 Nov 1915 Died Jul 1977 Residence: 42141 Glasgow, Barren, Kentucky Last Benefit: 42141 Glasgow, Barren, Kentucky Issued: Kentucky (Before 1951).

40 Federal Government, SSDI (Social Security Death Index), Clifton Lewis SSN 401-20-8814 Born 11 Aug 1923 Died 27 Sep 1989 Residence: 42141 Glasgow, Barren, Kentucky Last Benefit: (Blank) Issued: Kentucky (Before 1951).

41 Maxson Irsik, By an e-mail from DMJFACS540982247@aol.com, E-mail dated December14, 2001.

42 Charles Andrew Reynolds' Obituary (Dodge City Daily Globe, Monday, August 22, 2005), 3. DODGE CITY - Charles Andrew "Andy" Reynolds, 90, died Saturday, August 20, 2005, at the Kansas Soldiers' Home, Halsey Hall, Ft. Dodge.

He was born May 30, 1915, at Arlington, Kansas, the son of Joseph LeRoy and Sarah Walker Reynolds. He attended school in Arlington and moved to Dodge City in 1938, where he worked for Gum Motor Company until he was inducted into the Army. While in the service, he attended school in Omaha, Nebraska, Beverly Hills and Los Angeles. He served with General Patton's 3rd Army as a Tech Sergeant and received 5 Battle Stars and 3 citations. After 5 years of service, he was honorably discharged. After the war, he started farming, and for 22 years he worked for the Dodge City Co-op.

He was a member of the First Presbyterian Church, Dodge City, where he served as an elder and deacon and a member of the session and taught Sunday school for 25 years. He was a member of the American Legion, VFW Post 1714, RSVP and Masonic Lodge, all of Dodge City, and AARP and NRA.

On September 6, 1942, he married Edna Allen at Bellflower, California. She survives.

Other survivors include: a son, Dr. Allen Reynolds and wife, Barbara, Dodge City; a daughter, Carol Lynn Clough and husband, David, Hays; a sister, June Arline Dorman, Salina, Oklahoma; 5 grandchildren, Renae Ann Mercado and husband, Anthony, Kimberly Kay Padget and husband, Michael, Christopher Andrew Reynolds, Christina Lynn Lueth and David Andrew Clough and wife, Gloria; and 11 great-grandchildren.

He was preceded in death by a brother, James Walker Reynolds, and two sisters, Shirley May Heller and Maudell Kelly, and a granddaughter in-law, Tracey Renae Reynolds.

Memorial Service will be 10:00 a.m. Wednesday, August 24, 2005, at the First Presbyterian Church, Dodge City, with Rev. David Clipson presiding. Friends may sign the register from 9:00 am to 5:00 p.m. Tuesday at Burkhart-Ziegler Funeral Chapel, Dodge City. There will be no public visitation. Cremation has taken place. Inturnment.

43 Maxson Irsik, By an e-mail from DMJFACS540982247@aol.com, E-mail dated August 20, 2002.

44 Adam Fogleman, By an e-mail from fogleman1@hotmail.com, E-mail dated July 24, 2002.

45 Charles Andrew Reynolds' Obituary (Dodge City Daily Globe, Monday, August 22, 2005), Page 3. DODGE CITY - Charles Andrew "Andy" Reynolds, 90, died Saturday, August 20, 2005, at the Kansas Soldiers' Home, Halsey Hall, Ft. Dodge. He was born May 30, 1915, at Arlington, Kansas, the son of Joseph LeRoy and Sarah Walker Reynolds. He attended school in Arlington and moved to Dodge City in 1938, where he worked for Gum Motor Company until he was inducted into the Army. While in the service, he attended school in Omaha, Nebraska, Beverly Hills and Los Angeles.

He served with General Patton's 3rd Army as a Tech Sergeant and received 5 Battle Stars and 3 citations. After 5 years of service, he was honorably discharged. After the war, he started farming, and for 22 years he worked for the Dodge City Co-op.

He was a member of the First Presbyterian Church, Dodge City, where he served as an elder and deacon and a member of the session and taught Sunday school for 25 years. He was a member of the American Legion, VFW Post 1714, RSVP and Masonic Lodge, all of Dodge City, and AARP and NRA.

On September 6, 1942, he married Edna Allen at Bellflower, California. She survives.

Other survivors include: a son, Dr. Allen Reynolds and wife, Barbara, Dodge City; a daughter, Carol Lynn Clough and husband, David, Hays; a sister, June Arline Dorman, Salina, Oklahoma; 5 grandchildren, Renae Ann Mercado and husband, Anthony, Kimberly Kay Padget and husband, Michael, Christopher Andrew Reynolds, Christina Lynn Lueth and David Andrew Clough and wife, Gloria; and 11 great-grandchildren.

He was preceded in death by a brother, James Walker Reynolds, and 2 sisters, Shirley May Heller and Maudell Kelly, and a granddaughter-in-law, Tracey Renae Reynolds.

Memorial Service will be 10:00 a.m. Wednesday, August 24, 2005, at the First Presbyterian Church, Dodge City, with Rev. David Clipson presiding. Friends may sign the register from 9:00 am to 5:00 p.m. Tuesday at Burkhart-Ziegler Funeral Chapel, Dodge City. There will be no public visitation. Cremation has taken place. Inturnment.

46 Maxson Irsik, By an e-mail from DMJFACS540982247@aol.com, E-mail dated December14, 2001, E-mail dated August 20, 2002.

47 Social Security Card, David Andrew Clough 512-62-1418.

Index

L

M

N

O

P

Q

R

S

INDEX OF DESCENDANTS

79. Penn, Clark (son of Gabriel #37) 178
80. Penn, Frances R. (daughter of Gabriel #37) 179
81. Penn, Gabriel (son of Gabriel #37) 179
82. Penn, Ruth M. (daughter of Horatio #38) 179
83. Penn, Keziah S. (daughter of Horatio #38) 179
84. Penn, Gabriel (son of Horatio #38) 180
85. Penn, John W. (son of Horatio #38) 180
86. Penn, Horatio (son of Horatio #38) 181
87. Penn, Louvenia Foster (daughter of Mary #39) 181
88. Penn, Abram Foster (son of Mary #39) 181
89. Penn, Gabriel (son of Greensville #40) 182
90. Penn, Peter Phillip (son of Greensville #40) 182
91. Penn, Andrew Jackson (son of Thomas #41) 182
92. Penn, George Washington (son of Thomas #41) 183
93. Penn, Lucinda Susan (daughter of Thomas #41) 183
94. Penn, William Alexander (son of Thomas #41) 184
95. Penn, William H. (son of Abram #42) 184
96. Penn, Barbara Ann L. (daughter of James Francis #43) 184
97. Penn, Catherine Leath (daughter of James Francis #43) 185
98. Penn, James Abram (son of James Francis #43) 185
99. Penn, William Abraham Clark (son of Edmond #44) 186
100. Penn, Josiah Ferris (son of Edmond #44) 186
101. Penn, Sarah Elizabeth (daughter of Edmond #44) 187
102. Penn, Mary Ruth (daughter of Edmond #44) 187
103. Penn, George Stovall (son of Edmond #44) 187
104. Penn, Martha Luvenia (daughter of Edmond #44) 188
105. Penn, Gabriel Thomas (son of Edmond #44) 188
106. Penn, Charity Warren (daughter of Phillip #45) 188
107. Penn, Sarah (daughter of Joseph #47) 189
108. Penn, Mary Ann (daughter of Joseph #47) 189
109. Penn, Charles A. (son of Alexander #48) 191
110. Upshaw, John (son of Amy #49) 191
111. Upshaw, Sarah (daughter of Amy #48) 191
112. Stinchcomb, Mary C. (daughter of Mary #50) 192
113. Stinchcomb, Nathaniel (son of Mary #50) 193
114. Penn, Susanna (daughter of Joseph Roscoe #52) 193
115. Penn, Joseph (son of Joseph Roscoe #52) 193
116. Penn, Sarah (daughter of Joseph Roscoe #52) 193
117. Penn, John Anderson (son of Joseph Roscoe #52) 194
118. Penn, Sarah Jane (daughter of John #53) 196
119. Penn, John Wilson (son of William #54) 196
120. Penn, Thomas Lee (son of Moses #55) 196
121. Penn, Emeline (daughter of Moses #55) 196
122. Cashwell, Judith (daughter of Elizabeth #56) 197
123. Stewart, Thomas (son of Mary #57) 197
124. Stewart, William Blanton (son of Mary #57) 197

167. Barton, Caroline (daughter of Caroline Winston #142) 219
168. Barton, Martha Curd (daughter of Caroline Winston #142) 219
169. Barton, Elizabeth H. (daughter of Caroline Winston #142) 219
170. Barton, Clarissa (daughter of Caroline Winston #142) 220
171. Barton, Alice Forbes (daughter of Caroline Winston #142) 220
172. Barton, Sarah Frances (daughter of Caroline Winston #142) 221
173. Barton, Carrio (daughter of Caroline Winston #142) 221
174. Barton, James Terrence (son of Frances Burrus # 144) 221
175. Barton, Lee (son of Frances Burrus #144) 222
176. Barton, Charles Penn (son of Frances Burrus #144) 222
177. Barton, Robert White (son of Frances Burrus #144) 223
178. Barton, William Edmunds (son of Frances Burrus #144) 223
179. Edmunds, Mary Jane (daughter of Edmund Alexander #145) 223
180. Edmunds, Mary Diana (daughter of Edmund Alexander #145) 224
181. Taylor, Marion Gordon (daughter of James #149) 224
182. Edmunds, William Franklin (son of James Christopher #151) 224
183. Edmunds, Bennie R. (son of James Christopher #151) 224
184. Edmunds, Lizzie Dora (daughter of James Christopher #151) 225
185. Allen, James Crittendon (son of Catherine Eubank #153) 225
186. Allen, William Edmunds Gleaves (son of Catherine Eubank #153) 226
187. Allen, Mary Emeline (daughter of Catherine Eubank #153) 227
188. Allen, Katherine Edmunds (daughter of Catherine Eubank #153) 228
189. Allen, Hiram Perry (son of Catherine Eubank #153) 228
190. Allen, Frank Barton (son of Catherine Eubank #153) 228
191. Allen, Ora Laura (daughter of Catherine Eubank #153) 229
192. Edmunds, Callie Eubank (daughter of Charles Henry #154) 229
193. Barton, Mary Thomas (daughter of Elizabeth Frances #155) 230
194. Barton, Louis Hardin (son of Elizabeth Frances #155) 230
195. Barton, Charles Grigsby (son of Elizabeth Frances #155) 230
196. Barton, Richard Bethel (son of Elizabeth Frances #155) 230
197. Edmunds, Allen (son of William Persifer Smith #156) 231
198. Edmunds, James Buford (son of John Curd #157) 231
199. Edmunds, Leonard Matthews (son of John Curd #157) 231
200. Edmunds, Flora Laura (daughter of John Curd #157) 232
201. Willis, Jessie (daughter of Laura Wilson #158) 232
202. Willis, Kate (daughter of Laura Wilson #158) 232
203. Willis, Minnie Lee (daughter of Laura Wilson #158) 233
204. Willis, Mayme (daughter of Laura Wilson #158) 233
205. Willis, Pattie (daughter of Laura Wilson #158) 233
206. Holman, Henry Malcom (son of Martha Ann #159) 233
207. Holman, Paul Wilson (son of Martha Ann #159) 234

www.ingramcontent.com/pod-product-compliance
Lightning Source LLC
LaVergne TN
LVHW010608100826
845148LV00014B/2888

* 9 7 8 0 5 7 8 9 3 7 0 1 4 *